Graced by His Touch
My Story

HANYA GALITZEN

Graced by His Touch: My Story

© 2025 by Hanya Galitzen

ISBN 978-1-966866-78-7

Dedication

"We will use these stones to build a memorial. In the future, your children will ask you, 'What do these stones mean?' Then you can tell them."

Joshua 4:6-7a

Dedicated to my devoted husband, Don, of 60 years, who lived this BIG life with me.

Written as a legacy and for my son Aaron, his wife Melissa, my three grandsons—Coby, Brendon, and Dillon—and all the other children Aaron and Melissa have brought into their home to become part of our family, whether a few days or years.

Dedicated also to all who know us but need to know more about how God works and how he used Don and me in this life.

Man is like a breath; His days are like a passing shadow.

Psalm 144:4

Contents

A Tribute to My Husband

Don's 60th Birthday, October 2, 2002

Always safe,
Always safe with you.
Knowing that you are forever looking to our God for direction,
In that, I am safe.

You, Don, are a wonderful man. Not of yourself,
but because you look to our God.
In that, I am safe.

When we made decisions to "Go for God"
and knew the "cost" involved,
You never wavered.

You allowed God to use the vessel of your body to shelter not only me
but so many others, ignoring the cost of your fragile emotions.
In that, not only am I safe, but so many others are as well.

As Jesus poured out His life for many, I see Jesus in you.
You are strong but with a tender heart.
Loving not only me but so many others, wanting the best for them
and doing so much good to help make it happen.

Don, your mind has been called four-dimensional. I don't understand
all that means except it makes you different. Is that a flaw?
I don't think so. Sometimes, I have had to "Go in Faith,"
not seeing what you already know, and it has usually been bigger than
either of us thought. So forgive me as I put in my strong, logical, left-
brained, fleshly opinions.
Sixty, how did that happen? As we prepare for the years ahead,

*I look forward to the changes. I have already tasted being with you
in illness. I can say that the mixed blessing of peace,
along with the anguish, was worth it.*

*The years of recovery from illness have special memories of their own.
Camping by ourselves, seeing you enjoy God's nature with fresh eyes,
as though seeing it for the first time, was worth it.*

*I have enjoyed how life has taken on a new meaning
after each crisis in our lives, and there have been many.*

*Thank you for sharing your life with me.
You have been more than faithful to me.*

*I love you and am blessed to be your wife.
I am always safe with you.*

*Love,
Hanya*

Endorsements

The first encounter with Hanya Galitzen in 1991 reminded my wife Marianne and me of the living water Jesus talked about in John 7:37-39. Since then, we have watched her develop a constant balance between the fruit of the Spirit (Galatians 5:22) and the gifts of the Spirit (1 Corinthians 12:14). Hanya spends time listening to Jesus, hearing him speak, and obeying his words. Many times, my wife and I experienced her faithful commitment to God by serving people in an authentic, refreshing, and loving way. Her prophetic gift and lifestyle encouraged us to grow in the prophetic and finally write a book on hearing God's voice. We gratefully look back to all the Spirit-filled times we have enjoyed together with Hanya in California and Germany.

Wolfgang H.W. Peuster
Senior Judge Ret., District Court Freiburg, Germany.
Author of God's Angel Comes for Breakfast[1]
Bible teacher and preacher, Charismatic Renewal
Movement in the Protestant Church in Germany

Hanya Galitzen has one of the finest reputations I know. Her impact on her beloved husband and family, friends, and churches here in the U.S. and abroad is truly remarkable. As a friend of many years, I can say that Hanya's life memoir will be read and treasured. The book offers an intimate look into the life of a woman who hears God speaking and then does as He says.

Dr. Bette Bond, Ph.D.
Seminary and College Professor
Founder of Inspiration House International

3

The ministry that Hanya has had with nationals throughout the world is quite profound. On one trip, as we traveled near the Huangpu River, I was astounded. Hanya, with no fear, boldly prophesied over a group of Christian national leaders and led them as a group through healing prayer. I describe Hanya as bold, confident, yet gentle when she has a message to deliver. Whether speaking to an individual or a crowd, she is a messenger of God's love and forgiveness. Just like her husband, Don, both of them clearly hear from God. They traveled with me to many international mission conferences. They unabashedly broke strongholds and brought hope and light to many young leaders. Truly, I've watched them ignite many spiritual flames, and this book is a testament to her willingness to both serve with Don and follow Jesus. This book provides you with a taste of God's miracles!

Janet Moen Clough
Chaplain, Spiritual Director
Alumni of Campus Crusade for Christ (CRU)
Founder of International Impact, Overseas Worker

I've known Hanya since the mid-90s. During this time, my wife, Gunilla, and I have built a close relationship with both Hanya and her husband, Don. Through countless conversations, I have seen Hanya's heart follow the prompting and leading of the Holy Spirit. With her desire to hear God, her heart is undergirded with a deep sense of integrity, loyalty, and steadfastness. I have seen her watch and wait on the timing of the Lord, which shows me that her heart is surrendered and surrounded by grace. Hearing God is foundational for us as believers, and I am sure that every reader of this book will see the thread of listening and following as a major key in our walk with God.

Reverend Andy Glover
Revival to the Nations

As field missionaries, we receive many teams, and some are more memorable than others. I have known Hanya Galitzen for almost 20 years and have appreciated the wisdom, spiritual discernment, generosity, and character of both Hanya and her husband, Don. We received Hanya and Don with a team in 2017, and their ministry was such a fun, refreshing, and powerful time. They are definitely one of our most memorable teams. Hanya's compassion and prophetic insight were a huge contribution to our ministry at the many local churches that we served and the hundreds of people who we ministered to in our medical campaigns, seeing many saved and physically healed. I highly respect Hanya's knowledge of international cultures, church history, and her spiritual maturity and prophetic discernment. This book, as a chronicle of her years of hearing the voice of the Holy Spirit and obeying His lead, will prove to be a treasure for those who have a heart to do the same.

Reverend Jared C. Mueller
Regional Coordinator for Central America
Foursquare Missions International

Acknowledgments

I want to give a hearty thank you to Elizabeth Campbell, whom I have gotten to know not only as an editor but now as a faithful friend as she edited this, her first book, with me for six months. Also, thank you to Olivia Morgan, who stepped in to copy-edit this book and prepare the bibliography. To my dear friend Sherry Swier Johnson, who held my hand through prayer and encouragement all along the way. Deep gratitude to Corinne Livesay and Abigail Thranow, who assisted me in the publication process. To my loving husband, Don, who continually helped jar my memory, adding strength to my story and supporting this weighty endeavor. Thank you to the many people who gave their permission for me to use their names and their stories to bring glory to our Lord. To all of you, I am grateful.

Foreword

The weight of a book is determined by neither the sales at the bookstore nor the renown of its author. Its true weight is determined by the imprint it leaves on lives—through content that produces timeless and transforming results. By that measure, this book weighs a ton!

God spoke through the Prophet Jeremiah (9:23-24a *NKJV*), *"Let not the wise man glory in his wisdom, let not the mighty man glory in his might, nor let the rich man glory in his riches; but let him who glories glory in this, that he understands and knows Me."*

As the pastor to the Galitzens for over 20 years, I can vouch that Hanya and her husband, Don, know Almighty God.

I'm pleased to be asked to invite you to read these pages. As you walk through the chapters, you see firsthand how a faithful couple can change lives, communities, and the world. And we're asking, "Lord, do it again in me." As you enter these pages, I invite you to experience the promise of God's Kingdom, grace, and power in the face of profound need in our world.

Reverend Paul Harmon
Pastor, Hope Chapel
Huntington Beach Foursquare Church
(Chartered November 19, 1931)

Preface

"Return home and tell how much God has done for you."
So the man went away and told all over town
how much Jesus had done for him.

Luke 8:39 (NIV)

We all have a story to tell, and I have had a great urgency to tell mine, as well as the desire to give God all the glory for my life. The Lord spoke to me on May 21, 1988, that I was to "go tell my story to all the people he sends me to, that they need to hear my words and experiences. I gave them to you, and they are not yours. Handle the words carefully . . . ."

When God said that, a scripture and edict was given to me from Ezekiel 3:24, *Then the Spirit came into me and set me on my feet. He spoke to me and said, "Go to your house and shut yourself in."*

I was also challenged by my friend, Laurie Walz, who told me that I had a story to tell.

Since I haven't written a book before, you probably have no idea who I am, where I've been, and the works of God I have had the privilege of seeing and being part of. I pray that my story will fill you with inspiration to listen to the callings of God in your life.

The last paragraph of the Gospel of John tells about Jesus' work during His time on earth. *Jesus did many other things as well. If every one of them were written down, I suppose that even the whole world would not have room for the books that would be written (John 21:25 NIV).*

I have many stories to tell, just as Jesus did! The Bible calls them 'leaving monuments,' or our Ebenezer for our children and grandchildren. Ebenezer is a Hebrew word from the Old Testament book of 1 Samuel.

9

Samuel then took a large stone and placed it between the towns of Mizpah and Jeshanah. He named it Ebenezer (which means "the stone of help"), for he said, "Up to this point, the LORD has helped us!" (1 Samuel 7:12).

Telling our stories is a reminder of the battles God has won on our behalf. We are to "raise our Ebenezer," letting everyone know God is in our worldly accomplishments.

We will not hide these truths from our children; we will tell the next generation about the glorious deeds of the LORD, about his power and his mighty wonders (Psalm 78:4).

Our grandchildren know a lot about our present lives but probably nothing about where God has, in His graciousness, allowed Don and me to go and do His work. This story mainly glorifies the Lord and the ways He has seen fit to mold me more into His character. As I have obeyed and submitted to Him, I have seen and experienced many joys and blessings as well as frustration, grief, and sadness.

Sometimes, when we love something and give it up for God, He gives it back to us with a surprising twist of richness added to it that we would never think of. If we hold on too tightly to things and even people, we cannot go to the next level of fullness and fulfillment God has in store for us. In all of the twists and turns of this life, I am grateful for every hardship of refining. I celebrate the rivers of fire I have had to walk over that the Lord has allowed to purify me and bring Him glory.

In the middle of writing this book, I began doubting whether I was supposed to write it. People would ask me with surprise, "You're going to publish?" Another sincerely asked, "Hanya, do you have one person who would read it?"

During all these arrows of doubt that could bring defeat, I would receive promptings from the Lord that would confirm my word from

God to continue writing. One prompting was when President Netanyahu was being interviewed by a Christian television station regarding his newly published book called *Bibi: My Story*.[2] I realized I had 'My Story' in my title too. President Netanyahu was very glad he wasn't elected again since it gave him the nine months it took to write his book. Writing a book did, in fact, take a long time. All this encouraged me to keep going, no matter how tedious the journey.

The next day, I just happened to choose a movie to watch about Thomas Wolf, a contemporary of F. Scott Fitzgerald, both famous writers, and learned about the agony and hard work of bringing his book to fruition and the perseverance it took.

Recently, in frustration, as I was speaking with my friend Sherry, I said, "I need to pray." This was an impression that was placed upon my heart. As I prayed, I had a vision of a giant thumb coming down from heaven onto the cover of my yet unfinished book, leaving a golden fingerprint. I was frustrated and questioning whether I should even be writing this book, and having this picture gave me confirmation that God was definitely in this.

Join me as I tell my story and the plans the Lord had for me. What a surprise you will see! We all decide our minutes, hours, and days, not to squander them away, and I hope that by telling these exciting events, you will 'catch the bug' and do what the Lord has called you to do.

Lord, let my words be anointed, truthful, and inspiring as they are being told to glorify You and Your ways.

Come and hear . . . let me tell you what he has done for me.
Psalm 66:16 NIV

1

My Childhood

The lines have fallen to me in pleasant places;
Indeed, my heritage is beautiful to me.

Psalm 16:6 NASB

My full name is Hanya Petrovna Metchikoff Galitzen, and my middle name, Petrovna, means "daughter of Peter," Petro in Russian. For girls, Petrovna is the feminine version of Peter, and for boys, it is Petrovich. In Russian tradition, all our middle names reflect who our father is and which family we come from.

I was born on February 27, 1945, in East Los Angeles, California, the most famous city in the nation for gangs, the MS 13, The Bloods, and others. I lived near First Street, at 39 North Ditman Avenue, until I was three years old, then moved to La Puente, California, on a ten-acre small farm. The city is now called the City of Industry.

I remember my father purchasing a home in Baldwin Park, where the state was clearing the way for a freeway. The house was cut in half and moved during the night to our property in La Puente, where it was then reconstructed.

As a child, I always felt we were rich, seeing what seemed to me like a grand house, a very large white barn, and all that land in the middle of nowhere. And always proud for everyone to see when the school bus came to pick us up.

It was exciting when big rains came, and the ditch in front of our house overflowed. The water came up to our third step. We got to stay home, and I waved to everyone on the bus from the porch as it went by.

After dinner, most summer evenings, my parents would sit on the couch on our large front porch that had giant white pillars as we children spent a few hours playing games on our front lawn. We would play tag, jump the river, baseball, and kickball when, suddenly, someone would call out, "Dog pile on _____!" I would always be frightened by being called out as I was little and had small bronchioles, making it hard to breathe if they did that. My younger brother Peter, who was my best friend, only 18 months younger than I, would call my name out and shelter me, lifting the heavy load of the others off me.

My father was a real estate broker and gentleman farmer. I learned to answer our phone and take messages from prospective tenants wanting to rent from us and from current tenants calling with complaints. We raised goats, chickens, ducks, pigeons, sheep, and cows. Growing up, we would eat squabs, which are baby pigeons. They are considered an exotic delicacy and are very delicious. We drank goat's milk as it was very healthy, but we hated it, especially as we took it to school in little jars with waxed paper in the lid, and by the time it was lunchtime, it was warm and tasted so awful. When our goats escaped into our onion field, the milk was quarantined for about a week, so we got store-bought cows' milk. Oh, how rich, creamy, and sweet it was.

Then there was the day my father rented this stinky male Billy goat to come "visit the ladies," as my father told me! I was too young to understand why he would do this. This Billy goat stank up our whole property.

One of our dogs was named Rex. I remember him since he was kept on a chain, and even I couldn't come near him and needed prayer to get over the trauma of his trying to get at me even though he was tied up. This reminds me of the time when I was three and living in East Los Angeles. We had chickens and roosters in the backyard, and a rooster jumped up at me, leaving a scratch right down the side of my eye.

My father wanted to buy us a pony to ride, but my mother felt it would be too dangerous, so we used the cow instead. I have fond memories of riding that cow as my brother held a feed bucket in front of him to make him walk. We took turns doing that until we were in front of our kitchen window, and the cow bucked my brother high into the air with my mother watching! I'll bet my mother wished we had bought that pony.

I remember I would come home after school to visit my baby goat and allow her to chew on my dress until I looked at it and it was in shreds. From time to time, my brother and I would ride our goats, holding onto their horns, which was not a good idea. We would tug on their beards, abusing the goats to the max.

There was the time I climbed up a ladder onto the garage roof with my umbrella, and because of the many cartoons I saw, I thought that if I jumped with the open umbrella in hand, I would float down. What a surprise that was.

We kids would play hide-and-seek, hiding behind the bales of hay scattered in the field. I remember building a clubhouse in the middle of the large stack of baled hay, not knowing I was allergic to all that hay. There was the alfalfa field across the street where we would go to hide from each other, smashing the alfalfa down as we crawled through the field. The farmer came ringing our doorbell. After all, we were the only house on the street. What trouble we caused!

Other things we did included pouring tons of water into the many gopher holes, trying to get the gophers to pop their heads out. That was never-ending. When I skated, I used skates that needed a key to attach them to my shoes. Since there were many of us, I usually only had one skate and skated on our bumpy asphalt driveway. See how creative we were without cell phones and video games. Writing all this reminds me how fun my childhood was.

I do remember walking in our field and stepping on an extremely rusty three-inch nail embedded in a piece of wood. I immediately fell to the ground. Knowing what had just happened, I pulled the nail out, then had to soak my foot in kerosene! Yes, we went to the doctor, and I got a tetanus shot.

Every day, I would run out of our back door and jump over the three steps of our porch. One time, as I was in the air, I was hit smack on my cheekbone, full force by a baseball bat. My brother and some others were playing baseball. I graduated from the eighth grade three days later with a large shiner.

I remember the cesspool we needed to dig every so many years as we were not connected to city sewers. The grass grew very tall and beautiful back there. We learned to conserve water so only the dating-age girls could bathe more often with a small amount of water in the tub. Otherwise, every Saturday, we lit the outdoor wood-burning fireplace to heat stones on the inside of our Russian steam bath. We would go in and pour water over the hot stones to make the room steamy and very hot.

I'm the fifth of eight children having four brothers and three sisters, all living. In order of age, Mike (Mischa), Luba, Nadia, David (Davida), Me, Peter (Petsya), Nicholas (Nick or Nicolai), and Manya (Mary).

Being a religious family, we prayed before and after every meal. God and Jesus were spoken of regularly, and church attendance was a must. If we missed church because of sickness, we had church at home.

A Sunday I particularly remember was when I was five, and my father asked a question during our house church service, "Who was the first person on earth?" I was SO excited and raised my hand so high, shaking it. I knew, I just knew—I felt so proud! He called on me, and I said, "George Washington!" Everyone laughed.

At five, I fasted half a day as we celebrated many of the Old Testament holidays. My religion believed in Jesus Christ plus much of the law of the Old Testament and another holy book written by a relative of mine, the *Book of Spirit and Life.*[4]

I was also five years old when I memorized John 3:16 in Russian, but when I stood on a bench to recite it at Sunday School, I froze and could not speak! I was paralyzed with fear. The scripture is true when it says, *"Train up a child in the way he should go, and when he is old he will not depart from it" (Proverbs 22:6 KJV)*. I can still say John 3:16 in Russian. Here it is in English, *"For God so loved the world, that he gave his only begotten Son that whosoever believeth in him should not perish, but have everlasting life" (KJV)*.

In kindergarten, I was so shy as I was only exposed to my family and the Russian community and didn't know how people outside of my Russian community lived. I felt like a stranger in my class.

When I entered the first grade, my teacher called me Hazel. You need to know that was the name on my birth certificate. I was named after my mother but was called Hanya at home and in the Russian community. I was now called Hazel, and it seemed so strange to me, "Who is that?" I would ask myself.

Still in the first grade, a few of us were playing on the gym set and I was being teased as we were playing witch games when one young boy said, "You be the witch because your name is Hazel!" The next morning, when my name was being written on my lunch bag by my father, I said I wanted him to write my Russian name down, and he did. I asked again, "Is that how you spell it? Hanya?" He said yes.

I went to school and went up to my teacher and showed her my lunch bag and told her I would only be answering to that name from now on. When she called out Hazel later, I would not answer. My name was changed that day, I was six. Pretty determined little thing I was.

There was a time when I was about eight years old, and my father gave us a Bible study. He told us we were 'the chosen people' and that only the people of my religion would go to heaven. I remember not agreeing with him in my mind and I felt guilty about that. That was a new thing! Having an opinion that was not my father's, especially regarding God! I considered that if God created everybody, that He loved everybody and that heaven was a very large place that it couldn't just hold 'our people,' and that there was room for more people. I pictured our people in a tiny corner and that there was a lot more room in heaven. God would give me pictures in my mind like that often.

That same night my father also talked about burning in hell forever, at least that is all I remembered! I tried to go to sleep that night trying to imagine burning forever and how that would be. The fear of God was put in me good that day, and I needed to behave. I now understand the freedom that Christ affords.

As a child, I now realize, but did not then, that I had the gift of discernment, the ability to sometimes see into the spiritual realm. Usually, I saw the dark spirits and became fearful; I assumed everyone saw and felt these things. As I developed in that spiritual realm, I came to realize how to function in this gift with the spiritual authority we are given along with the power of the blood of Jesus. I have been able to help many to be set free from demonic influences and overcome past hurts. Just so you are not frightened of me, I use this gift when needed, and I also see many good things.

When I was eight, I remember not liking the name 'Jesus,' but I must have been thinking about Him! I just didn't like the name and felt guilty about feeling that way. I would say Jesus out loud many times. I feel the enemy was trying to get at me at a young age! I have since prepared and given teachings on the names of God, how interesting is that?

Decades later, it was 2014, I heard from God to tell my story by writing a book. I was sitting on a balcony in Kauai, Hawaii, and it was drizzling lightly. The name of Jesus and the power it holds spoke to me through a song. The song goes like this, "Jesus, Jesus, Jesus, there's just something about that name, Master, Savior, Jesus, like the fragrance after the rain."[3] So beautiful! If you remember, I struggled with liking the name of Jesus. This song was a confirmation from God telling me to write a book, and that it would be valuable to Him.

I am the fifth child, a middle child, and yes, the neglected one! My birthday is February 27, and there were two other siblings with birthdays that month. On my ninth birthday, I waited all day for a "happy birthday" from someone, but none came, and I was very sad. At dinner time my mother suddenly remembered, and someone quickly ran to the grocery store for soda and ice cream. My mom quickly baked a cake, called 'Busy Day Cake,' and I still have the recipe. My father liked it with bananas between the layers and frosted with vanilla cream frosting.

On my tenth birthday, my eldest brother got married, just two months after my oldest sister was married when she was only 17. There was a lot of fuss going on in our house that year.

My baby sister, six years younger than I, was doted upon by my aunt who had three boys. She always sewed beautiful frilly dresses for my sister, and I even remember my aunt asking my parents to adopt her or just raise her since my mom was so busy with eight children and was very tired all the time. That was hard for me to hear. For my eldest brother's wedding, my youngest sister's dress was very lovingly made for her by my aunt, but my dress was a bargain dress, very plain brown cotton with small polka dots, and had no frills like my sister's. I felt very plain and forgotten again and not very pretty—and to top it off, it was my tenth birthday.

When I was 13 years old and at our Sunday evening youth church, as we were worshiping God, I received a realization deep within me that the name Jesus was more than a word. I began sobbing and couldn't stop! It's interesting that He spoke to me regarding His name 'Jesus,' the name I didn't like! I, along with two others, was taken to the altar and prayed over by the elders. Jesus became more than a word to me that day. I accepted Jesus into my heart without yet realizing the fullness of what He did for me.

When I graduated high school, I couldn't find a job nearby and was only 17, so I had to apply in L.A. I worked at Pacific Telephone Company in the compilations department and proofread classified ads for the Yellow Pages. My father drove me across Valley Boulevard every morning to the bus stop and picked me up every evening. This street was very dangerous to walk across because of traffic. I eventually became part of a carpool.

After experiencing working life, I decided to go to Mt. San Antonio Junior College for a year while I dated Don.

I come from a humble, wealthy family; I don't mean opulent, but we had ten acres that eventually became the City of Industry, and companies began to build their corporate offices on the land around us. The land became more and more valuable, and I remember as my father was dying, he said to me during our last conversation, "One acre for each of us and two for Mama, Hazel," my mother—that was his wish. As time went on after he died, we never saw a will or heard anything. We discovered that all the properties were in the name of my mother and one unmarried brother as joint tenants. I never received any part of my family inheritance.

Do not remove the ancient landmark which your fathers have set.
Proverbs 22:28 NKJV

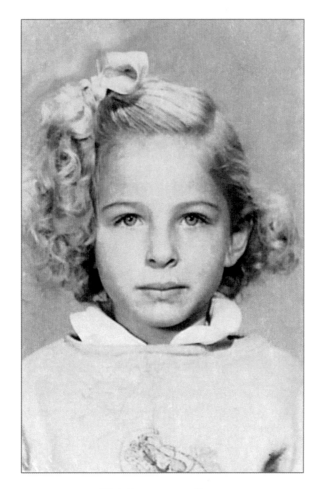

This is me at age five.

2

They Call Him "The Prince"

*Now we live with great expectation, and we
have a priceless inheritance—an inheritance
that is kept in heaven for you, pure and undefiled,
beyond the reach of change and decay.*

1 Peter 1:3-4

Donald David Galitzen was born in East Los Angeles, California, on October 2, 1942. Don and his family lived on Second Street in apartments his mother purchased when his father was at war.

Don learned to hear God during grade school. Living in East Los Angeles, it became crucial for him to hear from God as many of the kids in his neighborhood would walk in gangs. On his way home one day, he heard God tell him to cross the street. Don did not know that these boys who were always up to no good would be coming his way shortly, and because he had crossed the street, they never saw him. These boys would often frisk him for his milk money as he entered school, so he began folding his money into his sock.

Around the age of seven years old, Don was in a Japanese Boy Scout troop meeting held at a Methodist church where he felt he heard from God that he should become a pastor. After Boy Scout meetings, the other boys' parents took them to their Buddhist temple and Don was asked along, but he told them he was not Buddhist.

At one retreat as a young teenager, Don heard a stirring message. He was sure everyone was impacted by it and jumped up from his seat in the back of the room to go to the altar. Don thought everyone was also running to the altar but then realized that he was the only one. At the altar, Don recommitted himself to Jesus. The moving of the Holy Spirit in Don's life has resulted in a heart for the youth.

Don played the accordion and was in an accordion band from middle school through high school. Everyone wanted to play an accordion at that time. In high school, Don was on the varsity tennis team and became quite the skier, even skiing black diamond runs.

When Don was 18, he received his real estate salesman's license but continued his college education at Whittier College. Don was still deciding on his career; he inquired into becoming a dentist and also visited a pharmacy school but did not like working with the chemistry aspect of that field. He was also considering becoming a mortician! I said, "We need to talk about that." Don ended up graduating from Whittier College with a Biochemistry major.

Our Dating

I, Hanya, began dating when I was fifteen and a half years old and remember praying to God after a date, even though I was not taught to pray my personal prayers to God. I prayed, "God, who would you like me to marry?" I knew I could marry a poor farm boy, by fixing up a shack with cute curtains and be happy since I loved him, or I could also be happy with a city boy.

God answered my prayer by bringing me a city boy, an only child, and as I've discovered, a man with no guile—my precious Don, to whom I have been married for 60 years! I met him when I was 15; he was so cute with sparkling eyes and the perfect car, a 1957 baby blue Chevy. Don belonged to a Christian car club called the Crusaders. He had a club plaque that read 'Crusaders' displayed in the back window-ledge of his car; he had a car club jacket too!

Don was introduced to me and ten other girls by a friend at our Russian young people's church on a Sunday night. All I remember were his beautiful swimming eyes. I now recognize them as 'Jesus Eyes'; no other boy I dated had them. I was taken by him so much that when I got home I had to tell someone!! I told my nine-year-old sister, "I met the kind of guy I want to marry; I'll never get him, but that's the kind of guy I want to marry." It was love at first sight.

Don says he was driving home from a bad date one night and he felt lost, so he asked God, "What do you want me to do? This is a bad date; this is not good. Who do you want me to date?" God spoke to him with a picture; he says, "I saw the finger of God pointing in a certain direction right in front of me. Who is over there, God? There were two girls I knew, but then I thought, 'Ah, Hanya, yes!'"

We began dating when I was 17, Don gave me a Bible, and I began to read it every night. (Don has since read the Pentateuch, also called the Books of Moses, the first five books of the Bible, twice, which is read from the back forward.) One of our first dates was to Dana Point where he would surf with his longboard. Don asked me to make sandwiches for the day and when we arrived there, he left me on the beach and went surfing for a very long time, so long that other boys came to visit with me.

One of our dates was on a summer afternoon. Don had just finished his anatomy class at Whittier College and came straight over to my house. As we were sitting on my couch talking about his class, he just happened to mention that he was working on a cadaver that day! I pulled far away from him and said, "You didn't go home to shower and change?" He said he just turned his sweatshirt inside out!

Don didn't come to my church but was part of our Russian community; it was a requirement for me to marry a boy of our religious and ethnic background. He was a born-again Christian and attended YRCA, the Young Russian Christian Association. This organization was not accepted by my church or my family as they taught 'outside teachings.' My father wanted me to marry someone else, a preacher's son who was after me.

One night the pressure was so great from my father, and I was torn about honoring him as the Bible says, that I told him I would try to break up with Don, but when I tried, I couldn't. My older brother, who was nine years older than I, asked me what was going on regarding my dating Don. I told him of our father's pressure on me. He asked me if I loved Don, and I told him I didn't know but that I didn't want to date any other boys. Then I knew.

When my father asked me the next day about what happened about breaking up, I said, "When I date those other boys and talk with them, they don't understand what I'm saying but Don does. My father did not say anything about us breaking up after that. I didn't plan those words at all, they were from God.

Who can find a virtuous wife? For her worth is far above rubies.
Proverbs 31:10 NKJV

Don asked me to marry him in December of 1963 after we had dated for about a year and a half. I told him we could not let my parents know yet; otherwise, we would be married within two months. My father would not allow any funny business.

Don was graduating from Whittier College in June, so we planned on August 16, 1964, as our wedding date, and I received my ring in June. I was having finals after my first year of college and was busy studying and excited that I would get my ring on Sunday. Don told me that the ring was not ready and that made me cry when I told my sister. He was just teasing me, though, and as we drove on the freeway that day, he asked me if I wanted some gum in his pocket, the look on his face told me the ring was in his pocket. I didn't want to get it myself, so when we stopped at the A&W, he gave it to me. He was having so much fun; I didn't feel it was romantic. I guess I watched too many movies.

Our Wedding

A Russian wedding is a wonderful occasion. Once you are engaged there is a meeting of the families to get to know each other and to discuss the wedding plans, which is called 'Svyatetsa,' or something like that. Don's grandmother was named Hanya too and was thrilled we would marry.

Traditionally, there are two showers given, one for the couple and the other a personal one for the bride. No presents are brought to the wedding, they are brought to the wedding shower. Usually, there are about 200-300 women at the shower. The engaged couple comes to a front table where the elderly grandmothers are seated and present the couple to the group attending. This is done in the Russian language as well as a prayer for the food.

The personal shower is usually a home event with a luncheon, where many women outfit the bride with fun bridal essentials. Don's mother even gave me money for my honeymoon clothing, as well as paying for my wedding dress.

The night before the wedding, many young people come to the bride's house to gather outside and have a party. My best girlfriends spent the night with me as a last sleepover and helped me dress in the morning as they sang Russian songs to me.

The part I love about the wedding day is the goodbyes from each home of the bride and groom. The preacher, elders, and relatives from the church of the bride and groom go to each of their homes before coming to the church for the ceremony. Each one is prayed for, and we kneel before our parents and ask forgiveness for anything we've offended them for. They then lay hands on us, forgive us with a blessing, and release us from their care. As beautiful as I was, before the ceremony I needed to go back to my room to retouch my makeup.

The groom and attendants and a married couple, who are usually relatives of the groom, come to the bride's house to pick up the bride and go to the church. When they arrive, there is joyous singing, in Russian, and then when the song is over, the male attendant is asked who has come and they answer and ask permission of the bride's parents if they can take the bride. The bride then links hands with the male attendant, who places the bride's hand into the groom's hand, and all four go in a fancy borrowed car to drive to the church.

By then it's about eleven o'clock in the morning and the guests are waiting at the church. The groom's mother and father greet the couple and the bride's family with a loaf of bread with salt sprinkled on it. This symbolizes a welcome greeting in many countries. After greeting the bride's family with a holy kiss on the lips and a prayer, they are welcomed into the groom's church, which will become the couple's home church.

People are already in their customary places as the wedding party enters and the formal wedding begins with many different positions for the party of four always holding hands. The attendants are protecting the bride and groom from any ill will from anyone. They also do most of the speaking during the ceremony.

After the formal ceremony, tables are set up for a four-course feast for 300–400 people. Since I would be becoming part of Don's family, his parents paid for the wedding, and wedding feast.

Our wedding, August 16, 1964

The first course is traditional tea drunk from the bowl, bread with tomatoes and cucumbers sprinkled with lemon juice along with dates. The second course is soup, a Russian 'borscht,' or noodle soup; and the third course is meat from the soup presented on a platter with hard-boiled eggs and more bread. The fourth course is fruit, oranges, and bananas.

The tables are taken away and we again have prayers and then much joyful singing, all done in Russian. As Molokan people (a Russian sect) are 'spiritual jumpers' it can be a lively time. Usually after the wedding, family members go to the new home of the bride and groom to pray over it and then to a parent's home for coffee, tea, and pastries. Russian 'blinsi,' a crepe filled with cheese filling, melted butter, and cream over the top, and a side of soup are commonly served.

We honeymooned with a trip up north to Carmel, San Francisco, Clear Lake, and Monterey, California. Our first night was above a gas station; it was summer and there was no room at the inn anywhere! We were so young. I was raised kosher and had not found freedom from that yet, so I took my little cookpot.

Married Life

After our honeymoon in our 1963 white Volkswagen, we needed to stay a few nights at Don's parents' home since the utilities in our apartment were not yet on. A friend of Don's family, Stella Bogdanoff, called and I answered the phone. After a few words she asked me if I was born again. I was surprised and wasn't quite sure what she was asking me. I thought she was asking if I was a Christian. I said, "I think so," remembering my experience with Jesus when I was 13 years old. That question without her preaching anymore caused me to begin considering what that meant. I hadn't heard the words 'born again' before.

A funny story about one of my first experiences cooking was with a pressure cooker I received. Well, I had heard stories of them exploding, so I knew I would need help. I prepared the ingredients for a stew, put them in the pot, sealed the lid, and then put it on the cement ground of our patio. I wasn't going to have it explode in my house! I called for Don and gave him the little 'thingy' that you put on top of the lid and asked him to start it! He looked at me very funny, and I asked him again; he was speechless. Little did I know that the pressure cooker couldn't 'start' on its own, it needed the fire of our stovetop!

My first car was a 1949-50 dull steel gray Kaiser Frazer. We bought it from a little old lady from Pasadena for $50, so that worked. It felt like driving a boat on the water, but I did feel safe. This car company went out of business in 1953.

One day as Don and I walked on the Huntington Beach Pier, I remembered that he had told a woman, "You are doing great, you are right behind him (her husband)." We would counsel couples sometimes. I asked him if I was right behind him and he said, "No, you're right at my side." I answered, "Really, I thought I was behind you; I was raised that the man is the leader." He said "No," so I told him, "There would be changes." Boldness was on its way!

"That the woman was made of a rib out of the side of Adam; not made out of his head to rule over him, nor out of his feet to be trampled upon by him, but out of his side to be equal with him, under his arm to be protected, and near his heart to be beloved"[5] (Matthew Henry).

We lived in Los Angeles after we married. Don had applied and was accepted to University of Southern California Optometry College but discovered he did not like the calculations required for optometry. He finished the semester and didn't continue.

I worked at the Colwell Banking Company in the collections department. I made $320 a month, walked three blocks to work, and sewed my own clothes. We rented from Don's aunt and uncle right near Wilshire and Vermont in Los Angeles. They were very kind and gave us low rent in exchange for painting the entire inside of a very large apartment and doing the gardening for the four-unit complex. Early in our marriage, I also worked for Standard Packaging Corporation as secretary to the plant manager, then I became a legal secretary working for Ariey and Crow in Monterey Park, California. I was secretary to Mr. Crow, who worked with criminal cases as well as divorces, personal injury, and bankruptcies. Six months after I quit that job, I learned that Mr. Ariey, the lead attorney, was shot and killed by an irate husband of a woman getting a divorce. That was a sad thing to hear; the office was right down the street from where we lived.

Don went to a headhunter, a person who finds work positions for people, and was given the choice of becoming a traveling salesman over five states working for a pharmaceutical or cosmetic company or becoming a clinical laboratory technologist, now called a scientist. Don had read a book where it said whichever decision someone tells you to make, go the other way. He asked the headhunter which he should choose; well, Don went the other way and became a clinical laboratory scientist. The training was for a year at one dollar an hour, which was minimum wage at the time. The man had Don wait to start his training for two weeks which caused Him to be two weeks shy of the six months required to take the examination, so he had to work another six months because the test was given once every six months. We were not happy as Don could have been making eight dollars an hour if he had been licensed.

He worked for several hospitals for over 15 years, including Alhambra Community Hospital, Glendale Hospital, Fountain Valley Hospital, La Palma Hospital, San Gabriel Hospital, and Olympia

Hospital in Los Angeles. Don worked very hard. He took night calls, sometimes responding to several hospitals at a time. This became seed money for investing in property.

Don's heart was put to use through a variety of different ministries. I belonged to an Aglow group of spirit-filled women, and Don was asked to become our advisor. We, together, led a Seder, a ceremonial celebration of Passover.

He traveled to Mexico with YUGO Ministries—Youth with a Mission, whose mission is to mobilize and equip God's people to reach the forgotten. He slept on a church floor and was only allowed one shower for the week! Don also became a Bible Study Fellowship Discussion Leader for a men's group.

We took high school kids from The Evangelical Free church canoeing on the Owens River with canoes we had rented from Biola University. A near-tragic occurrence took place on the river. The youth were trained on how to stand in the river if they fell out of their canoe. One young woman, after falling out of her canoe, ended up being pushed against a rock with the canoe filling up sideways and beginning to crush her. She was in the center of the river and Don gave orders to break the canoe, they did, and she was rescued. That cost us $300, which was nothing compared to saving her life. As I always say about Don, "He's my champion." The next year, we took our son, Aaron, on the second canoeing trip with this youth group when he was four years old.

Throughout our marriage, Don was involved in other sports: he was part of a six-man outrigger canoe club, an "A" racquetball player, and I joined him on many skiing trips.

Interestingly, he has been in the business field, is a natural investor, and loves economics! His uncle, John Shubin, was an economics professor at New York University and wrote several textbooks. Quite possibly that should have been Don's major.

Early Days in Real Estate

While Don was working as a clinical laboratory scientist, we began the slow transition into real estate, purchasing a custom-built home with a duplex in Monterey Park after seven months of marriage. This was the beginning of our investing—using our $900 of wedding money, my $500, and help from Don's parents of $5,000 as a down payment, which we paid back quickly.

After a few years, we purchased the triplex next door. We continued saving money until we could buy six little houses in a row in Rosemead, California. We did most of the upkeep ourselves, except when we needed professional help. Even then Don would hire a plumber and get down on the floor under a sink with the plumber to learn how to do it. The same thing happened with carpet installation; we eventually had all the equipment for Don to do much of the work himself.

Many have said, "Don, I want to be like you." We answered back, "No you don't." People didn't realize the hard work it would take. I remember the time those six houses needed $10,000 worth of roof work. We ate very meagerly, Don hired one of my brothers, and they did the roof themselves.

We lived in Monterey Park, California, for about six years. Over a period of years, accumulating more property, we moved into Huntington Beach and became Galitzen Properties. After having a real estate license for many years, Don and I realized it was more beneficial to do business without the license and instead operate as private investors.

More than stocks, Don trades options and futures, as well as mentoring people in investing to become self-supporting to be able to serve God freely as we have. Whittier College, his alma mater, has asked Don to teach business several times now and continues to do so. They have invited our son, Aaron, to join Don to be on a panel for a simulation of Shark Tank as the student's final exam. It was such a success they are inviting them back. This is such a wonderful opportunity to be an influence in living a life for God as he is free to be who he is, taking ministry into the marketplace.

Don's Spiritual Side

Don has quite a spiritual side to him as well. He had an unusual dream one night that three demons (evil spirits) were trying to get into his chest, but when they tried to look inside of him, they realized that Jesus was there and they couldn't get in. They then jumped on top of our dresser. After he woke, we together, knowing the authority we had in Jesus, prayed and commanded them to leave our home in the name of Jesus.

"He will save His people from their sins" (Matthew 1:21b NKJV).

> Sin will be in us—it will never be utterly expelled, till the Spirit enters glory; but it will never have dominion. Christ will be Master of the heart, and sin must be mortified. The Lion of the tribe of Judah shall prevail, and the dragon shall be cast out.[6] (Charles Spurgeon)

Don, having accepted Jesus Christ as His Savior and Lord, protects his heart.

When Don told my older brother about this dream, my brother went to the book of *Spirit and Life,* and showed him a diagram at the back, asking Don, "Is this what you saw?" Don spun the book around so that the image my brother was showing him was now upside down, and said, "No, this is what I saw." My brother told Don, "That is satan." (I never capitalize his name, to never give him any honor). All three of the demons that tried to enter Don, had the same faces as the one shown in the book, known to be satan. The author of this book called himself the King of the Spirits, and this book is used next to the Bible in the church I was raised in.

> *Then He brought us out from there (Egypt) that*
> *He might bring us in [to the promised land].*
> *Deuteronomy 6:23a NKJV*

Another supernatural experience Don had was when he was struck by a light from above one morning around 5 a.m. as he was shaving for work, and he received a message from God regarding a relative. He came to me and woke me and kept pointing to his lips. I asked, "You're hungry?" He shook his head; I kept asking questions until I realized he couldn't speak. After about ten minutes he got his voice back and told me a very hard message regarding relatives of mine. Don tried going to work after that but about halfway there he was compelled to come back and said, "We need to talk to your mother." We called my mother explaining the message Don had received and she said we needed to talk with the couple, so we did. The man said, "Well, you had the vision so it must be about you."

The custom of our Russian culture was to invite the preacher and elders to the home for formal prayer in unique situations. They agreed to do so. This gathering of elders would also include a four-course meal. They had this prayer, but afterward one of the prophetic men came up to me and with his finger going in a circle said, "Whatever this was for, it did not work!" This relative was not living right and in the years to come it became obvious and sadly to say, they later divorced.

God has used Don in many ways throughout his life on behalf of many people to bring them success and closer to God.

Much later, Don and I were both water-baptized together in the ocean at Pirate's Cove in Corona del Mar, California. Two pastors put both of us under the water at the same time, it was very special to encounter that together. After many years, we both received the baptism of the Holy Spirit or speaking in another language (tongues).

A dear family friend was a strong woman of the faith, and I never wanted to be like her, strong and pushy. Wanting to receive everything the Lord had for me, I awoke one morning at 2 a.m., got on my knees, and asked forgiveness for my feelings towards this woman and told God I didn't want to 'throw the baby out with the bathwater,' so whatever He had for me, I was open and waited quietly. Then, "Oh no!" Strange words were coming to my mind and that was my reaction. I flowed with muttering them and came to realize that there is power in these words as well as great peace.

Don had a harder time and felt he had a knot in his tongue although flowing in many of the gifts of the Spirit. Moses spoke to God about having a hard time with his speech. *"O Lord, I'm not very good with words. I never have been, and I'm not now, even though you have spoken to me. I get tongue-tied, and my words get tangled"* *(Exodus 4:10).*

One day we happened to meet with Jack Hayford, who was then the president of the Foursquare denomination, and Don had the chance to talk to him about how he had not received tongues. Pastor Hayford's response was, "You have a problem with that?" Don said, "No, others do!" Because of our more conservative take on

Pentecostalism, we have been called to minister across denominational lines.

A word from the Lord in 1989 regarding Don was, "Hanya, you are there to keep him warm and healthy and satisfied. Don't deny him; my grace will help you to be everything I made you to be for him."

I remember these words and act on them to this day. King David in his old age had a young woman named Abishag to "keep him warm"; this was meant literally, as his aging body needed warmth (1 Kings 1:2). Helpmeet would be another good word for my role as Don's wife, a proper help, one particularly suited to Don's uniqueness. I see this word regarding Don as being a close companion to him and I know his love language is my presence.

Evidence of God

1. Don, as a child walking to school, heard God's voice to cross the street when a gang of boys would come to take his milk money, He would wrap it in his sock to hide it. They didn't see him.
2. Don asked God who he should date, "I saw the finger of God pointing in a certain direction right in front of me." He asked God, "Who is over there?" There were two girls he knew, but then he thought, "Ah, Hanya, yes!"
3. When my father asked me the next day what happened about breaking up with Don, the Lord gave me these words, "When I date those other boys they don't understand what I'm saying, but Don does." My father did not say anything after that. I didn't plan those words at all, they were from God.

3

Ancestors

Our children will also serve him. Future generations
will hear about the wonders of the Lord.
Psalm 22:30

Many of our Russian people left Russia between 1904 and 1912 and came to Los Angeles, California. They suffered tremendous persecution for their religion, refusing to bow to the Russian Orthodox church's rules and practices.

They were called Molokane, derived from the Russian word 'milk,' since they refused to adhere to the fasts of the Russian Orthodox Church by eating dairy foods, and were called heretics.

Courts were few, so the priests and police governed the people. Children were taken from their parents and put in foster homes to indoctrinate them in the orthodox ways. Tortured, imprisoned, and killed, many were sent to remote villages in the Caucasus mountains. They called themselves 'Spiritual Christian Holy Jumpers.'

The word 'Pahot,' refuge, is used for finding a place of destiny, away from the subjection of evil. A haven from harm until the second coming of Christ. Prophecies were given by a relative of mine in Russia regarding this exodus to America.

A story I once heard was that one wealthy woman from Long Beach, California, had a word from God to give property to these people coming from Russia. The property was oil-rich land in Signal

Hill located in Long Beach. Our Molokan Sect was very exclusive and did not trust many people as they had not been treated well in Russia or on their difficult travels to the United States. Some died along the way and their meager amount of money was gone from the bribes they had to pay along the difficult journey. They refused this property, which still contains five million barrels of recoverable oil. The field was enormously productive in the 1920s with hundreds of oil derricks covering Signal Hill.

The Molokan people settled in the 'Flats' area of Los Angeles, which had many factories for jobs for the new immigrants.

My Father

Peter Michael Metchikoff was born in Russia on July 25, 1909, and died in La Puente, California, on October 18, 1966. He is buried in the New Molokan Cemetery in Commerce, California.

About two years after Don and I married, my father died of brain cancer from breathing in creosote, a caustic chemical that burned his nose and caused cancer that went to his brain. Our family was very secretive; I did not realize the seriousness of his illness and was not told of his prognosis. I told Don I felt he had six months to live, when in fact, it was three weeks. We were called to come visit my father one evening and were there when the ambulance came and took him to the hospital; he died later that night. Family secrets are hard on children, and I have had to forgive family members, time and time again.

My father died when he was 57 years old. His funeral lasted three days and included a night viewing, prayers, an all-night vigil, a morning funeral, and three evening memorial services. The memorial services included prayers, singing, speaking, and a four-course feast. Russian Molokan people came from many places throughout the three days. One thing I learned upon the death of my father and in my grieving is that the mere presence of caring friends aand family brings solace even in their silence.

I loved my father; he was a good man and was one of the peacemakers in our church. He visited the sick, counseled people, and was a great man of compassion. I remember going with him when he visited an elderly couple caring for their adult daughter, Sadie. She had a very young spirit, and it was sad for me to see her bedridden in the living room. My father would visit them, often bringing food, companionship, and laughter. I remember singing in Russian for them. I saw what we did when we brought joy into their home, and it left a deep impression on me.

Peter Michael Metchikoff

When I was dating Don, I told him of an adopted auntie that my parents raised. That's when Don told me that my father was adopted too. I was surprised and told him that my father wasn't, but he said everyone knew it. Well, it was true—another family secret. My maternal grandfather told me that his adoptive parents, Michael Evanich Metchikoff and Hanya Evanova (Kobzeff), who had no children, were coming to America and that my father's birth mother had died.

My father's birth father had other children and was remarrying a

woman who also had several children. He felt it would be a good idea to give my father a good chance at life by giving him to this childless couple who were coming to America. As far as I know, my father was about a year old when he came to America. This is the story told to me by my grandfather. This was a family secret, but not really, as my father called his adoptive mother

My father as a child with his adoptive parents, Michael Evanich Metchikof and Hanya Evanovna (Kobzeff) Metchikoff

'mom druhoi' and his father 'pop druhoi'. 'Druhoi' means 'other' in Russian.

My father, Peter, became a real estate broker, supporting his parents who lived with us. My father's mother had relatives who were originally from Russia but then moved to Persia (now Iran). My father sponsored his mother's relatives to come to the U.S. When I was three, I remembered a lot of people in our house staying with us for quite a while. To be a sponsor, a person needed to be responsible for the immigrants either until they became a U.S. citizen, or until the immigrant earned approximately ten years of credited work toward Social Security.[7] We owned rental property in Los Angeles, and my father put them up for a time. It was a hard time for them, as these family members could not work in their professions as before and could only qualify for manual labor.

ПЕТР МИХ. МЕЧНИКОВ

Pete Metchikoff

Licensed Real Estate Broker

NOTARY PUBLIC   COLLECTIONS

Phone ANgelus 12489

39 North Ditman Ave.   Los Angeles 33, Calif.

My father's business card

As a teenager, I remember taking rental phone calls at home and helping my father with paperwork in our home office. I soon became tired of our tenants and their complaints and was glad to be marrying Don. A funny story is that my father highly respected his escrow officer and he would always ask my mother for some goat cheese or a little gift to give to her. As a little girl, I wondered how my father could have a girlfriend and be married! He wanted me to become an escrow officer like her or to become a linguist as I spoke a little Spanish and Russian.

My Mother

My mother Hazel Trofimivna Evanoff, daughter of Joe Evanoff (Kulikoff) and Anna Evanoff (Klubniken) was born on December 22, 1914, in Phoenix, Arizona. She died on March 24, 1986, in Western Australia and was brought to Los Angeles, California, to be buried next to my father at the New Molokan Cemetery. She never stopped grieving the loss of my father even though suitors would call her.

My parents, Hazel (Hanya) Trofimivna Metchikoff and Peter Michael Metchikoff, at Hollenbeck Park in Los Angeles

My father and mother married on November 12, 1933, in Los Angeles, California. My mother was called by her Russian name, Hanya.

A memory I had of my mother was that she was always tired caring for a family of ten, with the daily duties of cooking and housekeeping. I remember watching as she nursed my baby brother, born when I was only 18 months old, and remembered that I was still feeling very needy of her myself.

My father would take us children to the beach or Glen Ivy Hot Springs on laundry day, so my mother would be alone to enjoy the quiet as she worked. Even though my father bought her a new clothes dryer, she loved hanging everything out to dry enjoying the breeze and the smell of sunshine on the clothing as they dried.

My father would also help by taking charge of getting all of us off to school in the mornings so she could rest after fixing many lunches.

My mother would stay home from church often to prepare lunch for the widows my father would bring to our home after church. He would drive them back to Los Angeles in the late afternoon.

My Maternal Grandfather

My grandparents, after being married only three weeks, left for America along with the rest of the Tolmachoff family. My grandmother immigrated to the United States as a daughter of the Tolmachoffs. The group arrived in Galveston, Texas, and the authorities wanted to send my grandfather back because he didn't have money to enter. One of the women took a $25 gold piece out of her sock to pay his entrance fee. My grandmother came in free as the daughter of the Tolmachoffs. Grandfather became lonely after two years in America and wanted to go back to Russia, but he chose to stay instead.

As a younger man, my grandfather had to run across borders within Russia to escape serving in the army. He, along with a few other young men, ran during the night, hiding in ditches and being shot at. They had to pay off border guards using all the money they had with them. One of the young men in their group was shot and killed.

My grandfather, Joe Trofim Evanoff (right), his wife,
Onya (Klubniken), together with my grandfather's
sister, Masha (left), and her husband Petro Alexeivich
Tolmachoff, who had recently married

During my grandfather's later years, his brother, Taras, who worked for the Russian government, stayed in touch with him. Taras invited my grandfather and my mother to visit him in Moscow, promising them V.I.P. treatment. However, they declined the invitation, fearing what might happen to them because Communism was still in effect.

My Maternal Great-Grandfather

Taras Evanoff was originally a Kulikoff. His first wife was Dunya Nikolaivna Barisoff, granddaughter of Lukian Petrovich Sokoloff, also known as Barisoff, who was a martyr for the Lord. It is said that for his belief in Jesus and the Holy Spirit, he was in prison 62 times. When great-grandfather was a young boy, he broke horses for the military. Taras and Dunya had five children: Onya, Efeem, Trofim (my grandfather), Masha, and Taras. He died in 1858 when he was 105 years old and had four wives throughout his lifetime.

The Galitzen Family Line

Lithuanian coat of arms [8]

"Astride my brave, lightning steed, galloping across hills and mountains, I reach everywhere, indeed! My youth, my carefree youth! Where am I rushing? Where am I flying? Soon old age will be upon me, I should live more wisely and take life more slowly."[9] (Prince Vladimir M. Golitsyn).

Don and I always thought we were Russian until we gifted one another a D.N.A. test for Christmas. What a surprise it was to discover that we both had a high percentage of Lithuanian ancestry. If you look for the country of Lithuania, you will see it borders Russia and there is a Russian enclave near the border. Peter I of Russia permitted the Golitsyns to incorporate the emblem of the Grand Duchy of Lithuania into their coat of arms (pictured above).[10]

Galitzen History and Facts

The Golitsyn "Russian noble family descended from the 14th-century Lithuanian grand duke Gediminas. Three members played prominent roles as statesmen around the time of Peter I the Great (r. 1682–1725).

Vasily Golitsyn was chief adviser to Peter's regent, Sophia Alekseyevna.

Boris Golitsyn (1654–1714) was court chamberlain (1676) and Peter's tutor; he participated in the coup that placed Peter on the throne and was associated with the major achievements of Peter's early reign. Peter dismissed him after his despotic rule of a province in the lower Volga resulted in a major revolt.

Dmitry Golitsyn (1665–1737) held several posts under Peter from 1697 but opposed Peter's reforms and in 1724 was deprived of all public duties. In 1727, he became a member of the Supreme Privy Council, which governed for Peter II until his death (1730). He urged the council to offer the throne to Anna Ivanovna if she would sign a set of conditions transferring crucial prerogatives to the council. She initially agreed, then dissolved the council. He was condemned to death (1736) for his anti-autocratic beliefs, but Anna commuted his sentence to life imprisonment."[11]

"Anna Petrovna was the fourth child of the future Catherine I of Russia and Peter the Great. Although Anna was the fourth child and second daughter born to the couple, none of her older siblings survived infancy."[12]

"The House of Golitsyn or Galitzine was a Russian princely family. Among them were boyars, warlords, diplomats, generals, admirals, stewards, chamberlains, and provincial landlords. By the 18th century, the family was divided into four major branches. One branch died out while the other three and their subdivisions contained about 1,100 members.[13]

In the 1850s the Russian memoirist Filipp Vigel despaired: "So numerous are the Golitsyns that soon it will be impossible to mention any of them without the family tree at hand."[14]

"Of the numerous branches of the princely family that existed in 1917, only one survived in the Soviet Union; all others were extinguished or forced into exile. The Bolsheviks arrested dozens of Golitsyns only to be shot or killed in the Gulag; dozens disappeared in the storm of the revolution and the Russian Civil War, and their fate remained unknown."[15]

I have noticed that the name Galitzen has various spellings according to the country where people migrated. You will find it spelled Golitsyn, Gallitzin (Netherlands), Galitzine (French), Galitzin (German), Golicyn (Italian), or Golitsin (Spanish).

Gallitzin Borough on December 2, 1873, being named after Prince Demetrius Augustine Gallitzin, is situated atop the Allegheny Mountains, surrounded by Gallitzin Township and Tunnelhill Borough.[16] Prince Gallitzin State Park in Pennsylvania is named after Father Demetrius Augustine Gallitzin. Born in Holland (Netherlands) on December 22, 1770; he was the only son of Prince

Dimitri Alexievitch Gallitzin, Russian Ambassador to Holland, and his wife Amalia Von Schmettau Gallitzin.[17]

"Vir est Vis", or "man himself is power", is the Golitsyn family motto.[18] We do not claim this motto in our family line since Christ is our all in all.

Don's Father

Dave Galitzen served in WWII.

Dave Galitzen was born in Los Angeles, California, on December 17, 1912, while his parents lived at 150 S. Utah Street in Los Angeles.

Don's father, David Michael Galitzen, served as a translator during World War II due to his knowledge of the Russian language. He arrived in Europe three days after the invasion, serving under General George Patton, Jr.

Most of the men from our faith were conscientious objectors, meaning they would not serve in the war for religious reasons, one of which was not to bear arms. Don's father chose to serve and before leaving for war, he was given a formal prayer and a handkerchief that was prayed over by the Russian church.

Everywhere Don's father went, he was protected. As the troops were divided, some being sent to one area of combat and others going in another direction, he was always in the group that was neither killed nor wounded. Dave came back unscathed, except for the shell shock, or PTSD as it's called today. He was always protected, and I believe it's because of the prayed-over handkerchief he always carried with him.

He brought back some spoils of war; a sword was one of the items, but it was stolen when he put it down in Los Angeles to make a phone call.

Don's father's emotional issues from the war caused distress in their home during his childhood. Many young Christian men ministered to Don in his youth, taking him to retreats where he found Jesus. This mentoring experience impacted Don greatly, and he continues to have a heart for the youth.

Don's Mother

Vera Sasha Shubin was born on April 17, 1913, in Los Angeles, California. Her parents were living at 121 S. Clarence Street in Los Angeles at the time of her birth.

Don's mother was educated until the eighth grade. She became very entrepreneurial, went to beauty school, and owned and managed five beauty shops. The last was called The Leading Lady, in Monterey Park, California.

She first went to Los Angeles Trade Technological College for dress design and loved it, but her instructor crossed lines into her personal life; nothing happened, but she left and pursued a hairdressing career. Fashion design was her love; she always dressed fashionably and pursued design at home, I remember her matching beautiful laces together. She also invested in the stock market and real estate by purchasing three units in East Los Angeles, and after the war built three more on the property.

Don's parents, David Michael Galitzen and Vera Sasha Galitzen, in East Los Angeles

Don's mother was the oldest of ten children, and helping raise them turned her into a very capable woman. With her husband, Dave, away at war, she worked and kept the home fires burning.

Passionate about nutrition, she gifted us with gigantic jars of vitamins and enrolled us in a 12-week course in Pasadena with Nathan Pritikin. There, we learned about the benefits of a no-fat diet and attended cooking demonstrations. With these gifts came expectations that we would adhere to what we learned. Through my mother-in-law, I joined the Pasadena Nutrition Society where I heard noteworthy speakers such as Adele Davis, *Let's Have Healthy Children,*[19] Linus Pauling, 'the Vitamin C Guru', and others.

Sometimes Vera cooked delectable meals, but then she would bring us meatloaf made with ground meats like beef, liver, and heart—what an awful gift!

Vera passed away at ninety-six and looked beautiful even at her death. I loved my mother-in-law, and she dearly loved me.

Don's Paternal Grandfather

Don's grandfather, Mike Galitzen (*photo*), was born in Russia. He was 27 when Don's father was born. He was the head preacher of "Milikoi" church, one of the large Russian churches in Los Angeles, and we inherited the Bible, which was more than 200 years old, that had laid in the church.

Don's Paternal Grandmother

Don's grandmother, Hazel (Hanya) Orloff Galitzen, was born in Russia. She was 25 years old when Don's father was born. Don would go there after Sunday school, and he remembers her making hamburger drumsticks with a chicken leg bone.

Vera's Father, Don's Maternal Grandfather

Andrew Evanich (John) Shubin was born in Russia and died suddenly in his late forties.   On October 2, 1911, Andrew (18) married Alexandra (Sarah or Sasha) Vasilivna Shubin (15).

Andrew Evanich Shubin and his groomsmen

Vera's father, Andrew, owned the Russian market, Shubin's Store, on Clarence Street in Los Angeles (*photo*) and was a butcher. He and his family lived above the store. He died in his late forties, leaving Sarah with ten children to raise. The Russian people who owed the store money told her that those bills were buried with him. Don's mother Vera, the eldest child, knew she needed to provide for herself at a young age and that led her to become a business-woman, having only finished eighth grade.

Vera's Mother, Don's Maternal Grandmother

Alexandra (Sarah or Sasha) Vasilivna Vedenoff Shubin was born in Russia on May 4, 1897, and died on June 30, 1985, in Los Angeles, California. Sarah was 88 years old when she died of heart failure and is buried in the New Molokan Cemetery. Sarah's father, Don's great-grandfather, was Vasily V. Vedenoff and was born in Russia.

Sarah's mother's maiden name was Tanya Belikoff. Her mother died when she was a young woman and her father remarried a woman named Orloff, who had children of her own, which made Sarah feel like a stepchild.

Vera's mother, Sarah, had four brothers, Nick, John, Stephen, and Bill. Stephen tragically died of electrocution as a young man after a worker instructed him to cut an electrical line. The man had such remorse over Stephen's death that he served Sarah for the rest of his life.

4

Infertility

There are three things that are never
satisfied . . . The barren womb is one.

Proverbs 30:15-16

Instead of your shame you will have a double portion,
and instead of humiliation they will shout for joy over
their portion. Therefore, they will possess a double
portion in their land. Everlasting joy will be theirs.

Isaiah 61:7 NASB

After being married for a year, we thought it would be time to start a family, which ended up not working very well. I was raised with the assumption that I would marry, become a homemaker and a mother, but education was never factored in. After a year, I finally got pregnant, only to have a miscarriage at two months.

About a year later, I became pregnant again and had another miscarriage! Oh my, I thought, this is really happening to me. All my friends were having babies! I was being left behind. I prayed for every pregnant woman I knew every night to alleviate my sorrow, even praying for them through their deliveries.

As I compare myself to Hannah's plight in the Bible, reading of her barrenness and grief, I relate to how hard it was for her to go with her husband each year to celebrate God's abundant provisions, blessings, and goodness.

I don't know why I ever went to church on Mother's Day, when they invited each mother to stand and be rewarded with a rose. For 11 years, I felt as Hannah did: embarrassed, humiliated, and very barren, with all to see me sitting and not standing. Another miscarriage.

I was a praying woman and, at 21, prayed to God about the miscarriages and having a child. I had a dream that night that a car was driving into the driveway of the home where I grew up. The car was driven by Don's mother, Vera, and in the back seat was a little boy, about 18 months old, looking just like Don. The little boy was looking at me, and as I looked at him, I thought, "Are you for me?" He nodded. When I woke up, I was so excited, until a few days later, I realized he was brought to me! I didn't have him myself.

I then prayed to God that if, by the time I was 30, I didn't have a child, I would consider adopting. That would likely mean the child would not be Russian. I decided that if we adopted, we would not raise the child in our community, as he would be looked upon as 'ne-nash'—not ours. Families would not allow their daughters to date him, and rejection was not my wish for a beautiful child fresh from heaven.

Don and I began the long road of infertility intervention, which was very discouraging and painful, both physically and emotionally.

Still being in the Russian church, we called the elders to our home for formal prayer, which would include a four-course meal. During the prayer, one of the elders, a prophet, came to us crying and asked for one of the women to bring him salt.

Salt was used as a healing agent in the Bible:

> *Then the men of the city said to Elisha, "Look, this city is in a pleasant place, as my lord [Elisha] sees; but the water is bad and the land is barren." He said, "Bring me a new jar, and put*

salt in it." So they brought it to him. Then Elisha went to the spring of water and threw the salt in it and said, "Thus says the Lord: 'I [not the salt] have purified and healed these waters; there shall no longer be death or barrenness because of it'" (2 Kings 2:19-22 AMP).

It was comforting to be prayed for by the leaders of our church.

My doctor was Dr. Nakamoto, who was the head of the women's floor at White Memorial Hospital in Los Angeles. He had studied with Dr. Patrick Steptoe, a pioneer in fertility treatment.[20]

I had so many temperature charts from tracking my fertility that I could have wallpapered an entire room with them. I took pills that caused me physical problems, a half-hour-long injection, and several surgeries. One was an exploratory surgery after eight long, hard years of trying to conceive. There was hope when I would conceive, then depression when I would lose that pregnancy, as well as monthly discouragement when nothing happened at all.

I felt very forgotten by God and took on the belief that other young women were more valuable to Him than I was. I now know these were lies put there by the enemy, fitting my circumstances, and in my low state, they were easy to embrace.

How long, Lord? Will You forget me forever? How long will You hide Your face from me? How long must I wrestle with my thoughts and day after day have sorrow in my heart? How long will my enemy triumph over me? (Psalm 13:1-2 NIV).

In the Old Testament, there were many who felt forgotten by God. But God remembered so many:

- God remembered Noah, and the waters receded (Genesis 8:1).
- God remembered His covenant promise to Abraham, Isaac, and Jacob (Exodus 2:25).

- God remembered Rachel and opened her womb (Genesis 30:22).
- God remembered Hagar when she was lost in the wilderness; He saw her, spoke to her, and she named Him *El Roi*, the God who sees (Genesis 21).
- God remembered the thief on the cross: *"I assure you, today you will be with me in paradise" (Luke 23:43).*

After joining a powerful Bible study in my early twenties, I went home, knelt at my bedside, and gave God three things. One of those things was giving up my desire to have a child of my own and opening up to adoption.

"Lord," I thought, "What were they—the babies of my miscarriages?" I hadn't understood or thought about the embryos experiencing life and then dying. As I drove to Bible study one day, the sky was full of the largest white clouds, and I asked the Lord, "What were they?" He answered me as I was driving on the freeway, "You have three extra blessings waiting for you in heaven." This was such a delightful surprise that I never thought of before.

When I was 30, we had been married for 11 years, much of that time grieving the empty childless years, the painful procedures, surgeries, and miscarriages. I remember reading in the Bible where King David groaned. I immediately related to his groaning, and it helped me realize for the first time that I was not alone, that someone else grieved the way I had. Don and I had talked about leaving the country and living somewhere else in the world, but we realized that would not solve anything; we would be taking ourselves with us.

I needed a lot of encouragement during this time and was led to a scripture one day that reminded me of the promises of God.

Promises from God are for everyone; they are for those who are defective in different ways, as most of us are.

> *And don't let the eunuchs say, "I'm a dried-up tree with no children and no future." For this is what the Lord says: I will bless those eunuchs who keep my Sabbath days holy and who choose to do what pleases me and commit their lives to me. I will give them—within the walls of my house—a memorial and a name far greater than sons and daughters could give. For the name I give them is an everlasting one. It will never disappear! (Isaiah 56:3b-5).*

In the Bible, Jacob got very angry at his wife Rachel when she said, *"Give me children, or I'll die" (Genesis 30:1).* Jacob might have thought she was blaming him and came to the conclusion that he wasn't enough to satisfy her. He too was grieving, since a man without children is also barren.

According to Hebrew teaching, a woman has two purposes:

One purpose is revealed through the Hebrew word *ishah.* "In the Hebrew Bible's book of Genesis, the Hebrew for man is *ish* and woman is *ishah* because Eve was 'taken out of' the man's side:"[21] *"This is now bone of my bones and flesh of my flesh; she shall be called 'woman,' for she was taken out of man" (Genesis 2:23b NIV).*

Woman has a second Hebrew word *havah,* meaning "the mother of all living," or "life." Someone said barrenness affords "an extra ability." Many women never marry and do not become the *Havah,* the mother part of a woman. She can then pursue the *Ishah* woman and other areas of life more fully, as mentioned in Proverbs 31. There is a lot of purpose in being a woman outside of marriage and motherhood. The blessing will come as stated in Isaiah: *"I will bless those eunuchs who keep my Sabbath days holy and who choose to do what pleases me and commit their lives to me" (Isaiah 56:4).*

Proverbs 31:14-27 says:

She finds wool and flax and busily spins it.

She is like a merchant's ship, bringing her food from afar.

She gets up before dawn to prepare breakfast for her household and plan the day's work for her servant girls.

She goes to inspect a field and buys it;

With her earnings she plants a vineyard.

She is energetic and strong, a hard worker.

She makes sure her dealings are profitable;

Her lamp burns late into the night.

Her hands are busy spinning thread, her fingers twisting fiber.

She extends a helping hand to the poor and opens her arms to the needy.

She has no fear of winter for her household, for everyone has warm clothes.

She makes her own bedspreads.

She dresses in fine linen and purple gowns.

Her husband is well known at the city gates, where he sits with the other civic leaders.

She makes belted linen garments and sashes to sell to the merchants.

She is clothed with strength and dignity, and she laughs without fear of the future.

When she speaks, her words are wise, and she gives instructions with kindness.

She carefully watches everything in her household and suffers nothing from laziness.

I went to a conference on abortion at my church. I've never had one but wanted to learn about ministering to people who did. During worship, I began a gentle weeping which turned into gigantic sobbing, and I knew what it was—it was all the pent-up grieving I never had the chance to release. There was not enough tissue for me, and I could not believe how much tissue I needed—my nose just kept flowing. I was being delivered from my grief!

I learned I had carried not only life in my womb but also death in the nonviable fetuses. A miscarriage is called a spontaneous abortion. I received prayer to remove the spirit of death from me, and I learned I could name my babies. The Lord gave me three boys' names.

When I was recovering from exploratory surgery in the early seventies, the young girl in the bed next to me had an abortion, and they had to remove her ovary on that side. All I heard as I healed from my own surgery was loud, foul language as she was so angry and sad. On about the fifth day, she looked at me and said, "This bothers you, doesn't it?" I said it was her side of the room. We became friends, Rosie and I. I told her I was a Christian, and we talked about God. I prayed with her to accept Jesus, and she did. She had someone bring her grandfather's Bible to the hospital. God always provides joy in our suffering, especially when we look for it over and above our own. Rosie was my first convert.

After much treatment for infertility, a Pentecostal friend of Don's family, Stella Bogdanoff, came to my mother-in-law, Vera, sometime in the summer of 1975 and told her that we would be having a child in October. Mom told her, "She's not even pregnant." One day, as Vera was walking on the beach, she found a small toy car in the sand and took that as a sign that we would have a baby.

Vera, my dear, dear mother-in-law, was in my dream driving the little boy to me. She played a major part in the adoption process and stayed by our side throughout her entire life, raising him with us. Always there, always loving. A woman totally different than I, but stoutly loyal. She loved me and only wanted me to care for her in her last years. Vera died at 96 years old, although a strong woman, she and I had a sweet bond of love. I remembered Ruth's devotion to her mother-in-law and pledged in my heart her declaration, *"Wherever you go, I will go; wherever you live, I will live. Your people will be my people, and your God will be my God" (Ruth 1:16).*

On the first of October, I received a phone call from my infertility doctor that there was a child to be born from a marriage, and that this child was for us. I remembered my prayer of adopting by the time I was 30 and the dream I had about a little boy being brought to us. I knew the answer was yes but told him we would pray over the weekend. He said he would not tell the attorney yet so we could decide.

It is interesting how the attorney chose to call our doctor about a baby, and then he chose us. When the attorney got the call about a white, drug-free child from a marriage, to be born in two months from a woman in Michigan, he took his files of people who were candidates for this child. Unbeknownst to us, our doctor had this attorney make a file on us, and it sat in his office for ten years! The attorney opened the first file on the top—it was two doctors who had been married for ten years. Then he went to the next file, which was ours. He remembered that he owed Dr. Nakamoto, our infertility doctor, a favor. He called him, and Dr. Nakamoto immediately said, "The Galitzens," and he then called us. Our baby was due in six weeks.

Don and I had originally been planning to visit my sister, who lives in Australia. I prayed that morning that if God wanted us to go, I would find the Samsonite luggage I wanted. I took my mother with me, and we did not find the luggage. We then went to another sister's house for lunch, and that is when the phone call from my doctor came, telling me of this child to be born. He said, "This child is for us." We would not be going to Australia.

As we began to let the family know, the mixed reaction began. A brother-in-law came to my home while I was alone and said, "I come in love to tell you we will form a family 'spevka' (an evening singing Russian songs) without you on purpose, so you will know how it will feel to be excluded if you adopt this child." I smoothly got up, ushered him to the door, and told him, "That kind of love I don't need."

The family 'spevka' took place every Friday night, but while the meeting took place, special things would happen for us while we stayed home. One woman crocheted her very first baby blanket and brought it over as a gift. Another Friday night, the baby furniture was delivered, and yet on another Friday evening, a special friend came to visit.

Another friend said to us, "God has chosen not to bless you, and you should just accept it." A brother with six children compared us with another couple who lived happily without children and told us to "just accept it." An uncle of Don's told him, "You have grounds to divorce her."

Don and I called each elder of our church and went to speak to them individually, and most agreed that if we christened the baby in the church and raised him in the Molokan fashion, that would be fine. Some of my family did not agree. A brother of mine held a prestigious position in the church, and many people honored his viewpoint. Even my born-again family members, living just blocks away, took two weeks to come visit us after our baby arrived. A very bittersweet experience after waiting 11 years for a child.

When we spoke to our Russian preacher, he told us that he would christen our baby, but when we approached him about it after our child was born, he told us to go ask the associate preacher, which we did, but he never got back to us either. We did not beg.

There were also rumors from Australia that we were adopting a child of color, but this was a white, blue-eyed baby from a marriage.

All of a sudden, eight Russian churches in the Los Angeles area held meetings to make a new rule prohibiting non-Russian children from being christened within the faith. One elder, who led the Bible study group we attended, told us that some members (including cousins of mine) wouldn't receive us since we were adopting a "ne-nash" child. He stopped teaching the group and then offered to come to our home to privately dedicate our baby. As kind as he was, Don and I decided that our child would not become part of our church through the back door.

I prayed to God about how hard this waiting was for us, and the rejection we were facing was becoming stronger. God allowed our baby boy to be born two weeks early. Our doctor's brother-in-law, who was also the delivery doctor, kept the birth mother, Sherrie, in his home for the final two weeks before the birth. He never charged us. If she had given birth in Michigan, our baby would have to go through a state adoption process. A miracle was that airlines usually don't allow pregnant women to fly in the last few weeks of pregnancy, but she flew to California, and we never knew who paid for her flight. We were never charged for the flight, the stay, or the hospital and delivery.

We did have a group of Christian friends who stood by us during this time and kept us strong.

God had a bigger plan than we could have ever dreamed of. Sometimes, when we love something and give it up for God, He gives it back to us with a surprising twist of richness that we never expected. Deciding to adopt and the pain of rejection from many people opened the doors of the Kingdom to us around the world. I often tell our son that he was the key to our freedom.

It was hard trying to walk in love toward those who spoke against us and judged us, yet we still needed to interact with them in our lives and show God's grace. Jesus always walked in love—not just when people were praising Him and honoring His ministry, but also when He was bitterly rejected and mistreated.

"Who, when He was reviled, did not revile in return; when He suffered, He did not threaten, but committed Himself to Him who judges righteously" (1 Peter 2:23b NKJV).

In Luke 4:28-30, when the people of Nazareth tried to throw Jesus off a cliff, He simply walked through the midst of them.

Though Jesus was a man of sorrows, Charles Spurgeon says, "Down deep in His innermost soul He carried an inexhaustible treasury of refined and heavenly joy." And that "Christ had His songs, though it was night with Him; though His face was marred and His countenance had lost the luster of earthly happiness, yet sometimes it was lit up with a matchless splendor of unparalleled satisfaction."[22]

When we live committed to Christ and serving God, He will protect and bless whatever we do that glorifies Him, *"and the evil one cannot harm them" (1 John 5:18 NIV).*

Joseph said to his brothers,

"Do not be afraid, for am I in the place of God? But as for you, you meant evil against me; but God meant it for good" (Genesis 50:19-20a NKJV).

"I am the LORD your God, who brought you out of the land of Egypt" (Exodus 20:2a NKJV).

The Bible talks about God bringing His people out from Egypt, representing bondage, into the Promised Land, *He brought us out . . . to bring us in* (Deuteronomy 6:23 NIV).

After all tests were done regarding our infertility, the doctors told us there was nothing majorly wrong with either of us. There was one instance in my youth when I swung from a rope hanging from a tree and was hit squarely in my lower abdomen by a homemade, tall water faucet with a pointy end. I remember my mother asking the doctor, "Will she be able to have children?" He answered, "I don't know."

I believe we would not have discovered the abundant life in Jesus had we not faced 11 years of infertility. We truly believe that God allowed this course for our lives.

There have been many opportunities to forgive people involved in the opposition to our adopting a sweet, innocent baby. Forgiveness has since become one of my most powerful teachings.

> A pearl is a beautiful thing that is produced by an injured life. It is the tear that results from the injury of the oyster. The treasure of our being in this world is also produced by an injured life. If we had not been wounded, if we had not been injured, we would not produce the pearl.[23]

The story continues as our promise is born.

God Sightings

1. God placed Rosie in my room while I healed from surgery, and I was able to bring her to Jesus—my first convert.
2. My dream of a baby being brought to me by Vera.
3. At 30 years old, the call from my doctor when he said, "This baby is for you."
4. The attorney holding our file for ten years and choosing it, and us not even knowing a file ever existed.
5. Sherrie was allowed by the airline to fly here to give birth in her ninth month.
6. We were never charged for the flight, the stay, or the hospital and delivery.

5

A Blessing in Disguise

*To all who mourn in Israel, he will give a crown of
beauty for ashes, a joyous blessing instead of
mourning, festive praise instead of despair.*
Isaiah 61:3

*"Sing, O barren one, who did not bear; break forth into
singing and cry aloud, you who have not been in labor!
For the children of the desolate one will be more than
the children of her who is married," says the LORD.*
Isaiah 54:1 ESV

Hallelujah! Our child, Aaron Donald Galitzen, was born on October 31, 1975. On November 3, 1975, on a rainy, foggy morning, we waited at John Wayne Airport in Orange County, California, for an extra two and a half hours due to the weather. We then flew into San Leandro to pick up our three-day-old baby boy. Aaron's birth mother, Sherrie, wanted to hold him and spend a few days with him before we took him home.

As soon as we arrived, we told the airline desk that we were returning on the next flight with a three-day-old baby. However, we were told we couldn't do that because babies needed to be eight days old to fly. I showed her our diaper bag and told her that was all we had brought.

We first met our baby when a nurse brought him to us and unwrapped him for us to examine. All I saw were fingers and toes—somewhere I had heard you were supposed to count them.

The delay from Orange County caused us to arrive during the hospital administration workers' lunch hour. When we checked out, there was no one at the window to tell us how much we owed, so we carried our baby out, expecting that they would mail the bill to us. Later, we found out that the doctor who delivered Aaron was my infertility doctor's brother-in-law, who had housed Sherrie in the days before Aaron was born and didn't charge us.

What an enormous experience it was bringing Aaron home. When we returned to the airport, the flight plan had been changed to accommodate us. This flight would not be stopping in San Jose as planned, which was a miracle and a grace to protect Aaron's little ears. The announcement on the plane was that it would be a non-stop flight for the comfort of some of the passengers.

Aaron had jaundice from being born two weeks early, and we were told we needed to take him for a bilirubin test that evening. His sucking ability was a bit weak, so we immediately went to the hospital where Don worked as a clinical laboratory scientist and had them run the test.

Our great support came from my mother-in-law, Vera, who lived in Monterey Park but later moved right next door to us. As Aaron grew, Vera would take him on walks in his stroller with his bag of "junk food." Cauliflower was called "popcorn," carrots were "french fries," broccoli was "trees," and cabbage leaves were "potato chips." Vera would also fill an old paint can with water, give Aaron a brush, and say, "Let's paint the fence." What a wonderful, fun grandmother she was.

My own mother lived a block away but only came over when I told her Aaron was constipated. I had been preparing a goat's milk formula from a book by Adele Davis called *Let's Have Healthy Children*,[19] but I had put too much of something in it. She came right away and gave him an old-fashioned Carnation Milk enema, and it worked. I knew the pressure my mother was under from my family regarding our adoption, but I continued calling her every day as usual, keeping the communication open.

When Aaron was four months old, we received a phone call from an attorney saying that his birth father wanted him back. Apparently, he had never signed the release papers, and Aaron was from a marriage. For 18 months, we had to go to court four times, not knowing if he would be taken from us. The stress was immeasurable.

After the phone call, I immediately began to pull back my attachment to Aaron, but only for a moment. This was so hard after all we'd been through with my family and the church. A prophetic Christian man advised us not to rush to begin legal proceedings, since after a year, if the father hadn't contributed a dollar in support, it would be considered an abandonment issue.

This was agonizing for us, so I went to my knees and prayed to God, asking for Aaron to be returned to where he was supposed to go—his birth father, or so I thought. However, I had heard from God earlier that Aaron was meant to be ours. God confirmed this by giving me a specific vision of a very large hand moving people from one place to another around the United States, saying, "It is for me to put people where they belong." That was my answer: Aaron would be ours for sure, although the battle was long and very emotional for us.

In the end, the court's decision was that it was in Aaron's best interest to be placed with us. Aaron was 20 months old. His birth father only wanted money, but I said our son would not be bought. Many years later, we heard that a relative of Aaron's had told his birth father, "He could get a lot of money from rich folks in California." Aaron's birth father was not a good man and tragically passed away at an early age.

The official adoption was finalized in May 1977 at the Santa Ana Courthouse, with the judge and our attorney present.

If you noticed, Aaron's birth date—October 31—is my least favorite holiday: Halloween. I said, "Boy, God, you are funny." There were many people who prayed for us all these years to have a baby, only to have him born on this date. We enjoyed Aaron's birthdays by inviting all our friends' children to celebrate with us, keeping them off the streets on Halloween. The children dressed up in costumes and went home with bags of goodies.

Aaron went to Joyful Noises Preschool, a church school. His teacher, Kim Sotel, chose to write an extensive report on Aaron's development for her degree in Early Childhood Development.

Friends of ours lived across the street from us, and they had a little boy named Daniel, who became one of Aaron's good friends. Aaron attended his first birthday party at age three for Matthew Belikoff, and they were friends for many years. Matthew's mother, June, gave Aaron his baby shower when he was six weeks old.

One day, I was sitting in a comfortable chair in our family room, and Aaron, who was three, came onto my lap and asked me what I was doing. I told him I was studying about Jesus and that one day, when he was old enough to understand, he would ask Jesus into his heart. He answered, "I stan" (understand). I again said, "When you are older" but then realized what I was doing. I asked him if he wanted to pray to ask Jesus into his heart, and he said yes. He prayed the sinner's prayer, accepting Jesus into his heart.

Aaron just loved Papa's (Don's) red Toyota pick-up truck. He would sing happily in the driver's seat and tell me that he would take his wife out to "dinnoo," I assumed, in a red pick-up truck. Such a sweet boy, following his daddy.

Aaron was dedicated to the Lord in May 1979, at four years old, at The Evangelical Free Church, where we attended for about 13 years.

Around six years old, Aaron seemed very antsy to me, but I didn't think it was ADHD or any other ailment. I just knew he didn't need another sport—he already played T-ball. I prayed for two weeks about what he needed, and one day, I noticed a store next to my hairdresser that sold art supplies and crafts. I had never been interested in that store before, but when I went in, I saw a class of children painting with oils and pastels. I just knew this was what Aaron needed, and I signed him up without any discussion with Don—that's how strongly I felt. Aaron was a natural artist and had the extra gift of impressionistic ability, much like Van Gogh. According to his art teacher, only one in fifty children has this gift. He took painting lessons from the age of seven through his high school years. He loved it, and it calmed him.

One day, when Aaron was seven, he came home with a violin. Teachers of music had come to his school. He was tested and determined to be gifted to play the violin, which was also his choice. He played the violin, switching to viola in tenth grade, and took lessons throughout high school. Although he never became an expert, one teacher told us, "It was very good for him."

Aaron attended Copre Christian School, a private school in Newport Beach. This school impacted him in more ways than we could have imagined. His teachers included: Miss Evans in kindergarten, Mr. Wilcoxson in first grade, Miss Duncan in second grade, Mr. Miashiro in third grade, Mrs. Letterman in fourth grade, Mr. Pickens in fifth grade, and Mr. Lindstrom in sixth grade.

Miss Duncan and Mr. Miashiro got married and invited every student in both their classes and their parents to their wedding at the Newport Bay Club. It was fun and must have been expensive—all the boys dressed in suits, and the girls wore their beautiful dresses for the teachers' wedding. The children sat in front and behaved exceptionally well, while the parents sat in the back.

In first grade, Aaron had to stay home one day because he had swallowed a rock! We had a potted plant upstairs with smooth black rocks, and he accidentally swallowed one. I lifted this big boy and ran down the stairs with him, ready to call 911. He seemed fine, but we were on 'rock watch' for several days. We had a wedding to attend, and when Aaron had to use the restroom, we had to explain the situation to a long line of people and go to the front. There were lots of snickers. Mr. Wilcoxson sent a nice get-well card that said, "Rock of Ages" with musical notes all around. Fun teachers. We never did find that rock!

When Aaron was eight, we were sitting in our church one Sunday when our pastor, Bob Thune (whose brother, John Thune, is a U.S. Senator for South Dakota and was recently elected the next Senate majority leader), announced a water baptism being held soon. Aaron said he wanted to be baptized. I told him, "When you're older and understand," but he replied, "I understand." I realized what I had done and signed him up. We went to the house where the baptism was being held. The pastor was in the pool and said, "Don, come baptize your son." Don's heart was touched, and he went into the water to baptize Aaron.

Around this time, Aaron and I were shopping in Mervyn's, a small department store, when he became angry at something. I think it was at me, and he shouted for all to hear, "You're not even my real mom." It was time for "the talk." When Don came home, we sat down with Aaron, who laid on the floor on his back, with his arm under his head and his leg crossed. Apparently, some kids had been making fun of him for being adopted. We explained God's plan for his life and ours, and how he came to be with us. He was satisfied with our discussion.

At nine, we secured a few tickets to the 1984 Olympics and went to a soccer match at East Los Angeles Junior College. Aaron hadn't been feeling very well for a while. He was lethargic and not eating much. We were with people whose son had recently had mononucleosis and thought that might be what Aaron had. We took him to Palm Springs, thinking rest and sun would help, and I had to spoon-feed him. Aaron had taken riding lessons for two weeks during the summer, and he could have caught something from the horses. It took a long time for Aaron to regain his strength.

The Junior Lifeguard program was a big part of Aaron's childhood from age nine until he became a captain at 17. I remember his first jump from the Huntington Beach pier when he was nine years old. He was excited and said it was fun. His lifeguard instructors were waiting for him in the water, and he said it was the highlight of his year.

Our church had an "Awana" program, where children learned scripture mixed with fun, and Don became a leader. Their motto and scripture are:

"Approved Workmen Are Not Ashamed."

"Work hard so you can present yourself to God and receive his approval. Be a good worker, one who does not need to be ashamed and who correctly explains the word of truth" (2 Timothy 2:15).

This group aimed to train children in the gospel and teach them to serve Christ. Don served as a group leader for Awana at the Evangelical Free Church from when Aaron was seven to ten years old. As a young boy, Aaron was very proud to have his father as one of the leaders.

Some of Aaron's trips were to Mexico to give away things along the way, and we also visited orphanages through our church trips.

One adventure we had together happened at Moaning Caverns in Northern California. Don and I went to my twenty-fifth high school reunion and won a free pass to this adventure. One Thanksgiving weekend, we decided to take advantage of our free gift. The Caverns were owned by my friend's family from school. I couldn't believe that, at 42, I was putting on the overalls and lighted helmet for this adventure. I'm claustrophobic, and we would be descending the height of the Statue of Liberty—305 feet—into the caverns. They call it rappelling.

We had to go down bottom-first, single file, with ropes tied all over us, descending through two narrow vertical caves. We descended 20 feet and continued another 20 feet. Have you ever been scared spitless? I was. We were about to enter the gigantic open cavern. Once we reached the ledge after our 40-foot descent, I remembered the guide saying, "When you reach the ledge, kick off right away, or you'll want to stay there." We kicked off and continued our descent. Our guide made us feel better when he told us the ropes were fixed so that the descent was controlled, though we didn't know that at the beginning. What a relief that was! By now we were in the gigantic cavern and could see how far down we still had to go.

Don, Aaron, and I rappelling at Moaning Caverns.

When we reached the bottom, we went spelunking below the surface. If you don't know what spelunking is, it's crawling like worms through narrow tunnels underground. Aaron was ten.

Aaron was enjoying all of it, while Don was very quiet. We reached the floor of the cavern and, with no hesitation, continued spelunking. I was claustrophobic, and my heart was pounding. I began crawling and scrambling to keep up with the person in front of me. Sometimes we needed to use our entire body to rise to the next level; I felt like a rat under there. Occasionally, we would come to a room where we could stand up. The rooms had names, and when our guide told us there were two rooms left—the Pancake Room and the Meat Grinder—I told him I was very satisfied with myself. My heart was popping out of my chest, and I was ready to leave. There were exit options along the way, although we had to crawl to them without the guide, and they were farther away than I thought.

Six of us were done, and Aaron, not very happy, was promised a special private adventure with the guide afterward. We weren't going to leave him there alone. The owner's son took Aaron through the Meat Grinder and the Pancake Room. He was so excited! I have never felt such pain, soreness, and bruising in my life. That evening, we had dinner with the owners. I could barely keep my eyes open and hardly said a word.

When Aaron was 14, he discovered his powerful changing voice. He became very boisterous. He was frustrated one day and yelled at me, "I want my freedom!" I took a moment to think about it and then said, "Well, you can't move out, so if you want to grow up, you will now be doing all your own laundry." He looked blankly at me, thinking this was not what I meant. We also had him move his furniture around any way he wanted. That was all I could think of to give him freedom at 14.

A great joy for both Aaron and Don was bowling together at the Fountain Valley Bowl. That went on for years.

Refugio Beach—when I think of that name, it brings up wonderful memories of camping every year with friends. What a fun time that was! We camped there before Aaron was born and again when Aaron was 3 until he was 15 years old. We all remember when Don would collect cans, and all the kids would go along with him to find these treasures. Don still collects bottles and cans and enjoys the dollars he gets. He's quite a frugal man.

Aaron attended Fulton Middle School in Fountain Valley, then Foutain Valley High School, where he discovered water polo and

swim team and was involved in these two sports through his senior year under coach Ray Bray. The water polo team went to Hawaii in the summer of 1992. Aaron also received a Heritage Club Scholarship in his senior year.

Aaron's high school senior picture

With high school came the social dances. In ninth grade, his first dance was with a very sweet girl. We had them, along with Aaron's friend and his date, over for dinner.

The funniest story was when Aaron and his date, along with his friend and his date (a sweet Mormon girl), came for dinner before they went to the Homecoming Dance. I didn't see the pictures for quite a while, but when I did, I realized his friend had switched girls during the evening. The Mormon girl had to be home very early, so they just arranged to have another girl ready for the rest of the evening. How about that!

Aaron was accepted to five universities, including UCI, UCLA, USC, and UC Santa Barbara, but decided on Loyola Marymount University, known for its business program, as he was a business major.

Sam

When Aaron was about 19, he met a young woman online through a friend from Nebraska, named Samatha (yes, that's how it's spelled) Jones. They conversed many times a week for a few years, and then she invited him to her prom, and Aaron went. Over time, this relationship developed, with several trips back to visit her.

A day after Don and I returned from a ministry trip to Sweden, Aaron called and said he wanted to come over and cook us dinner. This was unusual, but we missed him not living at home anymore. After we prayed and began to sit down, Don said, "You're having a baby!" Aaron was so relieved and said, "Yes," and told us they were going to get married. Remember, Don and I had never even met this girl yet. We flew her to California to meet us, and we liked her very much.

We helped prepare them for their marriage in June by purchasing her wedding dress and registering them at several stores.

We then flew out to Nebraska with Grandma Vera for Aaron and Sam's wedding, which was to be held on June 13, 1998. It was a nice church wedding. No one told us how to get to the wedding rehearsal, and we didn't go, although we were dressed and ready and waiting for someone to contact us! Don and I hosted the rehearsal dinner at a restaurant near our hotel afterward. I even brought tablecloths and had flower arrangements made for each table after we got to Nebraska.

Sam and Aaron flew home with us after the wedding. We had a small house for them to live in on 12th Street here in Huntington Beach.

Don and I hosted a reception for Aaron and Sam here in California for 125 people at the Costa Mesa Country Club, and it was very nice!

My dear friend Marian asked me to go with her on a four-day cruise to Mexico. I was so exhausted from all the drama that Don let me go, but I didn't think it was very fun. I was experiencing total exhaustion—physical, mental, and emotional. We shopped, ate, and rested. A different environment for me, with a loving friend, helped turn my head around in another direction.

Close friends from the Vineyard invited us to join them at their cabin in Upstate New York for a week. What beautiful people they were, and so mindful of our needs at the time. What fun we had—we rafted, picnicked, rested, and ate a lot!

Coby Aaron Galitzen arrived on November 30, 1998. Aaron continued at Loyola Marymount University, where he had been attending.

After some time, we all knew Sam needed to go back to Nebraska—her heart and interests were still there. They divorced after 18 months, and sadly, Coby went with her. It's hard to know what was the right thing to do.

Aaron continued to be a good father and went several times a year to pick up his infant son for his visitation and do an immediate return flight with babe in arms. We are so proud of him for claiming his son like that.

Sherrie

Aaron's birth mother, Sherrie, found us when Aaron was 25. I was the first to speak with her, and with my pen and paper in hand, I learned a lot of history—especially health history. She kept saying we all have heart issues, and no one lives past their early 50s. I kept telling her not to say that, but she did, and she died in her early 50s. I firmly believe words are powerful, and we need to guard our tongues—something is released into the atmosphere where spiritual darkness lives.

Aaron and Sherrie spoke together for the first time, and she told him her story and that she loved him. She found us when he was 18 but waited until he was older to call, feeling he would be more mature then.

I never believed in divorce and remarriage but came to realize one can be chronically sinning and hurting another in terrible ways. I also knew the fate of a vital, young man in his early twenties would be more open to sinning without a wife, and knew we had a graceful, forgiving Father.

Melissa

Aaron prayed this time for a wife, seeking God's perfect one, so Melissa Michelle Tompkins, a delicate, sweet young woman, was the one. Melissa and Aaron met where she worked in sales for Kinecta Credit Union. She was promoted to branch manager shortly thereafter and then worked in both Long Beach and finally Lakewood before leaving banking to start her career as a mom.

Don and I first met Melissa at Chuck E. Cheese for Coby's third birthday party. She came fashionably late to not detract from Coby's celebration. What a beautiful, classy woman she was.

When Melissa visited our home for the first time, she didn't make it past the entry hall until Don asked her about her relationship with Jesus. She was a Christian—yes, that's my man!

Aaron and Melissa were at our house two weeks before their wedding, and Aaron needed to speak with Coby's mother, Sam.

Melissa and Aaron on occasion of their engagement dinner

As he chatted and laughed with her, I asked Melissa, "How can you do this?" meaning marrying a man with a child and needing to be in contact with an ex-wife. "Because I couldn't." She answered calmly, "Because I love him, and I understand." Wow, what an asset she has been to our family.

Their wedding was in our backyard, with only family and very close friends—27 in all. We took the entire wedding party to the Hyatt Regency Hotel after the wedding for a grand dinner in The California Room. The next day, there was a Luau in our backyard for 100 people. It was very fun, with hula dancers arriving to surprise everyone.

Aaron and Melissa had two boys, Brendon and Dillon, making them a family of three boys, including Coby. When Coby was nine years old, Aaron was given sole custody of him. He and Melissa were aware that Brendon, being their firstborn, became a secondborn, so Brendon was given added assurance of his importance in their family.

Eventually, Aaron, Melissa, and the boys all went to meet Sherrie, Aaron's birth mother. I was sad to have to share him with another mom. The night before they left, Aaron called to reassure me that I was his real mom. Aaron saw how his life would have been and why God opened the doors for Don and me to adopt him—God's plans are perfect. Aaron came back from the visit more my son than ever; it was powerful. Realizing what God had done, my vision of the Lord's hand moving over the U.S., saying, "It is for Me to place people where they need to be," proved true.

We discovered that Aaron's birth grandfather on his mother's side was French Canadian. At his birth, we were told he was German, Norwegian, and Dutch—and for sure, he does have that fair complexion of a Viking, probably coming from his father's side.

Eventually, Sherrie and her present husband, "Pa," visited here, and it was very hard to share Aaron. She asked Aaron beforehand what Don's favorite meal was and made a meatloaf for him. As soon as I walked in the door, Sherrie grabbed me, gave me a big hug, and said, "You did a good job." Wow, that broke the ice and made it so much easier for me.

After that visit, I made Sherrie a scrapbook album of Aaron from his birth to the present day, with a photo of Don and me at the end. She cherished that book. Sadly, Sherrie did pass away in her early fifties as she had proclaimed, but before her passing, Aaron and Melissa were able to lead her to the Lord. Aaron's half-sister called Melissa and asked if she could keep the scrapbook album I had made for Sherrie all about Aaron's life. It was treasured by the family.

It was prophesied by a friend of our family that we would be surprised at what would happen in our family, which moves me to explain the wonderful work Aaron and Melissa do.

What a wonderful God we have in giving Aaron a second chance to begin again, forgiven for his mistakes. I think of rejoicing as the father of the prodigal son saw his son coming home. God is the Father, and according to scripture, He leaves the ninety-nine for the one.

"If a man has a hundred sheep and one of them wanders away, what will he do? Won't he leave the ninety-nine others on the hills and go out to search for the one that is lost?" (Matthew 18:12).

Aaron and Melissa began taking in many wonderful children whose parents were not fit to care for them. They now have six teenage boys living with them, only two of their own. We always wonder what's next. I tell them not to take any more in since I can't even remember my own grandsons' names! I believe they have had 50 or more young ones live with them.

I had a vision during Aaron's teen years—a picture of him with a silver spoon in his mouth, representing wealth. I was angry at that since he was not behaving well, and I began praying against the vision I saw. I was not being very spiritual and was thinking with my emotions, but then I asked God why he would have a silver spoon in his mouth. He answered me, "He will be needing it." I can see now the need for Aaron and Melissa to be able to provide over and beyond for these special children. They always have another surprise child to announce to us.

As I look back, I realize there is a thread of adoption in my family line—my father's adoption, Aaron's adoption, and then Aaron and Melissa's desire to care for many parentless 'orphans.' God's ways are mysterious.

Aaron, our son, adopted through our infertility, held the keys to the nations and was our ticket to serving the Lord. We were released into a different way of living than we had previously known. This passion has continued throughout our lives, sending us to the far reaches of the world.

Miracle Sightings

1. The prophecy from our friend telling Vera of Don and me having a baby in October, when I wasn't even pregnant, and Aaron being born on October 31.
2. Walking out of the hospital without paying the bill and later finding out the bill was intentionally left out.
3. The airline changed the flight plan for us with a three-day-old baby.
4. My prayer to give Aaron back to "where he belongs," and then the vision of the Lord's hand moving over the United States, saying, "It is for me to place people where they need to be" proved true.

5. Aaron wanted to accept Jesus at three and asked to be baptized at eight years old, and his father baptized him.
6. Discovering Aaron's musical and artistic abilities.
7. Aaron makes peace with his adoption by meeting Sherrie, his birth mother.
8. Aaron prayed and found his true partner in Melissa and how their hearts are together helping young ones without families.
9. Aaron and Melissa bring Sherrie to the Lord, giving them peace that she is safe in Jesus' arms.

6

A Call to Learn and Teach

Your word is a lamp to my feet and a light to my path.

Psalm 119:105 NKJV

"Therefore prepare yourself and arise, and speak to them all that I command you. Do not be dismayed before their faces, lest I dismay you before them."

Jeremiah 1:17 NKJV

"For I have not shunned to declare to you the whole counsel of God."

Acts 20:27 NKJV

In 1966, when I was 21, and my Russian Molokan Church had a Bible study that met once a week. Don and I loved attending this Bible study and learning the Word of God, but it wasn't deep enough for me. When I heard about some women attending a Bible study called Bible Study Fellowship, I was intrigued. This group was considered an "outside teaching" compared to the beliefs of my church, and I hesitated to join. But I kept feeling a nudge for a deeper knowledge of the Bible.

In Isaiah 28:9 (NIV), it says:

"Who is it he is trying to teach? To whom is he explaining his message? To children weaned from their milk, to those just taken from the breast?"

Jewish children were weaned from their mother's breast at three years old and immediately went to school to learn.

In Matthew Henry's commentary, he says:

> What it was that . . . prophets and ministers designed and aimed at: It was to teach them knowledge, the knowledge of God and His will, and to make them understand doctrine . . . This is God's way of dealing with men, to enlighten men's minds first with the knowledge of His truth, and thus to gain their affections and bring their wills into compliance with His laws; thus, He enters in by the door, whereas the thief and the robber climb up another way.[23A]

I went to this Bible study with my younger sister and absolutely loved it. I couldn't get enough of the teaching. It was here that I learned the salvation story in its entirety. I would come home and read and study for hours each day. After dinner, instead of watching television, I would ask Don if it would be all right to spend time studying, and he didn't mind. I devoured the Bible, answered my questions, and read and highlighted about ten pages of commentary each week. This Bible study was a five-year program.

During my first year in this study, I asked the Lord what I could do for Him. I wanted to serve the Lord. Then, I received a call from the teaching director of the Bible study, who asked me if I would be the class administrator. This group had 450 ladies with a long waiting list, as well as a children's program with many children. I had already prepared myself to say yes to whatever was coming my way, and when she asked, I had this burning inside, as she did, a witness of the Holy Spirit. I said yes.

As I soaked in the Word of God, I began to pray and claim the truths of the Bible for myself, especially wisdom, over and over. Years later, a woman pastor from Sweden told me she had never met anyone with so much wisdom, which I can only credit to these prayers. The Bible states:

"And so I tell you, keep on asking, and you will receive what you ask for. Keep on seeking, and you will find. Keep on knocking, and the door will be opened to you" (Luke 11:9).

Being the class administrator, I was given keys to open the doors of a very large church every Tuesday and Thursday morning. I directed 30 leaders to set up 15 chairs in any space we could find. There were so many women that they even gathered under the stairwell and in a windowless storage room, bringing their own lighting. Groups met in the bride's dressing room, the ladies' lounge, and in many other places. One of my roles was to place women into their groups and keep the year's materials stacked high in a closet at home. I also had to lock up the church and make sure everything was left clean and better than we found it. What an amazing time this was, and I loved it.

This group was such a blessing to me. I learned so much about Christian living and the truth of the Word of God. I went to the first meeting with a prideful chip on my shoulder, telling myself that I wouldn't listen to that woman's words. If something I heard didn't align with my understanding, I would shelve those thoughts on a make-believe shelf at the back of my brain until the Holy Spirit or the truth of the Word shed light on them.

I learned how to live as an "American" Christian woman from these very sweet, godly women, who were considered "ne nash" (not ours). I completed the five-year program.

After some years, I discovered another study called Community Bible Study, which offered different books of the Bible to study. I began attending and was asked to be in leadership. I became a Senior Leader and the Treasurer—something I found amusing, as I didn't like math and didn't feel confident handling money.

I also had the opportunity to take a Precept course on the Bible and attended a few training weekends in San Diego to become a credentialed teaching leader. This took me to a deeper level. Before teaching each book of the Bible, we outlined the entire book by hand. I did my best. This course had different levels of study that women could choose from, depending on how much study time they could handle—either half an hour or an hour each day, which made it doable for everyone.

We moved to Fountain Valley, where my friend Marian Jamison, now Norkaitis, took me to a women's group called Aglow International. It was a lively group of Spirit-filled Christian women. Their scripture verse is:

Be aglow and burning with the Spirit (Romans 12:11b AMPC).

Don was asked to become the advisor of the Aglow group, where he and I led a Seder Dinner. A Seder recalls, retells, and reenacts the story of the liberation of the Israelites from slavery in Egypt—more commonly known as the Exodus. It was enjoyable to have Don involved in this group with me.

Marian and I are friends to this day, especially in deep intercessory prayer for one another. I remember the first time we met. We attended Church of the Coastland together, and she came up to me, this very tall, beautiful, powerful woman of God. I was shy, thinking she wouldn't want to speak to me. She said, "Hanya, I'm going to be your friend." I was embarrassed by her boldness and wasn't sure I wanted to be hers! A beautiful, prophetic woman of God, and here we are, very close friends.

I taught a Bible study for the first time on *'Becoming a Woman of Excellence'* for ten weeks. It was an enjoyable experience for me, as these women launched me with the confidence that I could do it. What a joy it was to discover a teaching gift that I truly enjoyed.

I was then asked to speak to the San Clemente Aglow group in September of 1999. By this time, I had a few stories to tell, as Don and I had been traveling for years in the Healing Prayer ministry to many countries, watching God perform miracles through us.

Here, I gave my testimony and spoke about becoming strong through our trials. I shared a vision the Lord had given me personally, which I call the *'rock vision.'* I had once asked the Lord, "When will my trials be over? Show me my path." Since I was praying, I thought the Lord would clear any debris away. But I was surprised to see in a vision many rocks on my path, with several large ones ahead of me! This was my path? Then, I saw two angels, one on each side of me, holding me up under my arms. I thought, "Okay, I can handle this life."

Since I saw many rocks, it became clear that God wasn't going to remove my trials. There were many rocks, and they were very large. With the angels still carrying me under my arms, I looked down and saw Jesus near my feet, placing each foot on each rock exactly where it needed to be. I realized that I didn't have to do this journey alone; Jesus would be there with all His angels to help me walk the road He ordained for me.

These few scripture references confirm this vision:

For He shall give His angels charge over you, to keep you in all your ways. In their hands they shall bear you up, lest you dash your foot against a stone (Psalm 91:11-12 NKJV).

He also brought me up . . . and set my feet upon a rock, and established my steps" (Psalm 40:2 NKJV).

The Lord GOD is my strength [my source of courage, my invincible army]; He has made my feet [steady and sure] like hinds' feet and makes me walk [forward with spiritual confidence] on my high places [of challenge and responsibility] (Habakkuk 3:19 AMP).

What Did God Do in This Chapter?

1. Called me into leadership through Bible Study Fellowship.
2. Placed me in leadership in Community Bible Study.
3. Made me a credentialed teaching leader for Precept International.
4. Launched me into teaching the Word of God through the Aglow group.
5. Don became director of the Fountain Valley Aglow group.
6. We led a Seder Dinner together.
7. I received the 'rock vision.'

7

Pier Colony

And get into the habit of inviting guests home for
dinner or, if they need lodging, for the night.

Romans 12:13 TLB

By January 1991, Don and I had become independent investors
in real estate and, by living in Huntington Beach, an up-and-coming
city, we found golden opportunities. We decided that it would be a
good idea to invest in a condominium on Pacific Coast Highway.
When we drove past a condominium complex called Pier Colony,
located across the street from the ocean and pier, deep in my heart, I
said to myself, "I want one here." I didn't mention this to Don,
thinking it would be too expensive because of the location.

Sometime later, one Saturday, I was packing for a camping trip.
Don came home and called to me, "Hanya!" in a voice filled with
excitement—a voice I don't think I've ever heard before from him. I
came to the stairwell, and he said with excitement, "I bought you
something! I bought you a condo."

I said, "You bought me what?"

He said, "Hurry up, you need to come pick one out—it's a condo
at Pier Colony!"

He had been having breakfast at the Sugar Shack, a well-known
breakfast spot on Main Street, when he heard God speak to him to go

buy a condo at Pier Colony. He got up and went to purchase it immediately.

I will hurry, without delay, to obey your commands (Psalm 119:60).

This was just before we went to the National Prayer Breakfast in Washington, D.C., held on January 31, 1991. We had been invited before, but Don had never wanted to go. This time, I said I did. Our friends, Sherry and her husband, who were also going, prayed with us, and during the prayer, I had a vision. I saw through an open window—very beautiful green trees, grass, and bluebirds singing. This trip would be an open window to something.

We were invited to stay with Bob and Bernie Strain, who became our dear friends. At the prayer breakfast, we were seated in the large convention room where President George H.W. Bush would be speaking. We sat with a diplomat from Africa and had interesting conversations with him.

We were divided into districts from around the United States for various dinners that would take place. Billy Graham was to be the speaker for our Western district, but the Gulf War broke out during our stay, and he was conferring and praying with the President. So instead, our speaker was Chuck Colson.

Through our meeting with Bob and Bernie Strain, we were introduced to The Fellowship, an organization of businessmen who were influential around the world as Christians in the political arena, bringing harmony to the world. Bernie managed The Fellowship House, a mansion called The Cedars, in Arlington, Virginia. We took a tour of this retreat house where people met with and advised Third World leaders, disgraced leaders, well-known people, members of Congress, and ambassadors. This was a place for leaders from around the world to meet, have dinners, stay out of the public eye, and be ministered to by Christians.

Young people would come to The Cedars to work as missionaries and live in houses across the street. Each house had a leader who discipled the young men and women. Houses like The Cedars are located near parliaments in several countries. We visited one in Bern, Switzerland, which was started by Bob and Bernie Strain, who spent a year in Germany setting up The Fellowship House.

I urge you . . . to pray for all people. Ask God to help them; intercede on their behalf, and give thanks for them. Pray this way for kings and all who are in authority (1 Timothy 2:1-2).

We caught the vision of ministry to leaders from around the world and told the Strains that if they had anyone coming to Huntington Beach, we would have a place for them to stay. This birthed a hospitality ministry in The Pier Colony condominiums, across the street from the beach and the Huntington Beach pier, which would last for 12 years, during which time we had-wonderful experiences hosting people in Pier Colony.

Friends of the Strains, Wolly and Marianne Peuster, called us from Germany and came to stay at Pier Colony. Wolly is a retired Senior Judge in the town of Freiburg, as well as a pastor and author. Wolfgang (Wolly's formal name) and his wife Marianne, "a reliable prophetic voice in the German-speaking countries" (as declared by the prophet and author Dr. H.C. Rust), wrote *God's Angel Comes for Breakfast—Discovering a Prophetic Lifestyle.*

Wolly was highlighted in the German news as the 'Sword of God,' because he preached in churches on Sunday mornings, and the criminals would expect leniency when he judged. What a safe haven our place became for them. Wolly was once shot at in the Black

Forest, in Germany, so the condominium's 24-hour security brought him comfort. The Peusters wrote the following poem in our hospitality book at the end of their stay:

"In Germany, we took off flying over to the ocean of California, where our hearts soon came into emotions. The Lord prepared his people to become new friends of ours; we won't forget, you gave us precious days and hours. This home has been a noble place to rest, we so enjoyed it. You did us the best!" April 1991.

Once, when Wolly and Marianne were visiting, they came to our life group, and we surprised them by learning three worship songs in German. You should have seen their faces as we began to sing.

Siegfried and Gudrun Koble, also our new German friends, came to stay in our condominium in April 1992. They came several more times after that. Siegfried is a retired President of the Judges of Freiburg, Germany. What humble friends they became to us.

Jorg and Sabine Dohnicht became dear friends to us and minister through The Fellowship even today.

After several stays in our condominium, each of our German friends invited Don and me to come and stay in Germany, and we eventually got to enjoy their hospitality. I had the opportunity to train and teach a few of them in healing prayer.

Eric and Isabel Noble from Scotland came to attend a conference at our church, The Anaheim Vineyard, and stayed at Pier Colony. Before their arrival, there had been a mix-up, and we had canceled their stay completely. Eric called, and things were straightened out. Don and I almost missed meeting these friends, who became dear to us. They became lifelong friends, and we visited them in Scotland a few times.

When people came from international countries to stay at Pier Colony, I would stock the refrigerator with food to help them have a bit to get by.

We would have our visitors over to our home for meals and fellowship, exchanging stories, laughter, and prayers. We shopped with them, showed them beautiful areas along the coast, and most importantly, we developed lifelong friendships.

One pastor told us he stayed in his pajamas all day. Some wrote worship songs, others' marriages were refreshed, and people came to fast and pray. At times, we had prophets come to rest, and we had the privilege of having them over for dinner. One woman, whose marriage was canceled at the last minute, came on the weekend of the intended marriage date with her bridesmaids to help her grieve and refresh. Part of a woman's study Bible was edited there by my friend.

A few chapters of the book *Taking Our Cities for God* [25] by John Dawson were written there. It's interesting that much prayer for Huntington Beach was done at Pier Colony as well.

There was a young couple who were both very ill and had a hard time having a family. They finally gave birth to a baby girl one early December, but the baby died on Christmas Eve. Their pastor called us and told us the church wanted to fly them out for a long vacation. They stayed for three weeks, the most we ever allowed. We cried with them, gave them time on the beach, had them over for dinner, and when they needed company, we were there to comfort them. We prayed for them and even laughed with them at times. The last I heard, they had two beautiful children.

Once, we got a call from a pastor who told us about a woman who was dying and had never seen the ocean. We welcomed her and her husband. What a blessing it was to meet them both. Her husband had quit his job to care for her, and despite the stairs, he would carry her to the bedroom. We learned so much from the wonderful people we ministered to—missionaries, prophets, and leaders.

Don and I entertained people from all around the world—Norway, Germany, Sweden, England, Scotland, Denmark, Austria, Iceland, and more. What a joy it was to have them in our home and condominium.

After I cleaned the condominium, I enjoyed the peace and quiet of the unit. I would lie on the couch with the ocean breeze coming through the door and fall into a Holy Spirit-induced restful sleep.

After 12 years of ministry, we realized that this chapter was over. When people began to request their "regular" week in the middle of summer, and things began to break down in our unit, as well as major issues in the complex, we knew it was time to sell. One week after listing it, we sold our Pier Colony condominium. We never charged anyone for their stay, and while there were expensive association dues each month, when we sold it, we received back not only the original price we paid but also 12 years' worth of association dues. No money was lost! How amazing is that?

God Working at Pier Colony

1. Don was very quick to obey when he heard God say to go buy a condominium specifically at Pier Colony. Remember, I never told him I would like one there. I believe God had planted that desire in me, already knowing the work we would be involved in that would impact the nations.

2. The many lifelong friends we acquired from serving in this ministry.

3. The ability to pray for and minister to many while they stayed in our condominium.

4. Receiving back all and more of the money invested over the 12 years.

8

So, You Want to Be a Landlord
(For Mature Audiences)

For all the animals of the forest are mine, and
I own the cattle on a thousand hills. I know every
bird on the mountains, and all the animals of the
field are mine. If I were hungry, I would not tell
you, for all the world is mine and everything in it.

Psalm 50:10-12

As the owner of Galitzen Properties, with many apartments and commercial offices, Don would often say when giving the rules of renting to the young ones, "What your parents didn't finish, I will. Do you still want to rent from me?" In other words, they wouldn't be able to get away with anything.

I remember a pivotal decision Don asked me to make one day: "We are going to be investing, choose Dana Point or Huntington Beach." Don was a surfer, and those were his surfing spots, so he had already 'walked the land,' or shall I say, 'walked the water.' I chose Huntington Beach since it was closer to my family and our church.

I always said I should have written a book about some of the tenants we've encountered, and here it is. I'll tell you some of our most interesting stories. You will find it both hilarious and appalling.

To begin telling our stories, I'll set the tone with one.

One morning, a radical Christian tenant of ours knocked on my side sliding door where our kitchen table was, not our front door, as I was eating breakfast in my bathrobe. He handed me his rent, but then said Jesus was coming soon and that he didn't have to pay rent anymore, and I couldn't make him, because he was a Christian. I quickly answered him, "Watch me"—it just came out. His attitude did not exemplify someone walking with God.

First Purchase

We purchased a tiny house in the 70s in Huntington Beach on the corner of 12th and Orange Avenue for $10,000 and used it as a beach getaway. After we bought it, we were told that a man had hung himself in the garage, and we prayed over the property. I had a miscarriage while in that house.

After some time, we began to rent the house out. I remember walking home after renting it out, carrying the 'for rent' sign to 13th Street where we now lived. On the way there, a person stopped their car and asked me what was for rent—that's how the rental market was at that time.

About three more tenants each told us they had miscarried when they lived at this property, along with a few divorces. We had had enough. Realizing the spiritual darkness of death still lingered on the property, we sold it. We were not yet trained in cleansing a dwelling place and sold it for $69,000. The last we heard, it sold for $1.2 million—that's Huntington Beach.

The last tenants to rent from us in that property left it in a trash heap. They went on a shopping spree and left all the boxes, bags, and papers scattered everywhere. The refrigerator was moldy, and the oven was gross. We cleaned our apartments ourselves for many years as we started our business.

Main Street

Don and I, shortly after moving to Huntington Beach, purchased six units on Main Street. A woman living in one of these units had been managing them, so we kept her as the manager. She became very controlling, as though she were the owner, and that was a challenge. We treated her as well as we could, knowing she was not well and on kidney dialysis several times a week.

One evening, I received a call from her asking me if it was alright to discontinue her medications so she could die and wondered if that would be considered suicide. She was a Catholic woman, and her priest would not give her permission. He believed that would be suicide and would leave her out of heaven, according to Catholic belief. I told her that taking the medications was only keeping her alive and removing them would be the more natural thing. I made sure she understood salvation and prayed for her.

She heeded my advice, and I went to her apartment to anoint her and pray for her with her family. She was giving precious jewelry to her daughter. It was a very touching time. Dying, for a person who has been on dialysis for many years, is not a pretty thing to see. She suffered a lot and died within a few days.

As I'm writing about our Main Street units, I recall the young man who was distraught after a breakup with a woman and decided to end his life. He opened the oven door with the gas on and placed his head in the oven, I guess to breathe in the gas, not realizing the water heater with a flame was nearby. Well, it exploded, blowing the back wall out. He survived with a seared face, but it left our apartment with a lot of damage.

Again, on Main Street, Don hired a Baptist young man who couldn't stop preaching to us as though we didn't know Jesus. He needed work and money and discovered an inaccessible garage on our property. He offered to help Don turn it into a studio unit. Of course, this would not be a legal unit, but remember, he needed work and money. I told Don not to do it, as God would not honor this idea. They proceeded anyway; it would be so simple—a sink area and a bathroom were all it needed. One of our tenants had been using it for her crafts room for free.

I fasted one morning, and at 9 a.m., I received a phone call from a friend saying she was glad I was home because there was a van just like mine on Main Street that had been in an accident. I told her Don took it that morning, and just then the Lord told me that Don was fine. She said it had a children's car seat in the back. I told her, "Yes, that was Don."

I sent my mother-in-law, who lived next door to us, to check it out as Aaron was still sleeping. Don came home and seemed alright. I told him I was fasting about the illegal renovation, but he left anyway to continue working on the property.

As soon as he was there in the garage, soon-to-be apartment, there was a 'knock, knock, knock' at the door. It was the City Inspector, who shut the project down.

God is so faithful, keeping us in check with His ways despite ours. Bless the Lord, O my soul.

Death in Huntington

One young woman, a free spirit, who rented an apartment from us downtown, went frequently to Perk's, the local bar in town. Our contractor talked to her and told her to be careful. One night, she brought a man home with her, and sadly, he murdered her. It was a horrific thing for us and everyone. The suspect disappeared, and the detective on the case was in an automobile accident and died the next week, which delayed the investigation. Our apartment was literally torn apart by the police investigators. Walls were sprayed with cancer-causing chemicals, which they left. Our plumbing was taken apart and not put back together. Doors were removed and left that way, flooring was damaged, and it was a mess.

When we asked for only $700 from the city to do some repairs, we were told that we would need to close the unit down, as it was an illegal unit. We hadn't made any changes to the property and needed to prove this by finding old documentation. We got help from our insurance company— a reminder to always carry insurance.

During the renovation, strange people came by dressed in black to "feel the energy," and told Don to leave it just as it was—they wanted to rent it. Of course, he told them to go away.

About 25 years later, we heard on the news about a cold case being reopened. It was the murderer of our tenant. The murderer had become a Christian and couldn't live with himself, so he confessed to his pastor, who told him to turn himself in. He's now serving his 25-year sentence.

The mystery of his disappearance was that he was a sailor on leave for the night. The ship left port that night with him on it.

13th Street

We lived on 13th Street in Huntington Beach for 13 years after moving here from Monterey Park and purchased a triplex across the street from us.

One day, I saw one of the front doors open, and a motorcycle drove right into the living room. Our tenant had been using the living room as a garage to work on his motorcycle. The tools were strewn about, and oil covered the carpet. They had also previously had a bonfire in the living room.

We always renovated our units with very new or clean carpets, so this hurt our spirits as we spent precious money on renovations. They didn't stay very long after that.

When we realized that many tenants were using the apartments wrongly—either for partying or foolishness—we decided to attract more mature tenants by renovating with higher-grade materials: wood floors, stainless steel appliances, granite countertops, etc. It worked; we raised our rent and got good tenants who had jobs and paid their rent.

Another Death

Over the years, we rented to what we called "trust babies," mostly young men who had physical or mental deficiencies that didn't allow them to work. Parents of these single adults would come and beg us to rent to them.

One day, a mother came and said she hadn't heard from her son for quite a while, so she called the police for a wellness check. The police went to check on her son. The mother was at the unit, and Don arrived shortly after, at which point the police officer told him to get away, even though he was the owner. This young man had been dead for weeks in our apartment. I won't get into the gory details, but it was very bad, and we needed to get a hazmat clean-up crew to rid the apartment of everything—from the flooring to the appliances. Our insurance company was very sympathetic to us. The poor mother.

It was the law at the time that if there was a death in a unit, the next renter had to be informed. This would be important to some people, and the other tenants would be sure to let them know anyway.

All in One Day

One morning, we received a phone call from our son, Aaron, that an apartment we had just finished renovating had been vandalized. A door had been left open, and someone sprayed black paint on the freshly painted walls, the brand-new stainless steel appliances, tiles, wood flooring—on everything. Aaron called the police, and they came to write a report. Everything needed to be redone.

We were leaving for our timeshare vacation to Hawaii early the next morning when, at 4 p.m., we received another call from Aaron. He thought a tenant who had cancer was dead in his apartment. Don told him to have Christi go with him and "handle it." He and Christi, our faithful assistant of over 20 years, went into the unit. Aaron went to the bathroom, and Christi went to the bedroom, where she found him lying on the floor, dead.

They called the police, who came, and guess what? It was the same officer that had met Aaron in response to his morning call regarding the vandalized apartment! He said to Aaron, "You're not having a very good day, are you?" Aaron and Christi were told that the police-would handle it from there.

Beach Court

The Beach Court property is a gem, and we are 'married to it' or 'it's a keeper.' That's what we call properties that we won't sell. One of the units has a bootlegging cellar with stairs leading into a small cave, and at the end of a hallway, there is a dumbwaiter that goes down into the cave. Bootlegging is a term dating back to the 1800s, when traders dealing with Native peoples carried flasks of liquor in their boot tops. During Prohibition (1920-1933), liquor was made and sold illegally. Some were selling adulterated liquor, which could have harmful and poisonous ingredients, leading to death.[24]

We had an elderly woman renting from us who had been scaring the other tenants. One of the things she did was slash all the screen doors with a knife at our 13-unit complex. The woman was on psychiatric medications and wasn't taking them. She did many other very unsightly things unbecoming to her.

We had to eventually evict her. We were in Israel that December, so my mother-in-law, our contractor, and the woman's daughter had to meet with the police at the apartment on Christmas Eve. The woman was nailing the door shut from the inside of her apartment, but the police told her they could get to her anyway and to just open the door. For her daughter to get her mother back on medication, the mother needed to be admitted to a mental institution. The only way the police could get her admitted was if she assaulted them and was arrested first. As the police broke into her apartment, the frightened woman raised a hammer as though to hit the officer, which allowed him to arrest her.

We thought we were done with her, but her Christian daughter asked us to help her with her mother. The woman's psychiatrist called me one day and told me he had her back on meds and that part of her recovery was to be in familiar surroundings. He asked if we would take her back. We did! She didn't stay long.

The Night Ladies

A young woman came into the office to pay her rent, dressed inappropriately, and leaned over Don's desk, showing him her tattoo, which was in an awkward place. He told her the next time she came into our office, she should dress more covered, as it made him uncomfortable. That's my man!

Don was known in town, especially at one complex, as a safe man to rent from. Many of our tenants were provocative dancers, and they found staying at our place brought them the safety, privacy, and rest they needed. He earned the privilege to speak into their lives.

The Man with the Gun

One man and his wife were not able to pay their rent, and the woman, who was a Christian, pleaded with us. The man refinished furniture, so we gave him some of our antiques to refinish in lieu of rent—one piece at a time, since I wasn't sure we would get them back. This man was troubled and called Don to come see him at his place of business. I told Don not to go or, at least, to take someone with him. Don went anyway, alone, and when the man, sitting behind his desk, began to talk, he opened his drawer and pulled out his gun. He was angry, not at Don, but I'm presuming at life. He said, threatening Don, "If you come again, I don't know what I'll do with this (the gun)." Don had to talk him down. We were never sure if he would have shot Don. I prayed through the visit. He was arrested soon after for growing marijuana where he worked. The police always told us, as landlords, that we were not to enter into domestic disputes since, in their anger, we would be the ones getting shot at.

Houseless Woman

Just recently, a woman came into our office, asking for a key to one of our units to see if she would want to rent. She viewed it and came back to return the key. The next day, our son received a call that there was a lot of noise coming from the unit she had viewed. This woman moved in and had a bed and a dog in there. Calling the police, we discovered she had made a copy of our key. I'm sure she had done this before, and that it worked.

Untangling a Mess

We own a very successful, large apartment complex in downtown Huntington Beach that we consider a gift from God.

Don heard about this property owned by three high-powered businessmen who were at odds. One had a gun and had threatened to use it to kill one of the men. We heard that no one could untangle their ownership of this property.

Don took it on. Bets were made in town that he couldn't do it! It took nine months of negotiating, and we were able to purchase it.

One partner was so grateful to Don that we were invited to his 60th birthday gala. He had a full orchestra as well as a smaller band. There were chefs grilling steaks on-site, and their palatial home had a man-made rock waterfall against the entire mountain.

We were invited to bring another couple with us, and when the hostess answered the door in her golden ball gown, I knew we weren't in proper attire!

Jewelry Store

One evening, we were watching the news about a man who was arrested for murdering a woman and wounding her baby, then throwing the gun off the Santa Monica pier. He went home afterward and barricaded himself in his apartment, and a SWAT team came to arrest him. As he was led out of his apartment, I said to Don, "That's our tenant who rents the jewelry store from us." He had murdered his business partner's wife and wounded their baby. This man owed us several months of rent and had given us two diamonds to hold as security.

We went to our rental property the next day, which by then had been cordoned off. Don explained to the detectives that we were the owners and that our tenant had given us diamonds until he could pay his rent. The detective told Don to keep them. This man's business partner was selling diamonds they owned together without his consent, and his rage got the best of him. When the investigation was completed and we were given permission to enter our store, we had a disaster to clean up, along with customers wanting to know where their jewelry was. We referred them to the authorities for months after.

Praying Mother

Don and I received a call one night from a distraught tenant whose son had just committed murder. She was a woman of prayer, and we had prayed for her son once before. We immediately drove to her house to console her after the police left her. Her son and a woman had been drinking in town, and they went to an open field in downtown Huntington Beach where she threatened him with ugly words. He became enraged and killed her. We drove the woman to the scene of the crime and prayed with her for her son, for her-family, and for a cleansing of the land which had been defiled.

I once asked my daughter-in-law, Melissa, upon a tenant moving out, "Does it need new flooring?" She answered, "No, we already did that when the last tenant's dog ran in with a running water hose, flooding the entire unit!"

I recently asked Don, regarding working with so many tenants and their problems, "Will I be doing this forever?" Don said, "No, you'll need to die one day!"

These are just some of our stories. Each unit has its own story—some hilarious, some tragic—and life moves on.

If you struggle with the fact that you aren't in a viable position in your church to minister, think of the opportunities that are available to you outside the walls of the local church. Your business could be your mission.

God Working in This Chapter

1. Having the authority to tell young ones, "What your parents didn't finish, I will. Do you still want to rent from me?"
2. The salvation, confession, and conviction of the man who murdered our tenant.
3. Being able to help 'trust babies' and their parents, who were extremely grateful to us. We had to keep an eye on them and sometimes tell them to straighten up—things their parents probably couldn't do.
4. Helping a desperate woman with her mother, who needed psychiatric help.
5. Earning the trust to speak into the 'night ladies' lives.
6. Taking a risk to help a couple get through a hard time by bartering and giving hope to the man with the gun.

9

Streetlight Espresso

And seek the peace of the city where I have caused
you to be carried away captive, and pray to the
LORD for it; for in its peace you will have peace.

Jeremiah 29:7 NKJV

In 1994, we received a golden opportunity to buy a coffeehouse for $7,500 with a friend. It was called Midnight Espresso and had gone bankrupt. Knowing that several churches had prayed for a coffeehouse in downtown Huntington Beach for about 25 years, we entered into a partnership with our friend.

Our goal was to make Midnight Espresso a Christian-friendly coffeehouse. Don had received a word from the Lord that a church would come out of it. The history of Midnight Espresso involved people playing medieval witchcraft games, so I had to do a lot of spiritual cleansing.

On Thursday nights, people from the LGBTQ+ community would come. We told all our Christian friends to come and mingle with them. We had worship nights on Friday evenings, as worship leaders came and filled the place. They said they were 'tilling the soil,' bringing the atmosphere of the Holy Spirit into the room.

We invited music groups to come on several Sunday evenings. Denny Correll, a singer in the 1960s rock band Blues Image and a touring member of the Jesus music band *Love Song*, came. A couple from Saint Mary's by the Sea, a local Catholic church, played their harp and guitar during Christmas time.

One particularly exciting evening, a dear friend from Perth, Australia, who was a professional musician, brought her violin and played for us. Her husband was the first chair flutist in the Perth Symphony. They were staying at our house, and he had a golden tip for his flute delivered to our doorstep, valued at $100,000. All these people performed in the coffeehouse for free, but we usually had a tip jar.

When our partner handed off our partnership agreement, one of the churches in town, Church 24/7, expressed interest in purchasing one-third of the shares of the coffeehouse. Don and I gave two-thirds of the shares to The Church of the Coastland in Huntington Beach. This brought a fresh flavor to the coffeehouse, and it was renamed Streetlight Espresso, a much brighter expression of being a Christian coffeehouse.

One of the churches began to have its own style of ministry, which affected the business. They needed to balance out their evangelizing style to avoid scaring customers away.

After several years, these two churches sold the coffeehouse to another local church, and a woman named Rose ran it very well.

Rose allowed a couple to hold a Bible study every Sunday morning before the doors opened to the public. The study grew to about 60 people, and the space became too small. They were offered a church building with five acres in Garden Grove, and of course, they accepted the generous offer—*a first church plant.*

As we shared our story about our coffeehouse in Huntington Beach, several churches were inspired by our model. One large church in Sweden even started their own. We visited it while we were there. We went down a very narrow staircase to a basement to get to the coffeehouse, which was full and lively.

One day, while we still owned the coffeehouse in Huntington Beach, a young German man with a history of drugs—who was now serving God—told us he wanted to go to Germany. Don told him he was going to be a pastor there. We gave him the contact information for our German friend, Siegfried Koble, the President of Judges in Freiburg, whom we had met and hosted at our Pier Colony condominium. Unbeknownst to us, Siegfried picked him up from the airport (a three-hour drive from his home) and hosted him for six months. This was a surprise to us.

The young German man began helping in the church Siegfried and his wife Gudrun attended, a Calvary Chapel, and eventually became one of the pastors there. Years later, we received a picture of him with a beautiful woman announcing their marriage. They now pastor a church in Switzerland that they planted—*a second church plant.*

It wasn't until after we were no longer owners of Streetlight Espresso that we heard of all the salvations and events that took place there. Friends we now know have told us they dated there.

The town was developing: Fifth Street (near the coffeehouse) was up-and-coming, and parking was sparse, making it difficult for people to visit Streetlight. The new Starbucks was opening, and it became harder to keep the coffeehouse going.

Rose decided to sell Streetlight Espresso and wanted to meet with Don and me to let us know she was offered a very large amount of money for the coffeehouse and asked if that would be alright with us. It was!

What Did We See God Doing Because of Streetlight?

1. The opportunity to work with many churches in Huntington Beach.
2. Salvations happened.
3. Bringing the light of Jesus into downtown.
4. Using people's musical talents to further the Kingdom.
5. Having a Bible study outside the walls of the church.
6. Many other churches caught the vision of a Christian coffeehouse, even in Sweden.
7. Two churches were planted.

10

Hebron House
A Place of Refuge

"But rise and stand on your feet; for I have appeared to you for this
purpose, to make you a minister and a witness both of things which
you have seen and of the things which I will yet reveal to you."
Acts 26:16 NKJV

His [Jesus'] one aim was to be "broken bread and
poured-out wine" for the Master. Early mornings were
given to prayer for others and receiving the daily anointing
which gave him such a skillful touch with souls."[26]
~ Oswald Chambers

November 11, 2003

In 1996, Don and I purchased offices for Galitzen Properties in downtown Huntington Beach at 218, 218 1/2, and 220 Fifth Street from a man we rented from, but he was going bankrupt. We saw this as an opportunity to begin using the building as a platform for 'business as mission.' When the 218 1/2 office became vacant in November 2003, I felt led to ask Don if I could use it for ministry. He said I could have it for one year.

My vision was to pray for the merchants in the downtown area and their businesses, that they may see the hand of God doing miraculous things in their lives through the prayers of His people. I also wanted to minister to people's needs and bring salvation, healing, and deliverance to our city.

In December, around five o'clock one morning, I turned on the television to watch a famous Bible teacher. Instead, I tuned in to Paula White, who started her message with a prophecy. She began by saying, "You thought you were going to see someone else," which made me listen intently, as I was expecting someone else.

She began speaking prophetically from Nehemiah:

> *"You are the LORD God, Who chose Abram, and*
> *brought him out of Ur of the Chaldeans, and gave*
> *him the name Abraham."*
> *Nehemiah 9:7 NKJV*

I wrote as she spoke:

> He brings you out to give you something. He brought Abram out and gave him the name Abraham. I will make you a great nation, I will make your name great, people will be blessed and will bless you. I will curse those who curse you. Don't worry. The answer to the world is inside of you—glory, goodness, and power. It is being obedient to it. The devil can tempt you but can't stop what is inside of you. He can hinder you, but you will go out stronger.

She continued,

> Everything God says I can do, I can do. Move into your purpose! Act out the Word of God. Get up! Do not sit in passivity—live! Do! Every day you have a new chance. There is a miracle with your name on it! A new day. New beginnings. What you do today changes the future. It's not your righteousness, it's God's. Leave your past behind, leave

and cleave. What is in front of you is to increase to thrive, not survive.

Stand up, who am I talking to? You need to stand up! You have one year! [This was speaking directly to me! Don had given me one year to use our vacant office space for Hebron House!] Proclaim your promise! No decision is a decision! If you don't do anything, you have sealed your fate. You must decide!

> *"You will also declare a thing,*
> *and it will be established for you;*
> *so light will shine on your ways."*
> *Job 22:28 NKJV*

Paula passionately declared, "You will be stronger this year than when you started—supernatural increase!"

> *Weeping may last through the night,*
> *but joy comes with the morning*
> *Psalm 30:5b*

The prophecy continued,

Morning is here! God will lead, blessing, magnifying, He is going before you. Abraham was given the opportunity, and he walked in it! Walk in your opportunity, don't miss the moment!

> *It is He who gives you the power to get wealth.*
> *Deuteronomy 8:18b NKJV*

What you do requires choice. Increase a thousandfold. Guard the Word. You have a year!" (She said it again!)

You can't sit, you must open the door, not your husband. Your hour of release! Don't let your miracle pass you by! God will open your eyes because you have obeyed. If the root is holy, the branches will be holy.

The super with the natural. The first determines the rest. Who am I speaking to? . . . Stand up!" [I stood up!]

The Bible called her great. She was not great. She had it in her. It was locked up inside. Don't miss your moment.[27]

These powerful, precise, prophetic words from Paula were the charge from God that I needed. They gave me a supernatural desire to take what had been given to me seriously.

On December 28, 2003, as I prayed regarding opening Hebron House, I had a vision of a homing pigeon and saw the words 'coming home.' In the vision, when the pigeon alighted at 218 1/2 Fifth Street, it turned into a dove, with translucent white wings opening and closing slowly as it came down, emitting a beautiful radiance. Truly a God-given picture.

After receiving the prophetic words and Don agreeing for me to use the space, I continued to receive confirmation. A pastor friend of mine said, "The Lord put it on your heart, I bear witness to that. Go forth." Don also said, "Go forward."

I opened Hebron House . . .

On February 8, 2004, Steve Purdue, our pastor at the time from Church of the Coastland, prayed over me. In a vision, he saw a white, radiant dove coming straight down onto Hebron House. When it landed, it exploded, emitting a great radiance—similar to the vision I had received! He also shared with me that about 26 years earlier, as he was riding his bike down Fifth Street, the Lord had him stop right in front of 218 1/2 Fifth Street. Steve told me that as he stopped, he received the call from God to start a church, which he did. I was standing on holy ground—this land was a place God used to speak to His people.

The office would officially become available on March 1, 2004, and it would take a few weeks to set up.

On March 24, 2004, about 12 pastors from our city came and laid hands on Don and me to anoint and inaugurate Hebron House. Our current pastor, Paul Harmon, as well as Steve Purdue, who has since passed, were there and prayed with these pastors regularly.

The name Hebron House was given to me prophetically when I asked a friend to pray with me about a name. Hebron House immediately came out of her mouth, and then she explained that it was one of the cities of refuge in the Bible. The words 'a place of sanctuary' immediately struck me, as this was a prophetic word given for our home. I have always strived to keep our home a place of refuge and sanctuary, and I wanted this for Hebron House as well.

The City of Hebron was not only a place of sanctuary but was also the place where David fled from Saul and was crowned king. Hebron was also known as a learning center.

In July of 2004, I wondered what God wanted through Hebron House and asked Him if this was to be a church. Instead, I saw a picture of the medical red cross, which "represents protection by international law for the wounded and sick and those caring for them in armed conflict."[28]

My friend, Janet Hall, had a picture of the emergency doors of a hospital with me standing there. All I had to do was push the button, and the doors would open. This was confirmation that people in distress would be able to come here for healing.

I set up a small Christian lending library in Hebron House for a season. Christian books poured in from people and churches, but it attracted few people.

On July 27, 2004, I received a violation notice, and then a second notice from code enforcement from the city. Someone had complained to the city that religious services were being held here. I had to fill out a form describing Hebron House activities: "Galitzen Properties private office, Bible study, prayer, and small gatherings." I was approached again in August and met with a licensing person at my office. I appeared before the Planning Department and explained to a very nice man that I had a Bible study and prayed for our city and for people at Hebron House. He smiled and said everything was fine and that I didn't have to pay any fees.

For over two years, I had an urge, a prompting, an unction, to go to Hebron House at 7 a.m., seven days a week, to pray for our city.

When I asked the Lord about praying there seven days a week, I received this scripture:

"When someone has been given much, much will be required in return; and when someone has been entrusted with much, even more will be required" (Luke 12:48).

Mostly, I prayed alone, but sometimes people joined me in praying for needs. When I was alone, I would pray a bit and then walk the downtown area, praying and speaking with owners and managers of establishments.

The Lord gave me these words from scripture to comfort me in my lonely, disheartened times when I wondered what was happening:

Jonah went out of the city and sat on the east side of the city. There he made himself a shelter and sat under it in the shade, till he might see what would become of the city. And the LORD God prepared a plant and made it come up over Jonah, that it might be shade for his head to deliver him from his misery. So Jonah was very grateful for the plant (Jonah 4:5-6 NKJV).

Praying one afternoon, I went into a bar on Main Street at 4 p.m. and asked for the manager. I told him that I was praying for him and asked if he had any needs. He began crying and told me his needs. I prayed for him right there.

In preparing to be at Hebron House every morning by 7 a.m., I moved all my toiletries to another bathroom so as not to disturb Don. I was waking up at 5 a.m. every day for two years. This had to be a God endeavor, to be given a supernatural desire and the energy for such a long period of time. I did this with only an occasional substitute.

While on Fifth Street, Hebron House was used by many churches and pastors for ministry. Our church, Church of the Coastland, had a weekly Bible study on Thursday evenings. We also did a Halloween outreach in downtown Huntington Beach, evangelizing on Main Street and using Hebron House as a refreshment site for the workers.

Pastor Paul Harmon from another church, Hope Chapel, reached out and used Hebron House for their first life group training. Another pastor, Greg Kruly, would disciple a man I brought to the Lord there.

When Don and I took a three-week vacation to China for our 40th wedding anniversary, our pastor, Steve Purdue, and friends kept morning prayer going. Now those are dedicated, devoted friends! Pastor Steve supported me 100 percent in this endeavor.

On March 1, 2005, the one year I was given by Don was up at the 218 1/2 location. I moved Hebron House next door into the back half of Galitzen Properties, as it seemed more economical, and I continued the work of prayer, Bible study, and outreach from there.

The number of people who joined me in praying had dropped off a bit, and I received this scripture promise from the Word:

"The latter glory of this house shall be greater than the former" *(Haggai 2:9a ESV).*

One day, Don received an email from a man who owned a 14-office complex, asking if Don would like to purchase it. Many real estate owners in the downtown area always wanted this prime piece of property, but this man only wanted us to buy it. We felt it was from God.

After purchasing, Galitzen Properties moved to this commercial building at 315 Third Street. We would still be downtown at this new location but now have a coveted parking lot, a rarity in this area.

I moved Hebron House to the large back room at our new location on Third Street, where we also used it for the life group we led through Hope Chapel, the church we were attending at the time.

When I was about ready to start a new project out of Hebron House, I was at our office when the man renting the space next door was telling Don that he would be moving out in two weeks. I happened to be there, and as he spoke, the man looked directly into my eyes and said to me, "You're going to be needing it."

I never knew this tenant, and no one knew his business. When I saw his eyes, which were a liquid, transparent blue, I could see into the depths of them. Who was that man who knew I would need this office?

So I sought for a man among them who would make a wall, and stand in the gap before Me on behalf of the land, that I should not destroy it (Ezekiel 22:30a NKJV).

This space became the new Hebron House meeting place and would birth The Nehemiah 52 HB (Huntington Beach) Project.

Nehemiah was the cupbearer to the Persian King Artaxerxes. When Nehemiah heard of the devastation of Jerusalem, the Holy City, and that it was in ruins, he knew that it needed to be rebuilt to protect the people from their enemies. Imagine asking your King for a leave of absence to go for who knew how long to work on restoring a city. He prayed and prayed before asking the King and was granted permission. It took Nehemiah 52 days to rebuild the city walls.

I felt the call to pray specifically to rebuild the brokenness of Huntington Beach. I'm always trying to hear from God on the decisions I make and to be obedient to the words I hear:

I will stand my watch and set myself on the rampart, and watch to see what He will say to me" (Habakkuk 2:1a NKJV).

One day, I was in my car, still praying about whether to do the Nehemiah HB Project, when the radio was on, and "Whose Lips Will Plead?" by Alexander Muir began to play:

Whose lips will plead, for the people of this land?
Who'll stand in the gap, and who'll build up the wall
Before the long day of God's patience is over
Before the night comes, when His judgment will fall.
And whose eyes will weep, for the people of this land?
And whose hearts will break, for the hearts made of stone
For those who are walking out into darkness
Away from God's love, without Christ so alone.
And whose ears can hear what the Spirit is saying
To those who are willing to watch and to pray.
Pray on till God's light, fills the skies over this land
The light of revival that brings a new day.[29]

This gave me the final confirmation and confidence that the Lord was in The Nehemiah HB Project.

The Nehemiah HB Project was a 52-day time of concentrated prayer for our city, counting back 52 days from Easter, which we did for several years in a row. I would assign different parts of the city to people, and they would prayer-walk their area or just pray as much as they felt led. Hope Chapel came behind me in a mighty way, supporting me in anything the Lord laid on my heart, and I am grateful.

On Saturdays, during the Nehemiah HB Project, we would caravan the city in a car or several cars, filled with people with cups of coffee in hand, following a mapped area of streets outlining the city.

We prayed specifically as we passed schools, businesses, neighborhoods, City Hall, churches, malls, people, and whatever came to our minds. The time flew by, and it was very satisfying. The first time we did this, it took 52 minutes. Remember, 52 days of Nehemiah's rebuilding the Wall? Incredible! Incredible Holy Spirit timing, God's fingerprints were all over this.

Rebuilding our city walls much like Nehemiah, treading the city (on wheels), through prayer. As the scripture says,

"Every place that the sole of your foot will tread upon I have given you, as I said to Moses" (Joshua 1:3 NKJV).

For a time, I held a monthly revival prayer meeting at Hebron House. Some friends held Monday night intercessory prayer, while others, including myself, would lead on Tuesday mornings, and yet another person led Wednesday evenings.

Hebron House was also used as a learning center, where Don taught classes on finance once a month for almost a year, having 35 to 50 people joining him. Don, now 82, recently taught Zoom classes for his alma mater, Whittier College, teaching real estate to senior students from Hebron House. Our friend and tax attorney, Ira Brodsky, taught classes on estate planning. I have also taught classes on healing there. I counseled couples, later officiating their weddings. Hebron House has been used to equip people, educate people, heal and restore, and to break chains over cities and people. Many young women came to me for deep inner healing prayer, and it was a joy to see smiles on their faces as they released their deep past hurts.

In the past few years, the Lord has been saying to me to take the dividing wall down. I had been functioning with Hebron House having two rooms. Since my only direction from God was to take the wall down, and it was going to cost about $4.000, convincing Don was a struggle. What was God's next plan for Hebron House? It's interesting that God spoke to me to take down the wall, considering Nehemiah's story. I know God has a divine purpose for this.

A new word from God, as I write this chapter, is "Revive." A word Don once had for me was, "Don't let anyone take the vision; you have been charged with this."

Two units of the Fifth Street Property that had once been filled with prayer are now leased to Surfing the Nations, a global humanitarian ministry reaching the surfing community. They have bases in Huntington Beach, Hawaii, Sweden, Sri Lanka, and Indonesia, with plans to open Surfer's Coffee.

God's Miracles Regarding Hebron House

1. The opportunity to purchase the Fifth Street Property.
2. My pastor, Steve Purdue's, call to plant a church was given right in front of where I was opening Hebron House.
3. Paula White's timely, succinct, and prophetic word confirmed to me the call to open Hebron House.

4. My friend immediately came up with the name for Hebron House.

5. The spiritual 'energy' to pray for two years, seven days a week, almost every morning.

6. Friends, friends, friends, who supported me in my endeavors.

7. The tenant just 'knew' I would need the unit next door to our office on Third Street.

8. The song "Whose Lips Will Plead?" began to play in my car, confirming The Nehemiah HB Project.

9. It took 52 minutes to drive around the city for the Nehemiah HB Project. It took 52 days to rebuild the wall around the Holy City of Jerusalem.

10. A continuation of God's service through Surfing the Nations at the Fifth Street property.

11

A Call to Healing Ministry

I will bring upon you a mighty anointing: the sick will be
healed, the dead in Christ will rise, the lame will walk. I
am doing this to you for My glory so others will see My
afflictions, My ways, and what I did for them. Wait, wait
patiently. I will drive the persecutor out from before you;
I will stop the hand of the enemy.

~ A word from God to me on September 19, 1995

With the power of His words,
Jesus said, "Let these go their way."

John 18:8

Out of slavery of sin and Satan, the redeemed must
come . . . from every cell of the dungeons of despair . . .
and forth come Despondency and Much-Afraid.
Satan hears the well-known voice and lifts his foot
from the neck of the fallen. Death hears it; the
grave opens her gates to let the dead arise."[30]

~ Charles Spurgeon

My River Vision

The Lord gave me this vision while I was praying and ministering
to people: I saw a moving river. At the beginning of the river, there
were steps to enter the flowing water. Three types of people were

waiting in line to enter the river: those with physical afflictions of the body—maimed and diseased; those with afflictions of the soul—torments; and those with afflictions of the spirit—demons.

On each side of this river stood those who prayed for the people needing healing. All they did, as the sick stepped into the healing waters, was hold their elbows to keep them stable.

A few days later, I saw the vision again, and this time it continued. The river ended with another set of stairs to exit the water. As the people stepped out, Jesus was there to help them, and then they too joined us at the sides of the river to help others.

I love this vision of seeing God heal. It is confirmed throughout Scripture that it is Jesus who does the healing. We are simply there to pray, encourage, love, and guide people.

Then great multitudes came to Him, having with them the lame, blind, mute, maimed, and many others; and they laid them down at Jesus' feet, and He healed them (Matthew 15:30 NKJV).

I consider this "my charge from God" to heal and pray for those in need.

The Vineyard

When Don and I had been attending a church for quite a few years, we felt the Lord leading us in a different direction. I made a list of churches to visit. When I shared the list with my friend, she told me I had it upside down. I had The Anaheim Vineyard at the bottom of the list. Not wanting to be legalistic, we visited there first.

As soon as Don and I sat down, the music began to play, and we both began to weep—not out of sadness but because the worship touched us deeply. As a result, we didn't want to visit anyplace else and could hardly wait to return. Still, we didn't want to be hasty, so we visited another church on our list. While it was fine, we could hardly wait to go back to The Vineyard, where we ended up staying for almost 15 years.

Driving from Huntington Beach two to three times a week took almost an hour, but for us, it was not too far.

The Vineyard was considered a "healing church," a term I had never heard before. I asked my friend what it meant, and we began learning about healing. We took classes on healing and joined the large Ministry Prayer Team after receiving training. This team prayed with people at the altar at the end of each service.

Eventually, we became coordinators for the small ministry teams and later their overseers. These teams provided private prayer appointments, each lasting an hour. We were the Sunday afternoon small ministry team coordinators.

We would attend church at 10 a.m., go to lunch with friends or take Aaron to Grandma's, and then return to lead our team for prayer appointments. What a wild, satisfying time of growth! We watched God heal many people in deep ways. We dealt with everything: divorce pain, physical illnesses, mental illnesses, multiple personalities, homosexuality—you name it. We even ministered to someone who came dressed in costumes, such as a chimney sweep with a tall black hat and a Civil War soldier. My pastor called him "histrionic."

We were dealing with significant issues, and I often needed to work with men. This required the protection and support of godly men. It had been prophesied over me several times that God would place "many strong men around me." My husband, Don, has been that for me, along with several others, in a pure, brotherly relationship.

What an education it was to see people healed and delivered from various afflictions!

"Most assuredly, I say to you, he who believes in Me, the works that I do he will do also; and greater works than these he will do, because I go to My Father" (John 14:12 NKJV).

God gave me these words on October 14, 1995: "I will bring to you, Hanya, many words for the nations to encourage tired, broken leaders—men of valor who have been robbed of their ability to function. Be faithful, listen to Me, hear Me; I am close to you. My people perish! Who will wake them up? Show them I care for them. Encourage, encourage. I see a basket of fruit in a time of famine. Their storehouses are empty, and they have no hope left. Dry their eyes; wet their parched lips. You are a torchbearer to bring light to the darkness, to wake up the sleeping."

I had always been involved with women's Bible studies and felt a pang in my heart about shifting toward healing prayer. Living far from Anaheim made it challenging to be closely involved with women there. Moreover, healing was now something Don and I were doing together.

12

Ministry to the United States

*At the Lord's direction, Moses kept a written record of their
progress. These are the stages of their march, identified by
the different places where they stopped along the way.*

Numbers 33:2

God called Don and me to ministry all around the world.
Amazing stories have been birthed, and Don and I have been blessed
to be a part of these beautiful stories. Believe me when I say, they will
not be boring.

Don and I were invited to help start a healing ministry at a
church called NewSong in Costa Mesa, California. This ministry
would be called MORE, led by Pastor Ed Salas, who later changed the
name to Sola Dei—God Alone. A very appropriate name, as we don't
want the glory that belongs to God. We are vessels to be used by
Him.

Stephen's Testimony

Below is a written testimony given to me by a member of Sola
Dei:

> *Bear with each other and forgive whatever grievances you may
> have against one another. Forgive as the Lord forgave you
> (Colossians 3:13).*

When Sola Dei first started over three years ago, I was just like anybody else who came to learn more about prayer. One day, I felt that God was telling me to forgive someone close to me who had hurt me deeply. "No," I argued. "I can't do it. There's too much pain that's been inflicted on me by this person." I dismissed it, left my home to attend prayer training and arrived at NewSong ten minutes early. When I arrived, the Sola Dei coaches were huddled in prayer, so I quietly took a seat.

One of the coaches later approached me and said, "We were asking the Lord whom we should pray for tonight when you walked in. Would you like to receive prayer? Tonight's topic is forgiveness."

At first, I resisted, but when the coach shared the verse above, I was convicted: "Forgive as the Lord forgave you." If God could forgive an unworthy sinner like me, who was I not to forgive others? It was like the parable of the unmerciful servant in Matthew 18:21–35.

There, in the Sola Dei hot seat, I went through the forgiveness prayer for the very first time. It led to one of my most significant and powerful breakthroughs ever. When I chose to forgive the person God had already placed on my heart to forgive, it felt as if a lead blanket had been lifted off my head—a lead blanket I didn't even realize was there until I sensed the freedom of having it gone.

While part of another church, the Anaheim Vineyard, we saw God work in mighty ways in the deep places of people's hearts. Miraculous healings took place as they yielded to the Holy Spirit.

Don and I served as healing prayer coordinators and later became healing prayer overseers for many years. This season changed our lives forever.

Debbie's Testimony

I once prayed for a woman named Debbie with a team for four one-hour sessions. She has given me permission to share her story.

Debbie was a 34-year-old married woman who held a ministry leadership position at her church as a worship leader. She had been depressed for over 30 years, with thoughts of suicide, and would beg Jesus to take her home—but she had never tried to take her life.

Debbie faced challenges from the start, when she was born three months prematurely and her father was not there when she arrived into the world and wasn't breathing due to mucus blocking her throat and lungs. Her father later committed incest with her though her family dismissed her claims as lies. She had asthma, was having nightmares and sleeping problems, and was questioning her femininity. There were sexual and financial problems in her marriage. She had been in and out of therapy for 12 years, but her problems persisted. Debbie came to our prayer sessions defeated, joyless, and hopeless.

I asked her if her therapist had helped her regarding her father's incest, and she told me that in 12 years she had not mentioned it. I was astonished and asked if she wanted me to pray about this issue. She said, "Yes!" My own inadequacies whispered, "Who am I to touch this?"

As we talked about her father not being at her birth, she realized she had rejected her father and made a death wish against herself, causing suicidal thoughts.

The Holy Spirit showed her a picture of the suction device used to clear her throat at birth. She felt the fear of not being able to breathe (we call this a body memory), which had caused a demonic stronghold that possibly resulted in the asthma. We brought all these concerns to the Lord in prayer, with her actively speaking to Him. After that first session, her suicidal thoughts and feelings were gone. Debbie shared this letter of response:

> Our Father used Hanya (and the team) to stand in the gap for me. God answered many of our requests for my healing, and we give Him honor and praise. Since the first session on October 5, 1996, I no longer want to die. Suicidal feelings plagued me for over 30 years. The hopelessness and helplessness of incest and other sick, sinful things to which I was exposed were covered in Jesus' blood. Soul ties and generational sins were broken. I think, feel, and act differently now that these are gone—I am truly a new person in Christ!
>
> The damage done to me pervaded every aspect of my life. In my sessions, I could forgive family members and ask God to forgive and heal them. Jesus is working in these relationships to renew and restore the years the locusts have eaten.
>
> *"So I will restore to you the years that the swarming locust has eaten" (Joel 2:25a NKJV).*
>
> The intimacy with my husband has greatly improved—I have more fun and less fear. Although I have labored in Christian therapy for many years on these and other issues, God used small ministry team prayer for major breakthroughs. I feel God's love and acceptance as I have never experienced. I can trust and rest in Him. I feel His joy and protection. I feel free for the first time in my life.
>
> One of the specific things for which we prayed was my sleep. For decades, I have had nightmares and fitful sleep. I am happy to report that I am sleeping better, which has affected my disposition. My husband has noticed that I do not get

angry anymore when I am awakened—I fall right back to sleep. He sees other changes in me as well.

I know this is a process, and sometimes issues cycle back. But now, I have hope. I no longer question God's love for me—especially when trials come or prayers remain unanswered. I used to think He was punishing me or didn't love me as much as He loved other people. I may not always understand, but I am not conflicted and stressed as much as I used to be. When He (God) says "No" to a request, it is for my own good. I now see Him as a loving, fair, and protective parent. This is a big change for me. He allows suffering, and He suffers with me to grow me into Christlikeness. He is sad when I am in pain but will work out the circumstances for my benefit and His glory.

My thinking is different and clearer now. I am worthwhile to Him. Although my birth was extremely traumatic, He (God) wanted me to be born and to remain alive! This is a major change in my thought process that continues to filter down into all areas of my life. *I am my beloved's, and my beloved is mine (Song of Solomon 6:3 NKJV).*

I have spent decades crying out to God for His healing. My therapist has counseled me to read, journal, study, pray, etc., for freedom, growth, and change. Many of her techniques and words to me were echoed by the prayer team. I was blessed by the many confirmations God brought and is still bringing. My therapist's hard work and the small prayer team's prayer dovetailed beautifully—so much came into focus.

Debbie did not mention the issue of questioning her femininity, so I will. It was such a wonderful transformation. She came plainly dressed, which I do not have a problem with—sweatshirt, jeans, no makeup—but she left with life in her face. I'm not sure if she realized she was now dressing very femininely, even wearing pink. A beautiful transformation took place in her through the work of the Holy Spirit and through the help of our team.

Kathilynn's Testimony

There was a time when I thought there would never be any hope. Fifteen years ago, I was in a cycle of addiction and was homeless. I ended up in prison, where I found God. He changed my life completely. I prayed endlessly and read my Bible daily. When I was released from prison, I went to a program that helped me figure out who I was. I went to church, started my own house-cleaning business, and gave back to my community. I am now a born-again Christian and teach in kids' ministry. God was the answer to all my prayers. I thank God for the life I live today and the person I have become.

What a privilege and honor to have been part of Kathilynn's healing process. She is a vibrant woman full of the Holy Spirit, and I gain life being near her.

What a privilege to serve God in this way.

God Sightings

1. The lead blanket Stephen didn't even know was there.
2. After many years with a licensed therapist, Debbie was majorly healed in four weeks of one-hour sessions.
3. Kathilynn's miraculous recovery from addiction and homelessness, being released into the fullness of life with God.

13

Austin, Texas

October 1997

Before leaving for any ministry trip, I go to the Lord in prayer, asking Him what is waiting for us there, what He might want to do, and I'm sensitive to any other impressions I might get from the Spirit.

When we are born, we receive natural talents and gifts—things we enjoy, things we are good at—and we produce fruit. When we become a Christian, we are given spiritual gifts in addition to those natural gifts. Some of my spiritual gifts happen to be in the seeing realm: visionary, impressions, teaching, prophecy, and words of knowledge.

In Christianity, "the word of knowledge is a spiritual gift listed in 1 Corinthians 12:8. It has been associated with the ability to teach the faith, but also with forms of revelation like prophecy. It is closely related to another spiritual gift, the word of wisdom."[31]

Our team from The Anaheim Vineyard came to Austin, Texas, to present a *Healing Prayer Seminar*. When we arrived, we were taken to our host homes. Don and I were taken to a beautiful home where we sat down to visit with our hosts—until I felt my face begin to itch. I had failed to ask if they had cats, to which I was highly allergic.

We were transferred to a smaller home and given the children's room with bunk beds.

Don was recovering from a serious illness from a prior ministry trip. He got the bottom bunk, and I climbed to the top bunk, which had a very deep hole in the mattress. I could not sleep, so I rolled up Don's jeans and stuck them in the hole. Yes, it was that deep—and I was one of the speakers the next day. When you think of speakers, you usually think of hotels and room service, luxury. Not us! Although we were treated very nicely!

At the conference on Thursday night, the team gave words of knowledge, using the spiritual gifts I mentioned earlier. Later during ministry time, people had the opportunity to receive prayer regarding the words that resonated with them.

Some of the words given were about oppression, healing for backs, people who wanted to commit suicide, ulcers caused by unforgiveness, and many more.

Regarding the church that invited our Anaheim Vineyard team to lead this conference, I saw the word "oppression" over it. I received a word that God would remove this oppression:

"The Lord will blow His wind through the corridors to cleanse the oppression out. (In the Spirit, I saw the Lord doing this.) The Lord's almighty hand will be on this church as a covering. Guard it well, like a watchdog." (I saw a bulldog at attention.)

I also had a picture of people holding hands around the church, and I received the word: "The enemy is looking for any crack in the circle. Unity is important. If there is any breach in the circle, fix it." This instruction would be called a word of exhortation.

I continued receiving words for this church. One was: "There is a lackadaisical spirit." The definition of lackadaisical is "lacking enthusiasm and determination; carelessly lazy."[32] My word continued: "Some of you think you are not important, so you have gone to sleep. I don't mean you are not doing anything, but there is no life in it."

I prayed over them: "Lord, break that spirit of sleepy eyes. Wake up! Everyone is important."

Prophetic words are for comfort, edification, and exhortation. With this invitation to minister at this conference, we were given the authority to move in the spiritual gifts God gave each one of us on behalf of their church. What a privilege to be trusted and used in this way.

On Saturday night of the conference, I received these words that I believe were from God:

"People, guard your leaders. They toil strongly and are tired. Uphold them. Charge them up. Help them to plug their batteries into the energy socket—some are too tired to do it themselves: 10-20-100 horsepower. Wash the feet of your elders. They serve well and are discouraged. Light a fire under them, Lord. Lord, give them new creativity to excite the people, to challenge them."

The following story was written by a woman I prayed for at this conference:

> I am the dominant being of multiple personalities and have been cleansed by the blood of Jesus during this seminar. I am not a stranger to renewal seminars and power revivals. I did believe in God. I do know in my heart that Jesus Christ of Nazareth is the Son of God, and I believed in the existence of the Holy Spirit. However, like Adam, I was hiding from God. Though I knew He could see everything, I was not comfortable talking about these compartments that housed fear, pride, deception, lies, talking about others (character assassinations), and using pain as a crutch to avoid becoming

an active member of any church. I had never confessed my sins openly.

Verses like James 5:16a—'*Confess your trespasses to one another, and pray for one another, that you may be healed*'— would be cut out of my "religious life." For the sake of not being shamed, condemned, or rejected, I would hold back and hide in the darkness.

I entered the seminar feeling a shroud of shame. As the first speaker began to teach, I started feeling the shroud falling off or being taken off. I felt vulnerable, but I was determined to accept Jesus for real that night.

I confessed my sins to my friend and a member of the visiting evangelists. On November 7 at approximately 9 p.m., I confessed my sins and am now a sister in Christ.

This woman told me, "I felt safe enough to confess. Today, I feel so free." I saw a picture of her heart, which had been broken, and the pieces were now put back together and held together with a net.

Dissociative Identity Disorder (DID) "used to be called multiple personality disorder (MPD). This is because many people experience the changes in parts of their identity as separate personalities in one body."[33]

Don and I have encountered people coming in for prayer who have this condition. For instance, one teenage boy, about 17 years old, was having problems at home with his mother, who was a dear friend of ours. We were meeting with him to help him cope with their family issues. His mother met with us one day to explain that she had multiple personalities, with 50 alters. Her pastor advised her to reveal her condition to us so we could better minister hope and healing to her son.

The poor young man was silenced regarding his problems to keep his mother's condition a secret. In time, as we met with her—and with the help of the Holy Spirit—she experienced the reintegration of her personalities, from fifty to two. It took her trusting us, knowing who she was in Christ, and the motivation to see her son healed to allow the perfect timing for her healing. The Lord is powerful and good. After several healing sessions, the young man let us know he would be pursuing a career in counseling.

I also knew another woman with MPD who had many personalities. She held a high-security position with our government. At home, one of her alters was a little boy, while her government alter functioned at an extremely high level of intelligence.

People with this condition have usually experienced great trauma and, to survive, were intelligent enough to compartmentalize parts of themselves. I have a high regard for people with this disorder, as the alternative can be going mad or committing suicide.

You probably wonder why we would be involved with such heavy issues. Don and I were lay counselors as well as overseers of the healing prayer teams at our church. For a season, there seemed to be an endless number of people signing up to be prayed for by our teams. If we knew of their diagnosis ahead of time, we would require them to also go to therapy, with signed permission for us to interact with their therapist.

We had specialized training and learned that you never cast a personality out as though it were a demon "in the name of Jesus." We also treated each personality as a separate person, even evangelizing each one within their system. What a privilege it is to serve Jesus in this unique, special way.

God Connections

1. The privilege of being given spiritual gifts as well as the tools to minister to the body of Christ.

2. Being allowed to be part of the teaching team at the conference in Texas, where we were all given complete freedom to function in the gifts of the Spirit.

3. The honor of being trusted by the woman with MPD who accepted Jesus into her heart as her Savior. She said to me, "I felt safe enough to confess. Today, I feel so free."

4. Being able to help the young man whose mother had MPD and then seeing him make the decision to become a counselor.

14

Arizona

*"Most assuredly, I say to you, he who believes in Me,
the works that I do he will do also; and greater works
than these he will do, because I go to My Father.
And whatever you ask in My name, that I will do,
that the Father may be glorified in the Son.
If you ask anything in My name, I will do it."*

John 14:12-14 NKJV

October 1999

We were invited to hold a retreat at a camp in the boonies of Arizona through a church connection. Don and I took a team of six to teach and minister on healing prayer.

The camp was really off the beaten track. We had to drive about 30 minutes on a bumpy dirt road, and even though we had a very nice car, my back was suffering with every jolt (I've always struggled with back issues). A deer even jumped in front of us on this bumpy trek.

A dried-up river ran through the road on the way to the camp, but when we arrived, the river was overflowing, and the road had turned into a river! We ended up needing to spend the night at one of the leader's homes nearby, traveling back quite a way. I wanted to go home already!

The next morning, we drove back to the river flooding the road, parked our car, and crossed the river on a plank with all of our luggage and food packed for the weekend. I was balancing two Marie Callender pies, walking across this plank, wondering if I would fall in. That was quite the adventure.

The following testimony is about a lady I prayed for at the retreat:

Her father was in prison for 90 years for abusing several children, and she was blamed by her family for his abuse of her. Some of the words her father said to her were: "You need to be submissive, or God will not work in your life. You shouldn't concern yourself with your own concerns."

Children of abuse often carry these pronouncements all their lives if no one helps lead them to understand the truth. If they are willing, healing prayer brings the Holy Spirit into these areas, bringing truth to their souls.

One of the team members saw in the Spirit that the family line had arrows coming at it, so our team prayed what we would call a generational curse off of her. Praying in the name of Jesus and by His shed blood is powerful in breaking sins and curses off of people.

"The name of Jesus grounds us in what is ultimate. His name secures us against the ever-shifting temporality around us—including our own incomplete perspective. Praying in His name is not a superstition, like knocking on wood or avoiding cracks in the sidewalk, but an expression of trust in His character. Trust that we receive when we pray as well as believe when we pray that His response, when it is not what we expect, is trustworthy." (*Foursquare 21 Days of Prayer and Fasting*, 2023)

She hated her family name, so we asked her what she would like her name to be in the spiritual realm. "Freedom" was her answer.

After going into great detail about the issues with her father and eventually forgiving him, we told her to take her shame to the cross, along with everything it represented. It was a beautiful thing to see the transformation take place.

The Bible says to honor your mother and father. We don't have to love them, especially when there is toxic pain and shame from them, but honoring them includes ensuring their care and safety.

With her lack of a father figure who could show her true love, we had her ask Jesus to come in and love her in the Spirit. We asked her, "How do you want Jesus to love you?" Jesus is a good Father. Afterward, she was in such a state of peace.

A spiritual vision I received for her after the cleansing, forgiving, talking, and praying was of her big toe entering the river of life. This represented the beginning of freedom, which is what she wanted her new name to be.

Because of the change that took place in her after the prayer, her husband came to us and received Christ into his life. He wouldn't come for a session with us until she shared what had happened to her. He told us he had never understood salvation before, even though his pastor thought he had already prayed the prayer.

Don and I went home via the Grand Canyon. We stopped at the El Tovar Hotel to ask if they might have a room available. Sometimes it takes a year to get a booking. It was Don's birthday, and we got a night in the presidential suite, where many presidents have stayed. Our room had a gigantic balcony and was situated right on the canyon's brim. A very nice gift from our Father.

Being Yielded to God

1. Don and I were blessed with the opportunity to lead this short trip to Arizona.

2. Our team member recognized the generational curse, leading us to pray and break it in the name and power of Jesus.

3. The new name, "Freedom," was given to the woman who was prayed for.

4. A husband came for prayer and received Christ as his Savior because of his wife's testimony.

5. Don and I were given the gift of a night's stay at the El Tovar Hotel on the edge of the Grand Canyon on Don's birthday.

15

Huntington Valley Healthcare

July–September 2018

I was invited as chaplain to take the place of a man who had been teaching the Friday afternoon Bible study at Huntington Valley Healthcare. I began doing so and really enjoyed it, as I taught through the book of Philippians. This was a church for many of the employees. The staff observed me and soon asked me to visit some of the patients to pray for them.

One request I especially remember was for a man who had been on life support for many years and was probably going to die in the next few days. This was the first time I went alone without anyone accompanying me. I was trusted.

I anointed him with oil and began to speak to him as though he could hear and understand me. I told him about Jesus and His provision of salvation, asking if he would pray with me. I proceeded to pray the sinner's prayer over him and then told him it was okay to release himself to God. He died the next day.

During that time, I tore my meniscus, so walking down those long hallways was painful. I was also scheduled to go to Washington State to do a women's retreat. While everyone there was blessed, it was not a very smart thing to do—I went limping. I came home to have knee surgery and did not return to the nursing home

16

Sequim, Washington

Healing Seminar, October 2017

My dear friend Sherry Johnson lives in Sequim, Washington, on the Olympic Peninsula. Through Sherry, we met Jonathan Simonson, a pastor and an anointed worship leader of the Sequim Foursquare Church. He presented me with an invitation to give a seminar at his church on healing prayer. Don and I believed we heard from the Lord and agreed to fly up to Sequim.

We stayed in a lovely bed and breakfast called Eden by the Sea, overlooking the Strait of Juan de Fuca, the waterway between Washington and Canada. What a beautiful place to refresh our bodies, souls, and spirits. The breakfasts were the epitome of a high-end restaurant, prepared and served with such grace by our host Evelyn, with the great help of her husband, Brownie.

This was a small church, and the seminar was sparsely attended, but the senior pastor told me he was powerfully impacted. As I gave my testimony about forgiving my mother regarding a certain situation, one of the young women attending was deeply touched and began crying as she sat next to her mother. Afterward, as I gave time for people to respond to my teaching and testimony on forgiveness, she and her mother spent time sharing things with many tears.

One gentleman volunteered and stepped to the front as a demonstration to receive healing prayer from Don and me. He needed help forgiving someone. As he was in the process of forgiving, the Holy Spirit brought another, more important issue to his mind. The prayer time with him had a tremendous emotional conclusion as he took everything to the cross of Christ. What a powerful public demonstration of how the Holy Spirit works, changing the direction of what we think is important, while God knows the true root of the matter.

The reward of seeing unexpected healing take place was worth all the effort it took to go to Sequim. Jesus knew exactly who we were there for, after all, Jesus went after the one, as this scripture proclaims:

"If a man has a hundred sheep and one of them gets lost, what will he do? Won't he leave the ninety-nine others in the wilderness and go to search for the one that is lost until he finds it? And when he has found it, he will joyfully carry it home on his shoulders. When he arrives, he will call together his friends and neighbors, saying, "Rejoice with me because I have found my lost sheep" (Luke 15:4-6).

I taught five topics regarding healing prayer on Friday evening and Saturday until noon.

During our last day in the Sequim area, we drove with Sherry and her husband, Charlie, to Hurricane Ridge, located in Olympic National Park. It was almost a mile high and covered with snow. This area gave us spectacular views.

Beauty in Freedom, September 28–30, 2018

The senior pastor's wife invited me to come and lead a women's retreat because of the healing seminar I had given the year before.

Before leaving for this retreat, I was struggling with a torn meniscus in my knee. I went limping and in pain but felt it was too close to the retreat to cancel. I coped by sitting on a tall stool through most of my teachings that weekend. I was scheduled for knee repair surgery shortly after returning home.

The retreat was held on Whidbey Island, in Puget Sound, north of Seattle, between the Olympic Peninsula and the mainland of Washington. It was a 35-minute ferry ride from the Olympic Peninsula to the island. This island is home to the Naval Air Station Whidbey Island, the premier naval aviation installation in the Pacific Northwest.

I created a weekend seminar entitled *Beauty in Freedom*, which about 30 women attended. On Friday night, I spoke on *The Beauty of the Lord in You*. Kenda Simonson, Jonathan's wife, was our worship leader and led us in a set of songs very appropriate for the weekend that included "Good, Good Father" by Chris Tomlin.[34]

On Saturday morning, I told them about a vision the Lord had given me a few years ago, for such a time as this. I call it *The Mountain Vision*. I'll share it with you:

> I saw a valley at the bottom of a very large mountain. People were sitting around campfires in the valley, quietly enjoying one another. Other people were climbing a very large mountain to get to the higher places of the Lord; some you could see, and some were hidden around the back. I could see myself about halfway up the mountain. It was an easy climb at the beginning, but then the path got narrower and harder as I climbed higher. Some people in the valley were waiting to take the climb, while others did not want to. It was too warm and cozy around the fire. I call it the valley of decision.
>
> *Thousands upon thousands are waiting in the valley of decision. There the day of the Lord will soon arrive (Joel 3:14).*

In *Matthew Henry's Commentary*, he calls this "The judgment day of the Lord, for the day of the Lord is near in that valley . . . we ought always to be ready for it because our judgment is at hand."[35]

I believe this valley is our life's decision place, where we determine whether to go to the higher places with the Lord—up to the mountain of the Lord—continually preparing for His coming. This change in us as we "go higher" can be called the sanctification process, which involves putting off our old self. It is a continual process as we proceed upward toward intimacy and maturity with God, our Father.

One thing King David said as he asked and sought the Lord was a desire:

To gaze upon the beauty of the Lord (Psalm 27:4b AMP).

There is a transformation happening within us during this sanctification process, which is between each of us and God. People only see us from the outside, but God sees everything—both outside and inside us. The decision to go deeper with God may require us to let go of some things to make room for more of God within us. He wants to fill us with the love given to Him by His Father.

In Jesus' last prayer, He says:

"O righteous Father, the world doesn't know you, but I do; and these disciples know you sent me . . . that the love with which you (God) loved Me may be in them, and I in them" (John 17:25-26 ESV)

While we are on the way up that mountain, there may be areas in our lives that hinder us from going higher and being able to walk confidently, steadily, and surely as the path narrows. We may want to stop and give up as we climb because of our fears and inadequacies, particularly in areas of unforgiveness and brokenness.

We need to go up to that mountain to seek His face. Are we living a *Coram Deo* life, or "life in the presence"? Are we living in the presence of God, under His authority, to the honor and glory of God? Are we living a life that allows His penetrating gaze to meet our eyes?

On Saturday morning, I taught *The Dynamics of Pain*, which included significant content about anger, followed by exercises to help us learn how to deal with pain. I also taught about forgiveness. In the evening, we went through my *Healing of Shame* teaching with a powerful time of ministry, where I, along with the senior pastor's wife, anointed each woman with oil, prayed for them, and gave them words we believed were from God. There were many, many tears—all good.

I gave the Sunday message entitled *Follow Your Dreams*, a sermon on finding our calling and responding to that calling. Jesus said in John 14:12 (NKJV):

"Most assuredly, I say to you, he who believes in Me, the works that I do he will do also; and greater works than these he will do, because I go to My Father."

Jesus is no longer here to do those greater works—He gives that to us to do.

When we don't respond to the call of God on our lives, we do often get second chances, just as He gave to Jonah (see Jonah 1-4). The second chance, however, may come with greater challenges that could have been alleviated if the first call of God had been chosen. Delay adds stress, and the atmosphere of this second work may not be as light and clear as the Lord had intended.

I spoke about a seed within us, planted by God, that needs to be discovered and then must die to grow into its intended, glorious maturity.

It was a beautiful time with these women from Sequim. The honorarium from the 30 women who attended my seminar was much more than expected. I even had checks on my bed when I got back to my room.

God's Gifts Given in This Chapter

1. My dear friend Sherry is always looking to increase my growth in God by presenting me with amazing opportunities. She has such a heart of love.

2. Watching the Holy Spirit change directions in our prayer demonstration, providing deeper healing to the man who came forward than he knew he needed.

3. Experiencing God's breathtaking creation as we visited Hurricane Ridge.

4. The honor and favor of being invited back so soon to do a women's retreat.

5. Having the opportunity to share The Mountain Vision. God gives us inspirational things to share with many audiences.

6. Seeing women anointed for the first time and having words of knowledge prayed over them—what a joy!

7. The encouragement of receiving monetary rewards. I was once told not to turn gifts down, as people need an outlet to give offerings.

17

Hotel Ministry

Abram was very rich in livestock, in silver, and in gold.
Genesis 13:2 NKJV

2006

There was a man from a church we once attended who impressed us greatly. He was a generous man of God who owned a hotel and wanted it to be dedicated to God's work. When we create a business plan and share it with God, He can ensure its success. There's nothing like inviting God to be part of a business.

This man invited Don and me to come to his hotel to pray over the rooms, and he then set up a prayer room right off the lobby entrance. He would often call me to come and pray for his employees when they had needs such as surgery or sickness. The Lord had told me I would be given a prayer room in this hotel.

One time, I was invited to minister in the prayer room for a man who was going to have surgery the next day. When I arrived, there were seven men in the prayer room. This was quite a surprise to me. I decided to show the men how to pray for their friend by having the hotel owner lay hands on the surgery area and anoint the man with oil. I directed the process, and the men were all eyes and ears, eager to learn.

One summer, I spent six weeks teaching Bible studies near the door to the hotel employee cafeteria so that any employee who wanted to join us could do so. I brought another man and woman with me in case anyone wanted prayer.

This generous hotel owner, with a beautiful heart, would hold elegant Christian events free of charge for many people. He loved to promote God's kingdom and served delicious food for free.

One day, we went to a home where there was a very sick dog on an IV that was not supposed to live. This dog was extremely important to its owner, so we prayed. Later, I found out the dog was healed. The Lord truly loves all creatures, great and small.

What a man of influence, using what God bestowed upon him to further the Kingdom. I was privileged and humbled to be a worker for Jesus in the marketplace through my dear friend. I learned so much.

As you read through Genesis 12-22, you'll see that Abraham had a thriving cattle industry that employed many people. His business flourished, and those in need of work found opportunities. When you develop a business idea and bring it to God, He will guide you to accomplish it. The joy of inviting God into your business will amaze you.

"Commit your works to the LORD, And your thoughts will be established" (Proverbs 16:3 NKJV).

King Solomon was also a wise businessman gifted by God who built the Temple of God (See 1 Kings 6 and 2 Chronicles 2-7).

And whatever you do in word or deed, do all in the name of the Lord Jesus, giving thanks to God the Father through Him (Colossians 3:17 NKJV).

We can call this 'business as mission.'

Glimpses of God

1. Meeting the hotel owner was a divine appointment from God.
2. Creating a prayer room in a hotel? Amazing!
3. Being able to pray for employees and train them!
4. Being given a room to teach the Bible, open for employees!
5. Healing a dog!
6. Mingling with people invited to fancy, free Christian nights with music and food hosted by the hotel owner.

18

Northern California

*Now God worked unusual miracles by the hands of
Paul, so that even handkerchiefs or aprons were
brought from his body to the sick, and the diseases
left them and the evil spirits went out of them.*

Acts 19:11-12 NKJV

One day, a Russian Molokan man and his son came to Don's office to ask him about real estate investments. He had heard about Don's business knowledge and wanted to meet him. When this man and his son arrived, he saw the name Hebron House written on our office window and was curious about what it was. Don explained what Hebron House was all about, and the man wanted to meet me. Hebron House is right next door to our Galitzen Properties office.

We invited this man and his wife for breakfast one morning. I did not know this couple and wondered how strict they were in their religious ways. Do they eat kosher? How do they dress? Will she have her head covered? Do I need to wear a skirt? They came dressed normally and brought another one of their sons and their daughter, Anastacia, to be mentored by us. I ended up having nothing to worry about. I made a nice breakfast for all of us, and we were delighted to have them in our home.

They were an amazing couple, and this meeting began a wonderful relationship. They have 13 children, all born at home, so this tells you they lived a very holistic lifestyle. I have a close relationship with Anastacia, who is like a daughter to me.

We were invited and agreed to do a healing prayer retreat in the couple's home for their family members, which also included some aunts and uncles. Upon our arrival, we were delighted to see that they lived on 17 beautiful acres, with their own large private swimming pond and a river running through their property. Our coming was a very big deal—they even killed a lamb to eat for the weekend. It was a blessing watching all their children participate in the weekend by serving and learning from us.

The father of these children took me to one of his daughters, giving me permission to have a deep prayer time with her. The trust and honor to do this were touching.

Their property had Native American roots, and Don and I were asked to walk around the 17 acres and pray over it. At one point in our walk, I stopped and had a powerful vision of a ladder from heaven with angels ascending and descending. I asked, "What happened here?" I'll let Anastacia tell her story, which she entitled "My Sanctuary":

> I was ten when my family moved from the city to a beautiful little farm in California just below the Sierras. It was a dream come true for my parents to raise their 13 kids. As one could imagine, with that many people in the house, I needed to escape for my prayer time. I was drawn to nature, and fortunately, I was surrounded by it. My daily walks, runs, and occasional moments sitting by the river were my times of solitude and prayer.

At some point, I sought a special place I could call my own. I searched every corner of the property until I found a little hillside with tall trees that overlooked the river and was within eyesight of the house. I hung a swing on the tree and cleared the foliage. This quickly became my place of solace, and I was drawn here increasingly as I prayed, sang praises to God, and cried out in times of need.

Once I got married and moved out, I passed on my treasured prayer spot to one of my younger brothers, who was struggling in his personal life and still lived at home.

Years later, Don and Hanya had become dear friends of mine and were invited to visit my family on the farm. Their time was full of teaching, prayer, and counseling. Later, my mom shared with me that while they walked around the farm, Hanya passed my prayer spot and sensed a sort of sacredness. Then, she had a vision of angels on a ladder going up and down in that spot. What a beautiful blessing this was for me to hear! I had never seen them, but I had felt the Lord's presence. A song I sang in my prayer sanctuary was this:

> My God is gracious, my God is gracious,
> He is merciful, He is kind,
> He is loving, He is wise.
> He is my everything, He is my King.

The next day, we presented another healing seminar to a wider group of Russian Molokan people about an hour and a half away. I had a dream of a man with a very long beard and the words, "Do not be afraid." The teaching I was bringing might not have agreed with the very religious Russian people, and it could have shaken my confidence.

Two things took place before my speaking time. First, the hosts wanted us to go next door to a family member's house and do a cleansing. I was in prayer and needed to stay focused for the day, so Don went, and everyone followed to watch him.

Second, while I was at the pulpit reviewing my notes, I saw through the window a car pull up. The man who got out had a very long beard! I remembered the dream: "Do not be afraid." He came in and sat down in the front row, about two feet from me. I was prepared. The spiritual gifts help in powerful ways, countering what the enemy might do in attacking any weaknesses we have.

I spoke, and then Don and I together held ministry times and gave the audience words of knowledge given to us by God. Someone's relative was gravely ill, so we gathered the group together to pray over a handkerchief. One couple then took it to the hospital and prayed over the sick person again. We prayed over a few more handkerchiefs for other sick people as well.

The Bible states that the Apostle Paul did unusual miracles, and Jesus said that after He ascended to heaven, we would do greater things (John 14:12):

Now God worked unusual miracles by the hands of Paul, so that even handkerchiefs or aprons were brought from his body to the sick, and the diseases left them and the evil spirits went out of them (Acts 19:11-12 NKJV).

Each time we follow God's leading, we leave so satisfied. Even though it seems our vitality has been taken, we are filled with another type of fullness.

I have a close relationship with Anastacia, and several of her 12 siblings have come to visit and be counseled and prayed over by both Don and me.

From Obedience Flows God's Goodness

1. The Russian man and his son sought out Don.

2. The Russian man's curiosity about Hebron House led us to host them for breakfast.

3. The amazing invitation to minister to their entire family with a weekend seminar.

4. Using the "seer" gift of God to see angels in Anastacia's sanctuary.

5. Being given a dream about the man with the beard and the words, "Do not be afraid."

6. Opportunity for Don to cleanse a house.

7. Opportunity to repeat some of this seminar to a greater group of Russian people.

8. Laying on of hands over handkerchiefs to give to a few sick people.

19

International Trips

"As You sent Me into the world, I also
have sent them into the world."

John 17:18 NKJV

"But you will receive power and ability when the Holy
Spirit comes upon you; and you will be My witnesses [to
tell people about Me] both in Jerusalem and in all
Judea, and Samaria, and even to the ends of the earth."

Acts 1:8 AMP

Ask of Me, and I will surely give the
nations as your inheritance, and the very
ends of the earth as your possession.

Psalm 2:8 NASB

I was called by God to international ministry. We developed friendships with people from different countries by hosting many of them at our home and ministry at Pier Colony condominium.

I set aside a special address box for our international contacts. I guess you would call this my "fleece" to God for international ministry. I began praying over this box of addresses regularly.

In September and October of 1995, God spoke to me:

"I will bring upon you a mighty anointing. The sick will be healed, the dead in Christ will rise, the lame will walk . . . for My glory. I will bring to you many words for the nations to encourage tired, broken leaders, men of valor who have been robbed of their ability to function. My people perish. Who will wake them up? Show them I care for them. Encourage! Encourage!"

I saw a basket of fruit in a time of famine:

"The storehouses are empty and there is no hope left. Dry their eyes, wet their parched lips. A torch bearer (me) to bring light to the darkness, to wake up the sleeping saints."

Scriptures That Encouraged Me

"Therefore prepare yourself and arise, and speak to them all that I command you. Do not be dismayed before their faces, lest I dismay you before them" (Jeremiah 1:17 NKJV).

"And you, son of man, do not be afraid of them nor be afraid of their words, though briers and thorns are with you and you dwell among scorpions; do not be afraid of their words or dismayed by their looks, though they are a rebellious house. You shall speak My words to them, whether they hear or whether they refuse" (Ezekiel 2:6-7a NKJV).

"How I kept back nothing that was helpful, but proclaimed it to you, and taught you publicly and from house to house" (Acts 20:20b NKJV).

I have not hidden Your righteousness within my heart; I have declared Your faithfulness and Your salvation; I have not concealed Your lovingkindness and Your truth from the great assembly (Psalm 40:10 NKJV).

Even with all these encouraging words and scriptures from God, I would become anxious about speaking, especially to the nations. One day, we had a prophetic man over for dinner the day before leaving for an international trip where I would be the keynote speaker. As he prayed for me, he said:

"Write as though you're not anointed, give it as though you are anointed, and while you are giving it, go fishing," meaning, look around to see what God is doing.

Our international travels have been filled with excitement, whether for ministry or vacation. Yet, in every journey, God worked through us for His purposes. Even on vacations like those to Jamaica and Puerto Rico, we saw Him move in powerful ways.

Jamaica

On one of our stops while on a cruise in Jamaica, Don told a woman who had an outdoor beauty shop to put little braids in my hair. My hair was very short, but I had one side longer than the other. As she proceeded to do this, Don spoke to the woman about Jesus. She was living with a man who had three women as wives. The woman knew it was wrong, but without this situation, she was financially helpless.

While Don was sharing the truth of the Word of God, people began to gather around. It didn't take long before we had a crowd of about 30 men and women listening to the gospel message.

After getting my hair braided, we walked on the beach and talked with three men about Jesus. Two accepted Jesus, but one was living with a woman and felt he was not worthy.

Later, on the same "vacation," as we walked through a marketplace, a very tall, skinny man approached Don and told him he had something for him. I think he meant drugs, but Don placed his hand on the man's chest and told him he had something better for him: Jesus! The man ran from us.

As we walked from stand to stand shopping, word went ahead of us, and we were asked to pray for the desperate needs of families.

Puerto Rico

During a timeshare vacation in San Juan, Puerto Rico, in June of 2006, we went to dinner near our hotel. As we spoke with the hostess, she seemed very down, so we asked her what was wrong. She told us her husband was very ill and in the intensive care unit at the hospital. We asked if we could pray for him. She bowed her head, but we said, "Oh, can we go to the hospital and pray for him?" She could not believe we offered and arranged to pick us up the next morning.

When we got to the hospital, we saw that her husband was very ill, and his appearance was pale. We asked him questions regarding his belief in Jesus, and he agreed to recommit his life to the Lord. We anointed him with oil and prayed for his salvation and healing.

It was a miracle that he left the hospital a day or two later! The day after he was released, they invited Don and me to go with them on a day trip to the Caribbean National Forest. We spent the entire day with them and could hardly believe that this man, who was near death's door, was driving us around all day and then took us to dinner. Seeing God's handiwork never ceases to amaze me.

What a joy it is to be a vessel, ready and willing in whatever time and place to be used by God. This is much better than lying around on the beach.

We later found out that this couple had been living together, and we later received a beautiful wedding picture of them. She wrote that she knew their marriage would make me happy.

Don and I have had the privilege of visiting many places in the world, and in the deepest banks of my mind, I have pictures of God's beautiful creation. I recall the wind creating waves across the wheat fields on the Caucasus Mountains in Russia while a row of men stood there with their scythes. Another moment was watching the vibrant sunset in Puerto Vallarta, with the sky emblazoned in oranges, reds, and yellows. A lasting memory was standing at the water's edge, gazing at the turquoise ocean in Jamaica.

There are many trips we've taken around the world that will not be mentioned as a chapter because they were vacation trips, but we never passed up an opportunity to minister Jesus when we could.

How God Used Us

1. I was inspired to create an international prayer box of addresses and dedicate it to God.
2. Having scripture as my strength when I became anxious about serving in public settings.
3. While in Jamaica on vacation, feeling silly having my very short hair braided so Don could testify to a woman.
4. Don brought two men to the Lord as we walked on the beach.
5. Don spoke to the tall man in the marketplace about Jesus being better, and people were drawn to us for prayer.
6. The miracle of praying for and witnessing the healing of the man in ICU while on vacation in Puerto Rico.

20

Mexico

When I was a young girl, my father took us to Mexico with our old pick-up truck, filled to overflowing with furniture and clothing to distribute to the poor. This impacted my life, giving me an understanding of a very different world outside of my protected one. I developed compassion for the poor as we went from community to community, giving away what was unnecessary to us but precious to them.

I can still remember standing in our truck, handing things out—what a good feeling that was. I remember a woman pointing at a crib she wanted, but we just couldn't get it out as it was covered by and filled with so many other items we had loaded into the truck. I was disappointed she couldn't have it. My father gave us a hands-on lesson in practicing care for people, as written in the Bible. I'm grateful to my father for imparting his gift of compassion to me.

"Blessed are those who help the poor" (Proverbs 14:21b).
"Helping the poor honors him [their Maker]" (Proverbs 14:31b).

Throughout the years, Don and I participated in various trips to Mexico, traveling to Tijuana several times with a church we attended to visit an orphanage. We brought lunch for the children and workers, played with the children, prayed for the sick, and prayed for those leading the orphanage.

Don and I also served a church planted by Hope Chapel in Rosarito Beach, Mexico. Later, we visited and served at various other churches. One church we visited was Pastor Daniel's Templo Christo Missionary Church, where we cleaned, evangelized in the neighborhood, and had dogs barking at our heels.

One distinct memory in Rosarito Beach took place during our daily time of worship and prayer before our service for the day. We talked about going on "treasure hunts," where we would pray and ask God what He wanted to do that day. As we prayed, a young girl received the name Rosa. We then walked the streets looking for someone with this name, expecting God to move.

We did, in fact, encounter Rosa on our walk, and I had the privilege of bringing her to the Lord. She was filled with such joy that her friends were in awe. We also visited an elderly man who accepted Jesus, and we prayed for him. We named him "Happy," as we would see him walking by the church afterward with a gigantic smile on his face. As tired as we all were, this brought such refreshment to us.

The greatest memory, however, was when Don and I took an epic road trip through Mexico early in our marriage.

Road Trip – May 1969

One adventurous thing we did early in our marriage, after Don and I had been married seven years, was take a round-trip road trip from Monterey Park, California, to Acapulco, Mexico. We were gone for three and a half weeks and drove about 5,000 miles!

When I think about it now, I am amazed that we drove our brand-new white Mustang with a black hard top on dusty, unpaved roads! We began this trip by driving to Arizona early one morning and entering Mexico through Nogales. Our car was filled with luggage and food, as I wanted to be careful about what I ate. Mexico was foreign to me, so I took a cooking pot and many cans of food.

Hermosillo. Our first stop was Hermosillo. The movie *Catch-22* was being filmed there, so we went to the filming site and met some of the actors. The movie is a satirical, dark comedy war film adapted from a novel by Joseph Heller. Alan Arkin plays a pilot and bombardier during World War II, trying to cope with the war and convince people he is insane. We saw the movie after we got home and were not impressed.

We stayed at a small beachfront hotel, where I learned how tasty lime is on papaya.

Guaymas. Guaymas, which means "a beach," is a gulf port and deep-sea fishing resort in the state of Sonora, Mexico. Don and I stayed at another beachside hotel and spent a few days visiting tourist stores filled with Mexican goods and walking through their many plazas.

After leaving Guaymas, we faced a very long drive to Mazatlán—about 11 hours—with nothing in between. I desperately needed a gas station, and when we finally found one, I hurried to the bathroom. To get there, I had to walk past what seemed like 30 men just sitting around and snickering at me. When I finally got into the bathroom, I found it riddled with peepholes and left immediately.

Mazatlán. Mazatlán is a large tourist destination. I remember Don and I renting a private fishing boat for an entire day. We had our own driver and spent eight hours trying to catch a sailfish but didn't catch anything. Determined to get our money's worth after paying $50, we went in circles all day. It was one of my most miserable days—the sun was so hot, and there was nowhere to go for shade.

Taxco – "Tass-ko." Leaving Mazatlán on our way to Mexico City, we stopped at a silver mine in Taxco, a city known for its silver and crafts. We took a small tour and purchased a few pieces of silver jewelry before continuing our adventure.

Guadalajara. Entering Guadalajara, we noticed a more modern, upscale, and very beautiful city, clearly geared toward tourists. We met many Americans who had made their homes in the Lake Chapala area. Guadalajara is known for its culture, Mariachi music, tequila, and charrería, a national sport of Mexico originating in Spain. Think of ranchers with their horses and livestock competing in various activities. A Mexican man who rides horses is called a charro, the equivalent of our cowboy.

It was refreshing to feel more at ease in these surroundings and to visit with Americans. After traveling for quite a while, we needed a taste of familiarity.

Mexico City. As soon as we arrived in Mexico City, we were immediately pulled over by the Federal Police, even though we knew we hadn't done anything wrong. The officer asked us incredulously, "What are you doing here?" and warned, "Park your car in your hotel garage and do not take it out until you leave." This put the fear of God in us. Maybe it wasn't a good idea to drive such a nice car in Mexico.

We stayed in La Zona Rosa, or the "Pink Zone," a district that is the center of the city's nightlife."[36] Today this area is also known as a hub for the gay community.

Looking very much like tourists (picture me with 70s platinum blonde hair teased as high as possible), we got into a conversation with a man who told us he could take us to a shopping center with good prices. Foolishly, we got into the back seat of his car with his driver and two other men.

We drove for a very long time, and I started feeling nervous, wondering where we were going. Anxiously, I asked, "When will we get there?" We didn't know these three men! How naive we were. Finally, we arrived at a deserted marketplace. We bought a lot of things—there were no other tourists there but us. Looking back, I now see how God's hand kept us alive.

One evening, we took a bus tour to see the Teotihuacan "City of the Gods" Light and Sound Show of the Pyramids of the Sun and Moon, which included dinner. The pyramids were illuminated as the story of the ancient people and the meaning of the pyramids was told.

While in Mexico City, we couldn't miss the Ballet Folklorico—no way! The ballet lasted 90 minutes and was filled with lively music and dances representing Mexican culture. The costumes were incredible and expressed the life and spirit of the Mexican people. What we know as the "Mexican Hat Dance" in English is called "El Jarabe Tapatío" in Spanish and is Mexico's national dance.

Mexico City is definitely a vibrant city. We enjoyed many tours of museums and, of course, all the shopping. Our car was getting filled.

Acapulco. Arriving in Acapulco was such a refreshment after all the dry land we had been driving through. We were now along the coast. Don and I checked into our lovely room and looked forward to a vacation after the grueling weeks of driving.

We went to see the amazing professional La Quebrada Cliff Divers. "These divers perform daily, diving up to 135 feet from the cliffs of La Quebrada into the sea below. The divers worked six days a week and were paid about $550 per month. This profession, which began as a dare, has been in existence for eight decades. The divers start training at age five, and the skill is only passed down through generations.[37]

However, we noticed a different attitude from the employees in Acapulco compared to those who had served us earlier on our journey. Don and I had so enjoyed the friendliness of hotel employees and shopkeepers in the other cities. In Acapulco, one man who brought something to our hotel room took his tip but then kept his hand out for more. We noticed this behavior repeatedly and were not pleased, so we decided to leave Acapulco after two days.

On our way back, we passed through smaller towns that we had skipped on our way to Acapulco, stopping in Guadalajara once again.

Puerto Vallarta. Puerto Vallarta is a beautiful tourist destination, where I saw what I believe to be the most stunning sunsets over the beach. It felt like such a luxury to push a button on our umbrella made of palm branches and have a waiter come to take our order. I could easily get used to this. We lounged on the beach, watching the sky turn shades of red and orange as the sun set over the water.

We met Mrs. Jacuzzi on the beach—she was the widow of the founder of Jacuzzi hot tubs. She invited some of us to her apartment for appetizers before dinner. It was a very nice time.

Early in the morning, we left Puerto Vallarta in our brand-new white Mustang, driving through several poor, small towns—a young couple, with me and my platinum blond hair.

Driving down one particular road, I had an unsettling feeling, like a man with a gun might come out and kill us. It crossed my mind that maybe this trip wasn't such a good idea after all.

The deserted town where I felt extremely uneasy

On the last stretch home, we planned to drive to California through the border town of Tijuana. As we were driving on a lonely highway, we noticed we were being followed—and then chased! Remember, we had this snazzy new car.

We found ourselves driving alongside an incomplete highway and decided to jump onto it. We sped up to one 100 miles an hour to get away from them. Shortly after escaping the other car, we were then followed by a police car. We stopped and explained to the officer that we had been followed. He told us to get back on the regular road.

We ended up leaving Mexico through Nogales into Arizona, and it felt so good to be back on American soil. I'm glad to have lived to tell you about our Mexico vacation!

21

Russia and Turkey Adventure

July 15 - August 9, 1974

Don and I were asked to travel to Russia with our Russian pastor, George Samarin, and six others. This trip would be for a month in Russia, including Armenia, followed by another week in Turkey. Several Samarin family members wanted to visit sites in Turkey where their families had lived, and Don's grandmother had also lived in Kars, Turkey. Kars used to be Russian territory but was taken over by Turkey through war.

I was 30 years old, Don was 32, and we would be celebrating our tenth anniversary on this trip. We didn't have any children yet, so we were free to go. We left on July 15, 1974, being sent off at the airport by a large group of friends and relatives, singing religious songs in Russian. There were prayers, tears, kisses, and well-wishes.

We flew to London, England, where we had a five-hour layover and took the opportunity to take a bus to the suburbs. While walking in a neighborhood, we met a couple, the Jennings, who then invited us into their tiny home for a visit. Afterward, we did a little shopping and returned to the airport. We then flew on to Helsinki, Finland, after being body frisked. From the plane window, we were welcomed by a lush green landscape, which was a beautiful sight after sitting on the plane for so many hours. It wasn't long until we would take off for Russia in an Aeroflot airplane.

Let's talk about the Russian Aeroflot planes. Oh, my goodness, they're not as modern-looking as ours, but they make up for it with impressive speed, being military aircraft. Up in the air, our ears popped, and the plane turned around in a split second to get us on course. Air conditioning didn't kick in until we were in flight. Hard candy was served first, followed by 'lemon juice' and 'chocolot,' and then more hard candy. Near the end of the flight, we were so tired that one of our group said, "Our toenails weigh too much!"

We need a bit of history for you to know about the political climate during the time we were in the country. Leonid Ilyich Brezhnev was a Soviet politician who led the Soviet Union as General Secretary of the governing Communist Party.

"While Brezhnev's rule was characterized by political stability and significant foreign policy successes, it was also marked by corruption, inefficiency, economic stagnation, and rapidly growing technological gaps with the West."[38]

While we called it Russia, during the time we visited, it was officially the Union of Soviet Socialist Republics (USSR).

We traveled to the USSR during the Cold War, which was an ongoing political rivalry between the United States and the Soviet Union.

"The term 'Cold War' was first used by George Orwell in an article published in 1945 to refer to what he predicted would be a nuclear stalemate between 'two or three monstrous super-states, each possessed of a weapon by which millions of people can be wiped out in a few seconds.'"[39]

"At home, our President was Richard Nixon, and our country was dealing with the Watergate situation, a major scandal during and after the 1972 landslide of his election. The Watergate scandal refers to the burglary and illegal wiretapping of the headquarters of the Democratic National Committee in the Watergate complex by members of President Nixon's re-election campaign and the cover-up of the break-in, resulting in Nixon's resignation on August 9, 1974."[40] While in Russia, we received no news of our country's situation.

St. Petersburg

After arriving in the USSR, going through customs was a frightening experience, as we were all bringing in too many Russian Bibles and religious books. Don and I were conservative about this, but remember, all our names were Russian, and all of us spoke Russian except for Don. When one of the members of our group had too many religious books, the officials would remove several, pile them up, and put a note in their customs declaration stating that these books had to exit the country with the people they belonged to.

I remember getting hot and pale at the same time. After the official took many of Jack's books, two more officials came over and tore through everything else he had packed—poor Jack! Our leader, George, had all his things taken apart and inspected. One couple with us brought a camouflage American Army duffel bag and got thoroughly targeted and inspected.

While all this was taking place, an official made friends with Don and me. We were at the end of the group; he took a very quick look through our things, not disturbing too much, and said we were fine. I knew God was with us. One inspector, among the many, found the

Mickey Mouse puppets I had brought to give to children, and he liked that. The whole ordeal was a shattering experience, but getting out of the country would be much worse!

We got to our hotel, had to turn our passports in to the front desk upon check-in, and wouldn't get them back until leaving for the next city. We were hungry, but the drama was so great that we just went to our rooms and slept.

The next morning, we had a typical breakfast buffet, which was cheese, bread, 'kislee malako' (think thin buttermilk), 'chi' (tea), eggs, and pastry.

We visited the Hermitage that day. The Hermitage has millions of dollars' worth of art and antiques, so if you stopped and looked at each object, you would be there for nine years. Each room in the museum has a woman sitting at a desk to oversee things. Well, my Don introduced himself as a Galitzen—our last name—and a Prince at that, and he proceeded to tell her that he was there to pick up the family jewels and asked where we should park our truck. I was horrified, but she laughed. I brought Earth Shoes to be more comfortable walking but had not broken them in yet, so my calves were screaming.

Russia has its own Intourist Travel Agency, but our group came in on our own itinerary, which technically was not acceptable. Once the officials realized this, they removed Kyiv from our itinerary. Rostov and Pyatigorsk were not included, so we revised our plans by adding these cities and had to pay more to do so.

You need to know this was 1970s Communist Russia. There we were—American Russians who spoke the language! We came in without a proper Intourist Guide, so we were assigned a guide for the first day in each new city we traveled to and were watched by the

KGB on the other days. They were not secretive; we were being tailed.

"The KGB, in Russian Komitet Gosudarstvennoy Bezopasnosti, in English Committee for State Security, foreign intelligence and domestic security agency of the Soviet Union."[41]

"Now, since 1995 known as the FSB, Federal Security Service of the Russian Federation, the main successor agency to the Soviet Union's KGB."[42]

The next day, we could not take any tours since we had a flight, so we wandered around the city for a few hours. A few of our men, Don included, put two watches on their wrists to attract street guys who bargained with them; no deals were made. Our guys were having so much fun!

Our group went to our first authentic Russian dinner in the hotel. The food was delicious. The fish at the restaurant was delicate and very thinly sliced, and all of us kept asking for more platters (up until this time, we had mostly been eating cheese and eggs). Not having any idea of what kind of fish we were eating, we asked! Our waitress told us we were eating 'kit.' "What is kit?" we asked. We were shocked to find out it was whale meat! You need to know we were kosher, and whale, a water-bound mammal, is not kosher as it does not have fins or scales and needs both to be considered kosher. We were horrified and giggled a lot at the same time. The cost was 76.97 Rubles (101.34 dollars), which was a lot of money in 1974.

The next morning, we went to the Peter and Paul Fortress, the original citadel of St. Petersburg. We then took a boat ride on the Neva River. As we passed a beach, we saw middle-aged ladies in their underwear, changing from their bikini tops very discreetly. And the men, wow! They were wearing little Speedos!

Moscow

On day one in Moscow, after breakfast, we took the required city tour and noticed we were being tailed by a man in a gray suit. After lunch, we went to the 'berioska,' which was the gift shop in our hotel—only tourists could shop there. The salesgirls could exchange currency from every country without batting an eye; it was amazing. Then, we went to the famous GUM (pronounced 'goom') department store.

We still needed to continue with our itinerary changes, and two of our men who spoke Russian were fighting to get Kyiv back onto our itinerary, which was causing a big fuss. I thought for sure we would be deported. Meanwhile, Don was speaking in English with our guide about how Russians live. Through this conversation, he discovered they could not have more than one item on credit at a time. She and her husband both worked full-time, had no children, and still didn't make enough money. We were hearing firsthand about the oppression of living under Communism.

Here are some day-to-day journal entries from our time in Russia:

July 20, 1974. We were supposed to tour the Armory to see the crown jewels, but it was booked for today, so we went back to the GUM department store where I purchased a Russian mink hat. We went to see the Eternal Flame at the Tomb of the Unknown Soldier. It is a Russian tradition for couples who have just married to cruise around the city, visiting different monument sites after their civil ceremony. While we were at the Eternal Flame, we saw 15 to 20 couples taking photos.

The men went to look for samovars (metal urns with a spigot used to boil water for tea), and the ladies went to Nora Ann's room where she fixed a tub with Hexol that she brought with her, and we all soaked our tired, blistered feet in the bathtub. My new Earth Shoes were not helping. The ladies took a nap, and later the men joined us for coffee.

We wondered why the women didn't wear hose until we found out they were ten dollars a pair. Their shoes looked like they were from Kmart but cost between 30 and 50 dollars a pair—a lot of money in 1974 Russia.

July 21, 1974. Don and I had a nice rest in our room last night. I took a hot bath. We finally took a tour of the Kremlin and the Armory. Nora Ann made friends with our 'dzeshoodnik,' room mother, Zola, the woman sitting at the desk overseeing our floor. We had to turn our keys into her each time we left our room, so we hid our valuables under the mattress. Nora Ann, our social butterfly, told Zola we were looking for samovars, and later got a call that she had a samovar that was 100 to 150 years old, gifting it to Nora Ann. Don took all the ladies to the Ukraine Hotel's 'beriozka' where we purchased souvenirs. After dinner, we went to the Russian Folk Dance and Choir—it was excellent.

The hardship of getting tickets to our desired destinations continued to be a hassle. So far, the travel agency only released tickets to Rostov; they were good at giving us the runaround.

July 22, 1974. We were up and packed early; it was getting hard to zip my mother's suitcase, which had a bad zipper. I left a few Christian paperbacks in our hotel—who has time to read them? Not me. As Americans, we are traveling with way too much. Getting taxis or anything is a hassle. We boarded our plane and were just sitting, waiting for it to take off, basically taking a 'banya' bath (Russian for steam bath) since the air conditioning wouldn't turn on until we were at a certain height. We were miserable.

We checked into our hotel, and Al was going to help us find our friend's cousins. We had a gift for them and needed a taxi, but when we showed them the address, none of them would take us. The taxi driver took us to the train station that would leave at 11 a.m. and arrive at 3 p.m. in the city where the Kasimoffs lived. It ended up that we were not allowed that far outside the city, so we mailed their package. We didn't have our passports either since we had turned them in to the hotel desk. The government knows how to keep us close to home.

Rostov-on-Don

July 23, 1974. While in Rostov-on-Don, we took a tour where we learned interesting information about the city.

Rostov-on-Don is a beautiful, green vacation spot along the ocean with cottages provided for families who work for industrial factories. One hundred and fifty thousand people could stay here at the same time.

The Amazon women (not to be confused with the women from the Amazon Rainforest) used to live in Rostov-on-Don. These Russian Amazon women did not like men and protected themselves by using bows and arrows; they cut off their right breast to be better archers. They fought against the Tartars, who were "people originating from the vast Northern and Central Asian landmass then known as Tartary."[43]

Cossack people lived here too; they were of Turkish origin and were known as the Don Cossacks. One telling story of the Cossack people is that when a baby boy is 40 days old, the father puts him on a saddle, and if the baby holds on to the saddle himself, he automatically becomes a Cossack.

The Cossack marriage ceremonies consisted of a circle of men along with the groom who would say his name and the soon-to-be bride's name to the Chieftain. The Chieftain would then declare, "Yes, you are married." A similar ceremony would take place for a divorce.

After our tour of the city, we had tea and cakes in town. The cost is on the honor system—you eat what you want, then tell the cashier what you had and pay for it. Don and I walked back to our hotel, and on the way back, we shopped and purchased six beautiful silver dessert forks and an amber ring. We then found children's blocks with the Russian alphabet on them with our future children in mind.

Later that day, we had Molokan visitors: Aunt Paula Valov and Aunt Katsya Babinko, who traveled quite a way to see us. We had all sent letters to our Molokan people and never knew who would show up. They gifted us with homemade jam, apples, cherries, and apricots. Our floor mother set up tea for all of us in the floor lobby, and we had a nice visit. One of the aunts had to leave as she had animals to feed; the other aunt had her very first restaurant dinner with us and stayed overnight. It was a great treat for these women to visit their people from America, and we enjoyed their company as well. The women who came were the only Molokans left in their city and were worried that there was no one to bury them in our Russian style. We had rain, lightning, and thunder that night—I've never seen the sky lit up so brightly.

Other visitors who came thought Don was a single young man around 18 years old and brought their niece to meet him. The Russian dream is to live in America. When I arrived, the aunt of the young lady asked who I was and was so embarrassed when she found out we had been married almost ten years; they left quickly.

July 24, 1974. More visitors traveled four hours by train to visit us. Some observations I made as we toured the city are that there are no billboards here, only communist signs. I have seen only five dogs in the country in a week and a half. We visited the Don Cossack Museum today.

We were at the airport awaiting our flight to Pyatigorsk. Everyone was worn out, but Don and I were alright—we'd been careful about our rest. We all had numerous carry-ons because we didn't want to pay the extra weight fee. We slept in the airport until 11 p.m., then arrived at Pyatigorsk at 3 a.m. We were so tired; it was the roughest plane ride yet.

Pyatigorsk

July 25, 1974. Pyatigorsk is a beautiful city with walnut, plum, and cherry trees. Mikhail Lermontov, a well-known Russian romantic writer from Pyatigorsk, wrote the book *A Hero of Our Time*.[44] He was sometimes called "The poet of the Caucasus."[45] In this book, Lermontov challenged the court aristocracy, which led to his exile to the Caucasus.

This city is known for its therapeutic mineral waters, with many sanatoriums used for therapy, healing, and long-term treatment. You cannot drink this water for more than 24 days because it deposits salt into your bones. You need a 12-month break between courses. This mineral water goes through the hills, flowing through hardened lava, picking up salts, valuable minerals, and gasses along the way. There is even radioactive water for varicose veins.

We are attracting more Molokan people. After breakfast, we had more relatives of our friends come to visit; this time, John Shivchikoff and Vasili Evanich Nemov were with us. Later, we took a long walk up a huge hill and then around town. We arrived for our 2:00 p.m. tour, and the guide said, "We will walk a little." After the tour, we were ready to relax and went for a mineral bath.

We had dinner with John and Nadya Conovalov. We were invited to a 'postayani' church and then again to the Conovalovs' house. 'Postayani' means a non-charismatic church; sometimes our Molokan people would have a lively time of worship, even jumping, but probably not in this church.

July 26, 1974. I needed to wash my hair this morning, and we only have a very large bathtub. I knelt down and bent over to put my head under the faucet, and as I was doing this, I saw a four-inch-long cockroach. It was so good to have Don around.

We took a public bus to another Molokan church and were crunched together, body to body. We needed government permission to go to this church, as well as any homes we visited, and could not spend the night outside of our hotels.

This was a registered church, meaning the government sent two men who were the only ones allowed to read from the Bible. The people were all old, as the younger generation would be persecuted if they attended. This was the government's plan to maintain control over religion. People could sing and worship but not read the Bible for themselves. We arrived and were greeted in the Molokan fashion with a formal prayer and a kiss on the lips. After the service, many samovars were lit up for 'chi' (tea). Then we ate, ate, and ate some more. The first course was bread, hard-boiled eggs, cheese, cucumbers, and tomatoes. Next, we had vegetarian borscht, then rice.

We were picked up by Yvonne Bogdanoff, who took us to his house. Having a car here is a very big deal. Yvonne told me he purchased his car with donation money given by the United States Molokan churches. Their home had running water, electricity, and television sets; he even had tape recorders. The toilets were outside. We ate lamb and potatoes, and they had two beautiful samovars. Yvonne was a block administrator, a government official, who took care of the needs in his designated area.

July 27, 1974. We were awakened at 6:30 a.m. when George knocked on our door, telling us people were here to take us to their home for breakfast. These people are 'prehune,' spiritual jumpers. When we arrived, we had a regular Russian Molokan 'malenia,' which is a formal church prayer. We felt very honored to be there, and they were honored to have us—it was touching. These were all very old people and wouldn't be here in five years, so it was wonderful to be visiting our historic heritage.

When we returned to our hotel, there were more Russian people waiting to see us off on our way to Tbilisi. We boarded the airplane and had an hour-and-a-half delay, another 'banya' bath, which meant sweat was pouring off us.

Tbilisi

July 27, 1974. When we arrived in Tbilisi, there were yet more people to greet us, and we were not very happy to see them as we were so tired. It was about 4 p.m., and they had been waiting for us since early morning. We were quite the attraction. We were on the thirteenth floor of our hotel and had a beautiful view of the city and the Kora River.

Everyone had relatives waiting for them except Don and me. Nora Ann had written to several relatives, and they were all there arguing about who would host her and her husband. We were invited along with them and took a taxi, which was a great luxury. We did not ask for government permission to go. This was a different city with a different language, and it didn't feel like Russia; we felt more freedom. I am platinum blonde and getting lots of stares here. Don is looked at a lot too; it's unusual for Americans this young to come to Russia.

We walked into our host's backyard, which had seven samovars lit for tea. Samovars have a wood-burning center cylinder to heat the surrounding water, which gives the tea a wonderful taste. We ate wonderful little pastries with apple and pear filling, along with stinky cheese, followed by thick 'lapsha' (noodle soup) with lots of butter, stew meat, and thin watermelon slices. There were lots of children here. We were treated so nicely. It was raining as we returned home in a minibus and then caught the subway. We came back to the hotel with a tub full of laundry waiting for me.

July 28, 1974. We had heavy rain off and on all night, and when we woke, I had to get ready for church. Usually, you wear what is called a 'Russian outfit,' which I made myself, but I wore a long skirt and a long-sleeve blouse. I was covered from head to toe and wore a lace 'kasinka' on my head. A man came to direct us to church, and as we walked to catch a taxi, many people stared at us. When we arrived at church, we were greeted by the people. This area of the city looked like downtown Los Angeles many, many years ago, where our people settled in, called 'the flats.'

The church was in a cellar with only three windows. We ladies sat in the front row where women singers usually sit. The women outnumbered the men two to one because of the war, and everyone attending was very old. Young people don't go to church because of the pressure from the government; they might lose their jobs and get beaten. These elderly people were very surprised that young people like Don and me were even interested in being with them, as their own children don't take an interest.

Church lasted so long; the first half had five speakers and a dozen songs. The speeches in Russian were very short and not very evangelistic. One woman reminded me of 'Ma Kettle,' a television actress known for her portrayal of an unrefined woman; she sang like a man and took over. There were prophecies given, and people spoke in tongues—a Pentecostal spiritual language—with no one to interpret. It became disruptive, but maybe this group needed the lively chaos.

Bread and salt were brought to the table; everyone stood, and a woman prayed. An offering was taken, with everyone putting their money under a handkerchief so no one could see what was being given. Every time "Amen" was said, everyone bowed very low together. I became very lightheaded as the heat was unbearable down there. There was only one course for our meal: 'chi' (tea), hard-boiled eggs, cheese, bread, and sweet bread. Church ended at three o'clock, and after the service, everyone came up to us, asking if we knew certain relatives of theirs in the United States. It was very hard to say "no" when we didn't; they were desperate to hear about their loved ones.

The same day, we were invited to another house for church, followed by another meal. Don made friends with a younger man, Vladimir, who kept winking at Don, wanting him to go upstairs and have Cognac with him and a few men. I think we could have gotten a samovar from him if Don had gone. He was offended that Don didn't join him, as it is a secular custom to drink together. He took us back to our hotel, and we gave him a sports coat. Then he wanted us to buy him a china set in the hotel store, which he could not enter. We didn't have enough American money for that.

The next day, we toured Tbilisi, a Georgian state. I was feeling very miserable and had caught a cold. People from the city we would visit next, Yerevan, didn't wait for our arrival but came to us. One of the couples looked like they had just stepped out of an old photo; both were 39 years old, and they had five children. One of their sons was a soldier. It is mandatory to serve in the war, or else you go to prison for many years and get beaten all the time.

I slept that afternoon, trying to get over my cold. Our friends were seeing so many people and giving out so many gifts. Our friend Vladimir came to see us again; we took him to eat, and he told us he had a gift for us. I hoped it was an antique samovar.

July 30, 1974. We were so tired that we slept late and didn't hear the knocking on our door. We were invited to go with the Kosareffs to their relatives' house for breakfast, then on to the Siapins' for another meal. I was not feeling very well, and we had to meet with Vladimir at 6 p.m., so we came back to the hotel. Vladimir gave us a samovar that was about 150 years old, just as I had hoped! I hope we can take it out of the country. We took him upstairs for dinner. Now Vladimir wants us to buy him a radio with American money, and he will give us equal rubles. Meanwhile, Nora Ann is being given so many things to take back to the United States that it's getting crazy. Someone named Fenya said she would bring me a 'chinick' (a teapot) tomorrow. I was very excited.

July 31, 1974. We were up at 6 a.m. and had to be dressed for the slew of people arriving. Someone brought us 'blintzi' for breakfast. Everyone was bringing us lunch for our trip and trying to help us, which was causing so much confusion. The maids just walked into our rooms, asking for souvenirs that we had brought. Don bought our friend Vladimir a portable radio from the 'beriozka,' and he gave us rubles in exchange. Now I must spend these rubles before crossing the Russian border.

Three men drove up from Yerevan to take us to a small village called Deleshan, in the Caucasus Mountains, where my grandfather Trofim Evanoff had lived before coming to the United States. We had to rent a third car, which cost us 55 dollars, before our journey to Deleshan could begin. The trip was so beautiful as we drove through the Caucasus Mountains that, although we were so tired, we needed to enjoy the majestic beauty. Don said we could become very spiritual out here; we felt close to heaven. A picture was forever impressed upon my mind as I saw the gigantic Caucasus Mountains, partially covered by a cloud and lined with men cutting its waving wheat with their scythes. We stopped for restrooms, which were just holes in the cement. We wanted to stop for pictures, but our drivers wouldn't stop and were hurrying us along. Somehow, there was now a fourth car following us; we were being followed all the way, and our drivers were nervous.

When we arrived in Deleshan, we were taken to the Evanoff home where my grandfather had lived as a child. I took photos of the Evanoffs still living there and went inside and took photos of all the rooms and the beds.

When I showed my grandfather these pictures in his late eighties, he cried and said that this was the home he was raised in and those were the beds he slept in.

We met with a blind man, Yvonne Samaduroff, my grandfather's half-brother's sister's son. We drove to a town called Ohta, where our Ohtinski people come from, as well as Don's family. I met a man named Alexi Evanich Seleznoff, who was 70 years old and was Don's grandmother Sasha's nephew. These names were all getting confusing; I heard all of these family details in Russian and only spoke enough of the language to understand and give simple answers.

We weren't allowed to continue our time in Deleshan since we did not register to stop there. So, we had to go all the way to Yerevan to get our paperwork processed and then come back another day.

Yerevan

We arrived at the Ani Hotel in Yerevan, and our friend was waiting for us. We are getting many stares from people. I was so exhausted, and we had to climb seven flights of stairs to our room with all of our luggage due to elevator trouble. These are the best rooms yet, with a regular shower. Our friend prepared fresh fried fish from the famous sea nearby, and we had to climb another four flights of stairs for dinner in Vera's room.

My luggage finally tore, and one of the men took it to get repaired.

August 1, 1974. We went to our friend Daniel and his wife Tania's house for breakfast and sat around the table chatting and eating for five hours. We were so full that we felt sick when we ate, but because they have really broken their necks for us, we must eat to be polite. They just can't understand, thinking food cures all ills.

We went back to the hotel to change into our Russian clothing to attend a formal prayer. Alexi Evanich Evanoff, my grandfather's half-brother, traveled from Deleshan to see us. I was so happy to see him, and he brought two photos, one of my grandfather Trofim before he was married.

We will see Alexi again in the morning.

Somewhere on this trip, I met with another relative of my mother's and gave him a Russian Bible, his very first. He cried and hugged it to his chest. I heard he passed six months after our trip.

August 2, 1974. After getting our official travel plans to Deleshan approved, we returned by bus. It was a very long, bumpy ride. Alexi Evanich was with us, along with the blind man Vanya Samaduroff. We arrived at Vanya's house and saw they were greeting us formally with bread and salt; none of us were dressed properly for this. I put on a scarf to cover my head. Our men were instructed by a Russian man to take their belts off and wrap them around their waists over their shirts that were hanging out. I thought our men were joking around, but the Russian man told us it was the proper thing to do.

We had lunch and returned once again to where my grandfather had lived. Then, we walked up a hill to the cemetery and saw where my great-grandfather and great-great-grandfather were buried. There were a lot of my Metchikoff relatives here (my maiden name).

So many raspberries grew here, and we were given raspberry jam to take home. We got back on the bus and went to Nikitina, then to Vascricenia, where Maxim Gavrilovich's house stands—a famous man in our Russian culture. Then we stopped to pray and sing in Russian for a sick boy along the way.

August 3, 1974. We were invited to a couple's house for breakfast with Vera. I joked with the husband about them having ten children and Don and me not having any. He said to take one of theirs! I was speaking in Russian and certainly thought I heard wrong, but his wife heard it and agreed that's what he said, and he meant it. They had two girls and eight boys; the youngest, a three-year-old girl with blonde hair and blue eyes, and the husband said right away, "We're keeping our girls."

They brought forward their seven-year-old, blond, curly-haired boy, who said he wanted to come to America, and I asked him why. He answered, "Because they have gum there." Okay, I thought to myself, "Is that enough to want to come to the United States?" When I had a chance, I took the wife aside and asked her in Russian why she would give one of her children away. Her answer was, "When they turn seven, they have to go to school, and then they are not ours anymore."

I understood what she was saying because we had heard stories about how the schools taught children to be loyal to the communist system and to reject their parents and their parents' religious beliefs.

Later, when we returned to the United States and tried getting passports for the mother and her son that the couple had chosen for us, we wrote in the application that they were cousins of ours. The mother had the same maiden name as Don's mother, Vera. The plan was to bring them to the U.S. for a vacation, and she would then fly home without him. Well, it ended up that obtaining a passport for a child under 15 in Russia was not possible at that time, and the adoption never took place.

Back in Russia that same day, we returned to the hotel where our Russian friends gifted us two small electric chrome samovars. That afternoon, we headed to Uraine's house for lunch.

We got ready for church and were picked up by some Maximist men (a strict Molokan sect). There were very few windows, and it was very steamy. We arrived very late, but they waited for us, and Don and I especially were stared at, as if we came from outer space. One lady kept pulling at my skirt, looking for my apron—a religious symbol I have never worn. They also told me I needed to move my hair and tried to move it themselves; I think it was too poofy! After church, we went to Sundikoff's house and didn't get back to our hotel until 2:40 a.m. When we got to our room, we were told that my relatives, Evan Evanich Evanoff (my mother's maiden name), his wife Olga, and his brother had waited for five hours for us. We met with them the next day.

August 4, 1974. The Evanoffs came again today. Evan is my grandfather's half-brother's son, a soft-spoken man like my grandfather. Olga, his wife, was very excited to meet us and brought us gifts and many family pictures, which will add to the records of my family history! These relatives are not the typical religious ones we have been seeing; Evan is a teacher working for the government. The other religious Russians visiting us in our hotel were not happy to share us with them.

On to another church service, where I needed to walk out as I almost fainted because I was overdone, and our friend Helen was too. Don and I left after the prayer, but before the feast. Don needed to visit his Galitzen relatives. When his relatives saw that I was sick, they thought I might be pregnant. I told them I was not. Knowing we had been married almost ten years, they began to give me 'cures' for my infertility. The cures were unmentionable—I had just met them a few moments before! I had lipsticks to give them and other little gifts. They wanted many different colors of lipsticks. I was so tired! We were driven back to the church, which had ended, and they were very angry we left. That was the only time we could meet with the Galitzen side of Don's family, and they traveled many miles to see us.

Nora Ann stayed at the hotel that day, exhausted. We were all worn out.

We went to Daniel and Tania's for 'shashlik,' which is BBQ lamb—they just bought the lamb yesterday! I mean a live one! Since we didn't attend church, the people just joined us here. The people are arguing over us all the time. We did come bearing gifts, including church money.

August 5, 1974. Evan Evanoff, my great-uncle, the teacher, came again, bringing his brother Alexander, who looks just like my uncle, my mother's brother Johnny, and talks like him too. Family traits sure show up in genetic makeup.

We had shashlik for breakfast in Vera's room again. Poor thing, traveling solo, her room was used as a hospitality room. We're getting ready to leave for Baku.

We'd been in the airport waiting for our flight to Baku for seven and a half hours. Vera passed out, and her lips were blue. It seems like the officials don't know what's going on. An entourage of Russian relatives were waiting with us. Finally, we were going to the plane, but guess what—it was the wrong plane. We came back into the building with another hour and a half wait.

Baku

We finally arrived in Baku and had dinner at 10 p.m., then went to our room, where I had to wash a tub full of clothes. We were outside of Russia and in another country. Baku is the capital of Azerbaijan, which borders Georgia, Armenia, Russia, and Iran. Baku is a city with a coastline along the Caspian Sea and is surrounded by the Caucasus Mountains, which span Asia and Europe.[46390]

"In 1723 Peter I (the Great) captured Baku, but it was returned to Persia in 1735; Russia captured it finally in 1806. In 1920 Baku became the capital of the Azerbaijan Republic."[47]

The old city dates from the sixth century and has a rich cultural past that includes Zoroastrian, Sasanian, Arabic, Shirvani, Persian, Ottoman, and Russian influences.

With Azerbaijan being a former Soviet republic and having a significant Russian population, they have adopted much of the Russian culture, including the food and the language. Azerbaijanis (ethnically) are Turkic people.

The population is 96% Muslim, with approximately 65% Shia and 35% Sunni.[48]

The language is Azerbaijani, which is part of the Turkic language family. Turkish and Azerbaijani closely resemble each other, so each language can be somewhat understood by the other.[49]

August 6, 1974. This morning we went to what we thought would be a nice, leisurely breakfast, but there were already two Molokan women here from Ashkhabad who were relatives of the Samarins. It took them two and a half hours by plane to get here to see us. They had waited two days for us.

We went shopping and found things to be very expensive—a very small towel cost $8 (U.S.). The women from Ashkhabad didn't think so; they were just excited to have something to spend their money on. Back to the hotel, and then we went to Zagulba Beach in the Caspian Sea to swim; the water was warm. We are being stared at everywhere. We took a walk after dinner.

August 7, 1974. I'm feeling out of sorts today, so I didn't go on our excursion. Don went and took pictures for me. I went shopping with two of the ladies traveling with us and purchased linen tablecloths, which are known for being from here. Back to the hotel, where I slept for four hours—so that's what was wrong with me. We had shashlik for dinner and took a walk along the oceanfront; it's raining now. We need to pack tonight and be downstairs by 7 a.m.

Yerevan

August 8, 1974. Up at 5:30 a.m. and took a bus to the airport for a 7 a.m. flight back to Yerevan. Our Molokan people met us at the airport, grabbing everything from us. I couldn't keep track of our belongings. They had lunch waiting for us at the hotel. After lunch, we went shopping since we didn't have time to shop the last time we were in Yerevan.

We went to dinner at the Minasheffs' home, then back to the hotel as we were leaving for Turkey that evening. The Molokans followed us to our rooms, where they gifted us with teapots, candy, and scarves.

We went to the train at 10:00 p.m. It was sad to know that we would probably never see many of them again. They said goodbye by waving white handkerchiefs and singing farewell songs in Russian.

Boarding the train, we were given our sleeping compartments. Vera, Helen, and I slept in one room. They wanted to change into nightgowns, and I advised them not to, but to sleep in their clothes instead.

August 9, 1974. While we tried to sleep, we felt every start, stop, and jolt of the train. Sure enough, we were up at 3 a.m., being given a ten-minute warning to get off the train. We threw our luggage out of the window to our husbands—us and our 50 pieces of luggage! We were at the train station and had five hours to wait until going through customs.

I dozed in awkward positions on the hard benches as we waited. I heard an American speaking and saw a few young men with a radio; we hadn't heard any news from the United States. It was President Nixon's speech resigning as President of the United States. We were all shocked, as we had not been able to keep up with the Watergate situation while we were in Russia.

I needed to use the restroom, so I took Vera with me. The bathrooms were open stalls and co-ed; one man was even reading the newspaper. I had Vera be my door; she stood in front of me, shielding me. To use the restroom, you put your feet on footsteps and squat, but people usually miss!

At about 10 a.m., we were preparing to leave Russia, traveling through Leninakan into Kars, Turkey, and began exchanging money. We had to show our customs declaration to the military officials. Don and I went first. Our group, because of experience, realized that the soldiers were easiest on us and pushed us to the front. Then he and I were sent to a room full of soldiers, where they began searching our luggage. The officials searched every little thing. Every book and any little pieces of paper I had put in my luggage were checked. They found Stella's relatives' address that we couldn't visit (four hours by train, out of our boundaries), so they photocopied her address and gave it back to me later.

The soldiers found our photocopied songs with Russian lyrics that we had practiced before going on this trip and asked who had a printing machine. I told them I brought them, that they were mine. They didn't believe me and snickered, telling me to read it. I read it to them, and they were very surprised.

They saw the samovar and realized it was very old, so I told them it was a gift. I don't think they liked the idea of us taking out an original antique relic from Turola. We had to show them who gave it to us, and they seemed to understand our interest in our heritage and let it go by.

Onya had given me a pillow, but I wanted to protect this couple, so I told the officials I brought it from home to sleep on. It was important that our camera film not be taken to the back to be x-rayed; we would lose precious photos. Thankfully, it was not taken. Many of the others with us lost their film. Poor Vera, I think she lost all of hers; she was seen as a risk to the Russian government. She brought a tape recorder and had to play it for the interrogators; it's a good thing that only silly things were on it. When they checked her purse, they found 200 U.S. dollars that she forgot to declare. They confiscated it all.

After being interrogated and searched, we were put on a single train car, not connected to any other cars, which was guarded by the military police. We were leaving Russia, traveling through Leninakan and heading to Kars, Turkey.

Most tourist groups don't leave Russia through Leninakan into Kars, especially by train, so this was unusual.

I wondered if they would take us all back into Russia, maybe to die! I'm sure they enjoyed putting us through all the drama. Don and I had a compartment to ourselves on the train and slept a little. We crossed the Turkish border and had to change trains.

Leaving Russia for Turkey, this saga continues in the next chapter.

How God Was with Us in Russia

1. Being invited to travel with this group.
2. The favor of God with the military guards.
3. The privilege of learning so much about my heritage.
4. Seeing the city where my father was born.
5. Meeting blood relatives of mine in person
6. Giving my great-uncle his first Bible.
7. Being given a child, though not being able to follow through in getting him to the U.S.
8. The farewell of the waving of white handkerchiefs and the Russian singing.
9. God's protection throughout our trip..

22

Russia and Turkey Adventure Continued

From Russia to Turkey

August 9, 1974. We changed trains and crossed the Turkish border. What a relief it was to see officials with big welcoming smiles. We had to go through customs again, but these officials were much more lenient and just put chalk marks on each piece of luggage, letting us through easily.

Traveling through the countryside was beautiful, passing by wheat fields, horses pulling large hay rakes, mountains shaded by clouds in the sky, and meandering old rivers where women were bathing children and washing their clothes. The women wore what I describe as gypsy clothes, with their faces partly covered. The opium fields were so green I can't describe the color—maybe emerald.

We entered the town of Kars, where Don's grandmother's family lived and owned a hotel. We got off the train with all our luggage and sat on it while people came up to us speaking Turkish, offering their horses and flatbeds. I took pictures all around the train station, unsure if the hotel was still standing, hoping I had something to show Don's 'baboona' (grandmother) when we got home.

We hadn't made reservations to stay anywhere for this part of our trip. We took taxis to a hotel that was not suitable, so we went to another hotel that was worse but had to settle for it. We got to our room and saw that the beds were not made, the sheets were extremely dirty, and there were no towels. We called for clean sheets and had to change the beds ourselves. The entire floor shared one bathroom.

We were taken to dinner and couldn't understand the menu, so Don went into the kitchen and began peeking into the pots. He was telling the cooks that we wanted "moo moo" or "pok pok," not "oink oink." They understood what he was asking and reminded Don that this was a Muslim city, so there was no pork. We had shashlik, Coca-Cola, and Pepsi. The sodas cost one dollar each, and we ordered so many that they cost more than the entire dinner. Russia didn't carry these brands of sodas, so it was nice to enjoy a bit of home again.

Frustrated that we couldn't be understood, Don stood up and yelled for everyone to hear, "Does anyone here speak English?" A few young men raised their hands and came to us. One man was named Ali, a soldier educated in South Dakota for four years. He had just arrived four days before and had been stationed in Kars for 14 months as an army officer in charge of 30 men. He was already wanting to leave.

Ali was available for us over the next few days while he was off duty.

August 10, 1974. We had wonderful omelets for breakfast. A man named Mehmet Kantar and Tuncau Babursah took us around the city today. We met Marfusha Bruhin (Samarin was her maiden name, and she was related to one of our travel mates) and Marfusha's daughter, Alichka Bruhin.

Upon arriving home, several of us joined together financially to bring this beautiful young woman, Alichka, to the United States, where she met her prince charming, and they married.

We toured Petrovka, visiting George's great-grandfather's flour mill that he built. Then we went to Chahmak, where we met a 40-year-old woman who hadn't spoken Russian in 13 years since her parents returned to Russia. She was delighted to see other Russians. We visited a cemetery where many of the Samarin family's relatives were buried, and George and Helen Samarin took many pictures of the wooden grave markers. We met a few older Russian people and then went to a very small town called Milikoi. Don and I were married in a church called Milikoi, one of our Molokan churches in Los Angeles, which was named after this city.

We were all very tired and had dust in our noses and throats from the dirt roads. I didn't know I had dust allergies and even needed medication. We had dinner at 8 p.m. and still needed to pack for our train trip to Ankara the next day. I was having stomach issues and needed to be near a restroom quickly!

August 11, 1974. It's 7:30 a.m., and I hear Nora Ann trying to take a bath with no hot water or electricity. This bathroom is so dirty that you must wear flip-flops even in the bathtub to rinse off with the hose. My hair is dirty, but I won't wash it here. The door lock didn't work, so I needed my guard, Vera. We all wanted to leave this town, but one member of our group wanted to meet more Russians. These Russians were the ones who did not return to Russia when Turkey won this area by war. Once the new borders were established in 1961, Russians in this area had the choice of returning to Russia or going to America. Russia offered them good deals on farmland, and many returned.

Later, we had dinner, which cost $18 for ten people. Breakfast only cost 90 cents each; it was omelets, chi, vegetables, bread, butter, and jam.

We were still in Kars and wanted to leave as soon as possible. We hadn't planned thoroughly for our next stop in Ankara, so things got a bit chaotic. Don went to check if we could change our flights from Ankara to Istanbul a few days earlier and found out we were booked on a hard-class train. Hard class meant hard benches with people carrying their pets, which could include farm animals on their laps, and we would be on this train for two days and one night. We realized that if we took this train, we would miss our connecting flight to Istanbul because the journey was so long. A bad deal all around. We decided to book a sleeper train, skip Ankara altogether, and go directly to Istanbul. We canceled our flight and avoided the hassle of going through an airport, greedy taxi drivers, getting a room at midnight, and so on. Taking a sleeper train to Istanbul sounded great.

We had the rest of the day and would stay another night in this fabulous 'otel,' then we would be off. Alichka took us to a 1,000-year-old ancient fortress where people took shelter when armies came, then to her house for 'chi.'

Back at the hotel, we had watermelon that the owner cut up and served to us. This was probably not a good idea for me or the others, with all our stomach issues. Vera was napping in our room, and both our stomachs were talking to us.

Did I mention how dirty the bathroom was and that the toilet was broken?

August 12, 1974. We tried cashing our traveler's checks, but the banks here wouldn't do that for us. Don wanted to buy me a bracelet—solid gold—but it was too expensive at 39 dollars for soft gold, so we bought a ring instead.

As we were getting ready for the train, we were concerned because some of the luggage was damaged or too full. Some people in our group mailed things home so they didn't have to carry as much, and they were not willing to help those who had more than they could handle. We're getting cranky! Alichka helped us get our taxis, which cost $3.50 each.

When we got on the train, we discovered we had two compartments to sleep six people, but there were nine of us! The men said they would sit in the hard seats and join their wives in their bunks later. We had a delicious dinner of lamb, soup, salad, and potatoes. The train porter discovered that Don and Phillip wiggled into our bunks late at night and kicked them out. Somehow, the porter put Don and me into another compartment with five bunks. Three of the bunks were occupied by drunken soldiers, and the two remaining bunks were for Don and me. The porter left and locked the door. Don immediately knocked on the door and told the porter he wasn't going to let me sleep there. Don went to the other compartment and told the men they needed to get out of the bunks and let me join the women. I slept terribly and woke up about a 100 times from the movement of the train.

Breakfast was bread, butter, jam, and tea. When Don asked for eggs, you should have seen the look the man gave him; eggs must have been a luxury.

We've been on the train all day. It's 4:45 p.m., and it feels like we're working, not on vacation. It's rough with nothing to do. We held our heads out of the open train window, and Jack turned to me with his face entirely covered in black soot—it was hilarious. We slept during the day but then couldn't sleep at night. Phillip got very sick, probably from exhaustion.

Don made another friend and tried to make a deal on a commemorative medal. He talked to a guy from Holland in English, who also knew German. The man from Holland then talked to a Turk who also knew German, and then the Turk talked to the guy with the medal in Turkish. Everyone in the car was listening to this conversation.

How hysterical—only Don can pull off this deal.

August 14, 1974. I had a good night's sleep. Phillip is better, it rained a bit, and the terrain is greener now. We passed the Sea of Marmara with its beautiful turquoise-blue water. I'm feeling slightly nauseous today. Everyone is cheering up a bit since our trip is almost over. We were supposed to be in Istanbul at 10 a.m. but arrived at 1 p.m.

Istanbul

It's raining buckets, so we all put on our raincoats. Our group was so indecisive we couldn't decide whether to take the ferry or taxis to a hotel. Our luggage was all wet, so we decided to take taxis. Al and Helen separated from the group and took the ferry.

When we got into our taxi, the driver was talking loudly in Turkish, waving his hands all over. We couldn't understand him. We finally figured out that the country was at war.

I remember thinking that it was good we didn't have small children.

A Turkish invasion of Cyprus began on July 20, 1974, and progressed in two phases over the following month. It was called the

Greek/Cypriot War. We arrived on the first day of the second phase when peace talks had failed.

I told everyone in our taxi that we needed to go to the Hilton Hotel, where we would register with the embassy as American citizens, and that they would have a ship in the Bosphorus Strait for us. When we made it to the Hilton Hotel, it was chaotic in the lobby; men were preparing to fight. We paid $31 dollars a night, adding Vera to stay in our room for another $10 a night. She was not doing well, and we took her under our wing.

People were in a panic to leave Istanbul and were booking tickets by bus and train to Sofia, Bulgaria, and then from there to other destinations by plane. Our group purchased bus tickets to Sofia.

We began conserving our money in case we had a long stay here or needed it for any reason. We went across the street for dinner instead of eating at the hotel. After dinner, we shopped next door, thinking it would be our only night in Istanbul. I don't know how we kept finding room for the things we bought, but we did.

No planes were leaving, and there was no telephone communication out of Turkey, but we didn't know this yet!

We returned to the hotel to register with the American Embassy in case the war situation got worse or if our families became worried about us. Everyone was going to see a show in the hotel theater on the top floor, but Don and I decided not to. We re-packed our luggage to make more room and prepare the value of our purchases for customs. After the show, everyone came to our room to visit. I was feeling queasy.

August 15, 1974. I'm still having intestinal problems along with nausea. I dragged myself to breakfast and ordered a hard-boiled egg but had to leave the table. There was no change in the war situation, but the American Embassy advised everyone to stay put. We realized we didn't have enough strength for a 12-hour bus ride to Sofia, and then we were told that these buses were being shot at. Don and I weren't too worried; I knew God was with us. However, we ended up canceling our tickets. We had a hard time getting our money back. Don worked on this and still came up short $7 per person.

We signed up for tours for the afternoon and the next day, counting on the tour agencies to keep us safe. We had lunch on the Bosphorus Strait, a waterway and boundary between Asia and Europe—beautiful. We took a boat ride on the waters where the Black and Mediterranean Seas meet. The boat ride reminded me of Italy. Then we visited the Blue Mosque. I was feeling sick all day, but there was nothing that could be done about it. Next, we went to the Bazaar and then back to the hotel, where Vera and I ordered dinner to our room, and Don went to dinner with the men.

I had the best shower in a very long time at the Hilton, especially because the hot water was endless. I then realized that Alichka's sister, Elizabet, her boyfriend, George, and their friend, Jack, were in our room. Here I was with wet hair, and they were giving us good tips about the city.

August 16, 1974. Happy Anniversary—ten years for Don and me!

We all had breakfast while Don was still trying to get the rest of our money back from the bus ride to Bulgaria that we never took. They were still refusing to reimburse us! Don then spoke with the manager of the tourist company and later the executive manager, but still no action. Finally, Don called the Consul General of the American Embassy, Mr. Amerman, who told Don he would help and that he had heard of the man who wouldn't give us our money back.

Mr. Amerman was very interested in how we got out of Russia and said that no Americans ever leave through Leninakan. So, that's why the officials gave us such a hard time when we were crossing the border.

We toured St. Sophia's Cathedral (Hagia Sophia Grand Mosque) and Topkapi Palace, where all the Sultans and their harems used to live. I'm feeling sick again. We ate lunch at a neat outdoor place overlooking the Sea of Marmara. Then, we returned to the Bazaar to shop. Wow, talk about a major shopping center! There were so many streets; it's like a maze! It would have been hard to find our way out without our guide, who was having a very hard time keeping all of us Russians together. The guide gets a cut of everything we purchase, so he was very concerned about not missing anything. As we walked, about a 100 guys bombarded us to buy slides, stamps, or whatever. By this time, I was swinging my arms to keep them away; they came so close. We had dinner downstairs in our hotel, our last night before going home to the U.S.

August 17, 1974. We were up at 5:30 a.m., and it was hard to get up, but breakfast was at 6:30 a.m. I couldn't eat much but made myself an egg sandwich for the airplane. They were allowing flights to leave now, just in time for our planned flight home. What a huge relief that airports had reopened! Our driver never arrived, so we had to take two taxis to the airport, at 80 Lira per cab, which was about $4.22 (U.S.).

It was crazy at the airport since it had been closed for three days because of the war, and everyone wanted out. All our luggage was mixed up with everyone else's, and we needed to go through customs, weigh our luggage, and then on to passport control. We were rushing as best we could, thinking we were going to miss our flight.

We were going to miss our connecting flight from Frankfurt, Germany, to Washington, D.C. Our flight was rescheduled from Istanbul to London. As we finally boarded the plane, our 100-year-old samovar was taken from us. They told us we would get it when we arrived; however, on our arrival, our samovar was nowhere to be found. We tried to locate it—where was it? I guess it was stolen! We had carried that samovar on planes and trains all the way from Tbilisi. Don went ahead and scheduled a flight from London to New York instead of Washington, D.C. We were exhausted, as usual, and should have been sleeping. Vera was very sick again. We were set to arrive in New York at 8:30 p.m. Eastern Standard Time.

Upon arriving in New York, there was an amazing storm, with lightning striking the sky, and it struck our airplane. I was sure we were going to die. The storm made our airplane circle for a very long time, delaying our landing. We had a two-hour layover that was being used up, but at least we wouldn't need to deal with our luggage.

I don't remember the rest of the journey home except that I was overjoyed to be back on U.S. territory. I needed major chiropractic work and over a month of recuperation. We had the family over to view our slides. My grandfather cried when he saw his childhood home and the bed he slept in as a youth. Don's grandmother also cried when she saw the slide of her family's hotel at the Kars train station, which was also her family home.

23

Israel

For Zion's sake I will not hold My peace, and for
Jerusalem's sake I will not rest, until her righteousness
goes forth as brightness, and her salvation as a lamp
that burns. And they shall call them The Holy People,
The Redeemed of the LORD; and you shall be called
Sought Out, a City Not Forsaken.

Isaiah 62:1,12 NKJV

What a blessing it was for Don and me to be able to travel to
Israel twice. They were different experiences since our 1986 trip was a
private trip hosted by our friends, and the 2011 trip was led by Elias
Malki of Middle East Gospel Outreach.

December 1986

Our friend Bill Brooks and his wife were going to Israel for six
months so Bill could study at the Institute for Holy Land Studies,
now named Jerusalem University College. He asked Don to watch
over their property while they were away and offered to do
something in return. We told Bill that we'd like to visit Israel for a
week while they were there and asked if it would be possible for us to
stay with them. They said yes.

It was Christmas time when we visited Israel. Our son, Aaron, was ten years old, and I brought small Christmas gifts I knew he would like. Israel provided free Christmas trees for Christians, so there would be a holiday atmosphere for us while we were away from home.

We arrived in Israel in the evening, but Bill wasn't there to meet us. We picked up our luggage and went outside to wait in the cold December night air. We waited a very long time, tired and hungry, and weren't allowed back into the building. Bill had thought it would take an hour for us to go through customs, but we were already cleared before landing.

Each day, we ventured out in the blustery December weather to see the sights. Bill was our private guide, freshly filled with six months of Bible history from his studies. Aaron was attending Copre Christian School in California, and we were surprised by how much Bible history he remembered. That school had its benefits! Ten-year-old Aaron taught us Bible stories alongside Bill at the sites we visited.

Some of the historical places we visited on our first trip included the following:

Tel Megiddo. Known in Arabic as the "Mound of the Governor" and in Greek as "Armageddon," Tel Megiddo is an archeological site referred to as a Tel. Tel Megiddo was considered a royal city in the Kingdom of Israel. Armageddon is mentioned in the Bible only once, in the Revelation to John (Revelation 16:16):

"In the New Testament, [Armageddon is] the place where the kings of the earth under demonic leadership will wage war on the forces of God at the end of history."[50]

King Herod's Palace. Known as "the second most important building in Jerusalem, after the Temple itself, in Herod's day . . .

Herod lived in it as a principal residence, but not permanently, as he owned other palace fortresses, notably at Masada, Herodium, and Caesarea Maritima."[51]

Masada. Don, Aaron, and I were especially astonished when the tour guide told us the story of Masada as we stood atop this historic site. Masada, one of King Herod's palaces, is located near the Dead Sea with picturesque views. "Its uniqueness is expressed in the fact that Masada is a king's fortress in the desert surrounded by a complete Roman siege system, the only one of its kind to survive. Masada, integrating these elements, is a unique phenomenon."[52]

After the Romans captured Masada, they controlled the city for two years. Nine hundred and sixty Jewish zealots held out. "The leader of the Jewish inhabitants decided that instead of being captured by the Romans, then brutally tortured and tossed in the Gladiator games, suicide would be a better choice. The Jewish Zealots literally gathered straws, the ten with the shortest straws killed everyone else. Then the last two survivors killed the rest and then killed each other. That night 1,000 men, women, and children died. The next morning, they were found by the Roman legion."[53]

Solomon's Pool. King Solomon built the pools for his wives in 950 BC so they might bathe and enjoy the gardens.[54]

Tel Dan. At the time we visited this site, we were able to stand on the exact spot where the Exodus 32 Golden Calf once stood, but today the area is blocked off and can be viewed only from a distance. The story of the golden calf takes place after the Israelites escaped Egypt. Moses went up Mount Sinai, where God gave him the tablets with the Ten Commandments written on them. The Israelites, tired of waiting for Moses, went to Aaron, Moses' brother, and said,

"Come, make us gods that shall go before us; for as for this Moses, the man who brought us up out of the land of Egypt, we do not know what has become of him" (Exodus 32:1 NKJV).

Aaron, yielding to the people, told them to gather all the gold objects they had taken from Egypt. They melted the gold down and created a golden calf, which then became their god.

Then they said, "This is your god, O Israel, that brought you out of the land of Egypt!" (Exodus 32:4 NKJV).

The people worshiped this new god. When God saw this abomination, He told Moses He would consume the Israelites and make Moses a great nation. After 3,000 people had already been destroyed, Moses pleaded on behalf of the Israelites, and God stopped the destruction.

Tiberias. We stayed at a kibbutz hotel, Nof Ginosar Hotel, which means "View of the Sea of Galilee," located on the shores of the Sea of Galilee. We experienced kosher dining here and visited the Jesus Boat, also called the "Ancient Galilee Boat," a first-century A.D. fishing boat that is preserved by keeping the frame underwater to protect the ancient wood.

Bethlehem. It was a cold and rainy day when we went to Bethlehem. We were able to get into Bethlehem with no problems and visited the Church of the Nativity, then went down into the cave where Jesus was born.

Caesarea. On the day we visited what is also known as "Caesarea by the Sea," the waves were wildly breaking, with the wind blowing so hard we could hardly stand. It was still beautiful.

Caesarea carries a lot of importance in Roman history, but it also has significant biblical importance: "Events in Caesarea sparked Gentile inclusion and the hope of the Gospel for all people. It was here that the Apostle Peter met Cornelius, a Roman centurion who became one of the first Gentile believers. Peter also baptized Cornelius and his two servants."[55]

At this time in history, there was a great divide between Jews and Gentiles. Both groups were just beginning to realize that the power of the Holy Spirit and Jesus was for all people, not just the Jews. God revealed Himself to Cornelius (a Gentile) through a dream and to Peter (a Jew) through a vision. Cornelius' dream instructed him to send for Peter, while Peter's vision gave him permission to intermingle with "unclean" Gentiles.

Once Peter arrived at Cornelius' home, he shared his vision and began to preach the gospel to Cornelius and those gathered. The Spirit of the Lord fell upon them while Peter was preaching, and the Jewish believers accompanying Peter were amazed. God poured out the Holy Spirit upon the Gentiles! They were speaking in tongues and praising God (Acts 10:44-46). Peter then went to the Jerusalem Council to try to convince them of the Gentiles' inclusion and God's miraculous presence among the Gentiles as well as the Jews.

> *And after there had been much debate, Peter stood up and said to them, "Brothers, you know that in the early days God made a choice among you, that by my mouth the Gentiles should hear the word of the gospel and believe. And God, who knows the heart, bore witness to them by giving them the Holy Spirit just as he did to us, and he made no distinction between us and them, having cleansed their hearts by faith" (Acts 15:7-9 ESV).*

The Dead Sea. Even though it's called the Dead Sea, it's actually a lake with high amounts of salt and minerals. Since it's so concentrated, you float easily, and the further you go out, the easier floating becomes. Something important to remember is never to allow your head to touch the water because the salt content will burn your eyes, and the density of the water can drag your head under. I wore a silver necklace, and it was destroyed by the saline. The combination of salt and minerals, including magnesium, sodium, and bromide, is considered healing relief for many chronic conditions. I came home with several tubes of bathing gel made from elements of the Dead Sea, which caused the authorities to tag my luggage, checking to see what I was taking onto the plane.

Jethro's Tomb. Our trip was coming to an end, and as we were driving around after a big storm, we stopped a man on a street off the beaten path and asked him if there was anything of interest to see in the area. He pointed to a driveway right across the street that would lead us to Jethro's Tomb. Jethro was Moses' father-in-law; his story can be found in Exodus 2:16-22; 3:1, and 18:1-27. This site was not on any travel brochures.

We drove up the driveway to some buildings, and a small man came out of a house wearing black, very baggy pants. He told us that he was part of the Druze religion and took us into a building where the marble tomb of Jethro lay. Jethro was not a Jew but a Kenite and was one of the most important prophets of the Druze religion—a shepherd and priest of Midian. As we entered the building, we were not allowed to step on the threshold, as part of Druze practices:

"Apparently there were residents of Judah in Zephaniah's day who were leaping over thresholds because they had been influenced by the pagan religions around them. They believed that by not stepping on the threshold of the door, they could protect the space they were entering from evil spiritual forces."[56]

Don and Bill needed to cover their heads with scarves. In many cultures, men cover their heads for certain special circumstances. The prophet Muhammad wore a cap with a piece of cloth on top; it's called Sunnah. It is a common practice among Muslim men from various cultural backgrounds. The kufi holds cultural significance and is considered a modest and respectful head covering in many Islamic traditions. Some African Christians wear a kufi to symbolize their status as wise elders, religious people, or family patriarchs.[57]

We walked through a large room into a smaller one that held the remains of Jethro in a large white marble casket, which we were allowed to touch. Afterward, we were invited into the man's home, which consisted of one large room with benches lining the walls, where the family sat during the day and slept at night. Their sleeping blankets were neatly rolled up along the walls.

While visiting, he explained why Druze men wear baggy pants. Although his explanation is not part of known Druze doctrines, he may have genuinely believed what he shared: Druze men think the Messiah will be birthed through a man!

He also served us coffee that had been boiled for 24 hours! When Bill hesitated and whispered to me, "I don't drink coffee," I replied, "Today you do!"

Wadi Cherith. We visited Wadi Cherith, the place where Elijah—a mighty prophet and one of only two men in the Bible taken directly into heaven without experiencing death—was sent by God to stay for three and a half years after proclaiming a drought to King Ahab.

> *And Elijah the Tishbite, of the inhabitants of Gilead, said to Ahab, "As the LORD God of Israel lives, before whom I stand, there shall not be dew nor rain these years, except at my word." Then the word of the LORD came to him, saying, "Get away from here and turn eastward, and hide by the Brook Cherith,*

which flows into the Jordan. And it will be that you shall drink from the brook, and I have commanded the ravens to feed you there" (I Kings 17:1–2 NKJV).

The brook dried up as Elijah had prophesied, and God spoke to him once again:

"Arise, go to Zarephath . . . and dwell there. See, I have commanded a widow there to provide for you" (1 Kings 17:9 NKJV).

Elijah was used mightily as a prophet of God, and God showed His care for him by hiding him and providing for his physical needs of rest and sustenance.

Israel in December was very cold, rainy, and windy. Aaron caught the flu, so we gave him medicine, bundled him up to lie in the car, and one of us would stay with him while the rest of us did quick visits to the sights. He wasn't happy to be away from home during Christmas.

Having a ten-year-old use the restroom when they were available was a chore, so we told Aaron that we were writing a book called *Toilets of the World*. I would take pictures of each toilet along the way, which Aaron was then eager to visit. This was so much fun for Don; each toilet was so unique, and Aaron enjoyed the ploy.

On our way home to the U.S., we decided on a last-minute visit to a site. As we turned left, our car was hit from behind by a sherut (a shared taxi). I hit my head on the window, making me a bit dizzy, but I was fine. A tourist bus that saw our accident stopped, and army officers arrived, directing the bus to take us to the airport. They also gave Bill a ride to the car rental company since we were driving a rental vehicle.

Upon arrival at the airport, we were led into private rooms to be searched to ensure we weren't taking anything illegal onto the airplane.

Our trip home included a few nights in Amsterdam, which was just what we needed to refresh ourselves before the long flight home. Our hotel room had the largest bathtub I have ever seen. We took turns in it, and it was so much fun!

September 20-29, 2011

Don and I were privileged to go on Hope Chapel's church trip to Israel with Evangelist Elias Malki (Middle East Gospel Outreach) and Pastors Paul and Ainsley Harmon. There were 21 people in our group.

We arrived in Tel Aviv, stayed overnight, and drove to the house of Simon the Tanner, then on to Caesarea by the Sea. We saw the place where Elijah challenged the prophets of Baal on Mount Carmel. You will remember from our first trip to Israel that God sent Elijah into isolation to Wadi Cherith during a trying time as the Wadi ran dry. God allows us to go through dry seasons in our lives to be alone with Him, depending upon Him for our very existence. This was a long season that prepared Elijah's faith and dependence on God for the next greater challenge ahead, which was Elijah's confrontation with Baal's prophets at Mount Carmel.

We took a boat ride on the Sea of Galilee, where Jesus walked on water, then went to Cana of Galilee, where Jesus performed His first miracle by turning water into wine at a wedding. We visited Nazareth, Jesus' boyhood home, where He was rejected for preaching in the synagogue.

Next, we visited Caesarea Philippi, where Jesus asked His disciples, "Who do people say that I am?" and where Peter declared that Jesus was the Christ, the Son of the living God. We enjoyed standing where Jesus preached the Sermon on the Mount on the Mount of the Beatitudes, hearing the echo of our voices as Jesus might have when He spoke to the great multitudes of people.

We saw Jericho, the city mentioned in Joshua 6, where "The walls of Jericho fell after the Israelites marched around the city walls once a day for six days, seven times on the seventh day, with the priests blowing their horns daily and the people shouting on the last day."[58]

Some of our group took a swim in the Dead Sea, while most took a hike to Ein Gedi, where King David fled to hide from King Saul, who was pursuing his life. Although Psalm 23 speaks of walking through the "valley of the shadow of death," there is an actual Valley of the Shadow of Death, now called Wadi Qelt—a wilderness with a harsh climate known as a place of danger. Some say this is the area where the parable of the Good Samaritan took place (Luke 10).

We visited Mount Tabor, where the Transfiguration occurred, and Jesus' human body changed into a radiant, glorious one. Mount Tabor is also the site of a battle between the Israelite army and the Canaanites. We went to the Wailing Wall, the Rabbi's Tunnel, and the Garden Tomb, where Jesus had lain before He rose, folding the handkerchief that had covered His face, signifying, "I am coming back" (symbolically, when a napkin is folded, it means you are coming back, and when it is wadded up, it means you are finished).

We saw the Pool of Bethesda, where Jesus healed a paralyzed man; the Garden of Gethsemane, the place where Jesus suffered His agony and was arrested before His crucifixion; and we walked the Via Dolorosa in the Old City of Jerusalem, where Jesus walked on the way to His crucifixion. We also visited Emmaus, where Jesus appeared to the disciples, and then went to the Mount of Olives and the Lord's Prayer Church.

Another city we toured was Bethlehem, where we, as tourists, entered through guard inspection, showing our passports, but Israelis cannot enter so easily. It was here in Bethlehem where our group shopped and went to a believer's home to watch Elias' (Elias Malki, our friend and tour guide) daily television program. Don and I once had the opportunity to visit his tapings at his Upland, California, studio.

Since we were traveling with Elias Malki, a well-known evangelist in the Middle East, our day was not finished after touring and dinner. We met most evenings after dinner for a worship service. It was very hard to do all of this and feel spiritual—I could barely stand at the end of each day from exhaustion. On our way to dinner one night, we drove by the Stars and Bucks Café, an offshoot of Starbucks, which had a copy of the Starbucks logo on their sign. What a funny surprise!

Several times throughout our lives, Don and I wanted to go to Israel for a few months to study at the Biblical Institute or an actual Jewish school to learn the original Jewish theology, but having an elderly parent and a teenager at the same time made this impossible.

Both trips were quite brief, but we learned so much and visited so many historical sites with our dear friends. It was amazing to set foot on the exact spots where biblical stories took place.

God's Blessings in Israel

1. The opportunity to travel to Israel with Aaron and stay with our friends.

2. Aaron and our friend Bill were full of biblical knowledge to share with us.

3. Visiting Caesarea, the place where the Gentiles were included in the final plan for salvation, meaning that salvation is for everyone.

4. The *Toilets of the World* (pretend book) was fun for all of us.

5. Being able to travel with such amazing people like Elias Malki, Pastor Paul Harmon, and Pastor Ainsley Harmon, and getting to glean from their anointed knowledge.

6. All the biblical sites we visited, knowing that Jesus is truly exalted in the land.

24

South Africa

*And Jesus answered and said to them, "Have faith
in God. Truly I say to you, whoever says to this
mountain, 'Be taken up and thrown into the sea,' and
does not doubt in his heart, but believes that what he
says is going to happen, it will be granted to him.
Therefore, I say to you, all things for which you
pray and ask, believe that you have received them,
and they will be granted to you."*

Mark 11:22-24 NASB

Healing Conferences

We were new to The Vineyard Church in Anaheim, California, where John Wimber was the Senior Pastor. Don and I had just completed our first Ministry Training class when an invitation to take a ministry trip to South Africa was announced. I felt a stirring in my spirit as I heard about this trip and went home to pray, waiting expectantly for God to speak. While washing dishes after lunch that day, I saw a vision of a green traffic light with all three lights blinking! This was a "Go" to me, and Don agreed.

God confirmed and strengthened our decision through a few scriptures:

In Matthew 9:37-38 (NIV), Jesus says, *"The harvest is plentiful but the workers are few . . . send out workers into his harvest field."*

This reminded me of God's need for workers to go out into the world.

Genesis 28:20a (ESV) says, *"Then Jacob made a vow, saying, 'If God will be with me and will keep me in this way that I go, and will give me bread to eat and clothing to wear.'"* This told me we would have provision from God.

Acts 14:21-22a (ESV) says, *"When they had preached the gospel to that city and had made many disciples, they returned to Lystra and to Iconium and to Antioch, strengthening the souls of the disciples, encouraging them to continue in the faith."* This spoke to me that we were to go to encourage and strengthen people's faith.

As soon as we made our decision to go on the ministry trip to South Africa, one of our Christian tenants told us that her son had murdered a woman. This would be one of many spiritual attacks to try to discourage us from going, as we liked to care for our tenants. We went to her home, heard the story, and took her to the field where the murder happened in downtown Huntington Beach. We prayed cleansing prayers over the field, for our tenant, and for her son.

Good things also began happening to confirm our decision. Money came in that we didn't even need, and when we attended our friend's son's Bar Mitzvah, we were seated with four South Africans. One of them was named Hazel. She was going to be in South Africa when we were there and invited us to their home. I felt so confident in our decision to go—her name was Hazel, my birth name, and she was from South Africa! How much more confirmation did I need?

Don and I continued to receive Healing Prayer Training at the Vineyard, and we began to move in more anointing, which means to have more effectiveness in ministering in the presence and power of God. This was very necessary in preparing for our trip.

April 20, 1988. The day before the trip, I woke up to the words, "The glory of the Lord is on you," which was very good news after a day of spiritual warfare. We took Don's mother, father, and Aaron to Sizzler for dinner since we were leaving the next day. We prayed over our house, "Holy Spirit, come upon this house and surround it, keep any evil far from it." We prayed for Aaron, Mom, Dad, and Misty, our Whippet dog.

That evening, I had a vision that I was praying for deliverance for people. I saw spirits leaving them, freeing them to rejoice and worship God. I remember once, as I walked into a prophetic night at the Vineyard, the man prophesying began to talk about a woman in a striped shirt, which I had on, saying I would be surprised at the people I would be setting free. I received an anointing for praying for the deliverance of the demonized and the gift of healing.

For Don and me, this trip would be life changing.

April 21, 1988. About 20 of us left for South Africa, with Pastor Bill McReynolds as our leader. We arrived in Zurich, Switzerland, for a 10-hour layover, then took another 13-hour flight to South Africa. We had warfare on the plane; a drunk man cursed our team members and touched our women. Aside from the man, it was the best flight I've ever taken—we had a high-end, restaurant-quality dinner.

Upon arriving in South Africa, we refreshed ourselves, slept a while, met with our team for worship, and then prayed together.

During our visit, South Africa was under Apartheid, a system of institutionalized racism, defined as "a former social system in South Africa in which black people and people from other racial groups did not have the same political and economic rights as white people and were forced to live separately from white people."[59]

People who have these belief systems may feel they have the right to abuse people through murder, extermination, enslavement, deportation or forcible transfer of population, imprisonment or other severe deprivation of physical liberty in violation of fundamental rules of international law, torture, and more. These are crimes against humanity and genocide, as stated by The International Criminal Court in The Hague, which prosecutes these crimes.[60]

The United States is not part of the ICC (International Criminal Court), as that would mean this court could prosecute people from our own country, where we already have our own judicial system in place.

On one of our bus trips near the beach, as Apartheid was easing up during our stay, one of my friends pointed out the "colored beach," which was strewn with trash, compared with the pristine "white beach" right next to it.

A sign posted on a beach in Durban, South Africa, stated:

"CITY OF DURBAN UNDER SECTION 37 OF THE DURBAN BEACH BY-LAWS. THIS BATHING AREA IS RESERVED FOR THE SOLE USE OF MEMBERS OF THE WHITE RACE GROUP."

Pieter Willem Botha was the Prime Minister of South Africa while we were there. He was a South African politician and served as the last prime minister of South Africa:

"Botha was an opponent of black majority rule and international communism. However, his administration did make concessions towards political reform, whereas internal unrest saw widespread human rights abuses at the hands of the government."[61]

Apartheid ended in April 1994, and Nelson Mandela was elected as South Africa's first black president.

We were strictly told not to involve ourselves in the politics of Apartheid in any way. We were there to promote the Gospel of Jesus Christ and to promote healing.

Johannesburg

Two women on our team were riding a bus to get to their host home when they encountered a black woman in deep distress. Our women asked her what was wrong, and she opened her coat to reveal that she had been stabbed, with the knife still in her back. Our friends told the bus driver to take the woman to the nearest hospital immediately, which was a white hospital. This act put them in big trouble with their host for breaking the rules about not becoming involved in Apartheid issues. It jeopardized their host's position in the community. We weren't sure if the woman would continue hosting them, but she did.

Our team often gathered to worship, pray, minister, and prophesy to one another. One song our worship leader played was about being God's bond-slave. During this song, God showed me that Don and I had been obedient to Him but were lonely and didn't have much joy. This song touched our hearts, and we teared up.

A word given to Don during this time of worship by our friend Sandy was, "Do not be afraid; you are equipped. Do not hold back in ministering to women." That must have been a word from God because Don is extremely effective in ministering to women. Women are not afraid or threatened by Don, and our strong marriage helps us minister together (we've been married 60 years!). I am not bothered by having Don join me in extremely sensitive sessions with women, as he represents the opposite of abusive males. His compassion is often accompanied by tears for women's situations.

We were preparing to attend our first conference, centered around healing, in Johannesburg, which would last several days.

Before the conference, we did some shopping and purchased ostrich wallets, leather belts, sweaters, and a few other things. While speaking to a shopkeeper about why we were in town, she told us how a man had said bad things to her. We explained that she didn't have to live according to the pronouncements made over her. She allowed us to pray for her, and we prayed three separate times. The peace of the Lord was very present, and she loved it. This encouraged our faith and prepared us for what was to come.

We prayed for so many people during the conference. One woman, Mary, had back spurs and pain. We prayed for her, three pastors, and many others. The power of God was so great—it was tangible.

Before leaving the U.S., we had been asked what we wanted to see happen on this trip. Don said he wanted to see blind eyes healed. During the conference, John Stone remembered Don's words and came to take him to join a team praying for a young blind woman. John's face was shining brightly as he led Don to this moment.

This young woman had been dropped as an infant by her uncle, severing her optic nerve. The team began the healing prayer by asking her to forgive her uncle. In the process of forgiving him, her eyesight began to return—in black and white. With more prayer in the following days, she began to see in color.

People often ask us if we pray for physical healing. Yes, we do! In this case, as the young woman forgave her uncle, she was healed.

Dealing with our issues in life is more powerful than we think, freeing us in many ways.

The healing of her blind eyes was considered a creative miracle of God—creating nerves where there were none, specifically in the severed optic nerve. Several family members were at the conference to confirm her blindness and the validity of her story. She later followed us to Port Elizabeth to receive healing prayer for infertility.

One of our teammates was planning to propose and needed an engagement diamond, so Don called a diamond factory. The factory arranged to send someone to pick us up during our lunch hour. As we waited for the car, a gold limousine pulled up, and I wondered who in the world it could be for. Yes, it was for us!

Our friend found the diamond he wanted, and Don handled the bargaining, reviewing several diamonds with varying colors and flawless characteristics. As Don was finishing negotiations, he said, "Now, how much will it be for these two?" I got to choose one, too.

As we moved throughout the city, we experienced a boldness that came upon us during our preparations for this trip, which only increased over time. Shopkeepers recognized we were on a mission. Many welcomed us with openness, though some immediately rejected us and didn't like us.

"The righteous despise the unjust; the wicked despise the godly. (Proverbs 29:27).

There were two team members who felt uneasy regarding the power of God, but God used one of them to pray for four people who were slain in the Spirit. This means they fell by the power of God as she prayed for them. I'm sure she learned that God would even use someone like her.

We were like the disciples of Christ, each with different character traits—Peter the bold, peacemakers like Barnabas, and even Mark, who caused problems, just as in Paul's day. Other prayer ministers at the conference watched us and tried to emulate how we ministered, but their own issues held them back from moving freely. We showed them how to break away from the things holding them back by praying for their personal healing.

April 27, 1988. We are now fully into the conference in Johannesburg—what a long day it had been. The presence of the Holy Spirit was so evident during worship and prayer times, with so many people being touched and going to the altar. I prayed for a woman named Sally who had diverticulosis, and she was ecstatic. I don't know what happened, but she was experiencing the Holy Spirit. The evening worship was powerful, and the entire Vineyard team danced with joy while worshiping. Our team was joined by other members of our church who had first gone to England and then came to South Africa. Together, we were a very large group.

April 28, 1988. We went to a leather factory in the morning, and Don ordered a coat.

During the conference later in the day, people were receiving the gift of healing for the first time. John Wimber had those who had just received the gift of healing pray for the sick. We need to put our gifts into action.

John Wimber spoke, and his message was a rebuke, given in love. He addressed us all about loving our fellow man—English vs. Dutch, Black vs. White. There was an altar call after the message, and ten people came forward who felt defeated. One woman had rheumatic legs, and her feet were tapping the ground very hard. Then we found out she was also blind, and we began praying for her. Our pastor, Bill, prayed for a man whose crooked legs were healed. People who needed prayer for their legs to be the same length lined up at the front. One leg I saw grow did so in three small spurts.

John Wimber announced that he was giving his mantle away, and if you wanted it, to come forward. Don and I didn't know what that meant, but one of our team members said, "Just go up there, he's never done this before." We did, and he prayed over all of us.

As I said before, this was a life-changing trip for us—the mantle of healing was being placed on our lives!

In the Bible, Elijah passed his prophetic authority (mantle) over to Elisha. After Elijah was taken up into heaven:

Elisha picked up Elijah's cloak, which had fallen when he was taken up. Then Elisha returned to the bank of the Jordan River. He struck the water with Elijah's cloak and cried out, "Where is the LORD, the God of Elijah?" Then the river divided, and Elisha went across. When the group of prophets from Jericho saw from a distance what happened, they exclaimed, "Elijah's spirit rests upon Elisha!" And they went to meet him and bowed to the ground before him (2 Kings 2:13-15).

This passing of John Wimber's mantle could be symbolic—representing a purpose or calling being passed on. I believe the passion Don and I have could also be what John Wimber had for healing the sick and praying prophetically. The passion we received on this trip for healing the sick is still alive in us today.

Years earlier, a Pentecostal Pastor, Mike Pavloff, came over to our house and laid hands on us, praying for our infertility. This man would cry as he prayed, and now Don often cries as he prays too. When Don tears up as he's speaking, it usually means these words are from God.

A young man came to Don one day and said he had gone to Pastor Mike, asking him for his mantle, but Pastor Mike told him he had already given it to Don Galitzen—we never knew that. I believe who you associate with is who and what you become.

There was a girl watching me as I was ministering to others. I asked her if she wanted prayer, but she said she just wanted to watch. I asked her again, and she wouldn't answer, so I prayed for the Holy Spirit to come upon her. She told me she really loved Jesus but wanted to love Him more. I prayed that she would become more devoted to Him and prayed over any brokenness she might have. I received the word "children" from the Lord and asked her about it. She said she had one child but had been trying for three and a half years for another one. I told her a bit of my testimony about barrenness and how if I had had a child of my own, I would not be here in Africa. One of my prayers in my distress while trying to get pregnant was to surrender to serve God in Africa.

A man I had prayed with earlier came and told me God had something special for me. He prayed, and one of our teammates joined in—she prayed the sweetest prayer for Christ's character over me. We were all moving freely, blessing whoever we could.

Soweto

April 30, 1988. We arrived this morning in the township of Soweto, where 5,000 people were expected to attend the next conference we were a part of, which was to be held at a soccer stadium. Due to fears of an uprising because of Apartheid, only about 1,500 people came.

There was an uprising in 1976 led by black school children called the Soweto Rebellion, and many deaths occurred because of it. The government was insisting that the Afrikaans language be used in Soweto's high schools, and the students refused. The languages mostly spoken in Soweto were Zulu, Afrikaans, Sotho, and English. This rebellion spread to other parts of the country.[62]

"This rebellion marked the end of submissiveness on the part of the black population of South Africa and the beginning of a new militancy in the struggle against Apartheid. South Africa would never be the same again."[63]

We came in by van, which needed to be driven by a black person for our protection, and we needed to be out of Soweto by 5 p.m., before dark. Once we arrived at the conference, we were told to stay with our team and be in groups of two.

Right away, I met Lilly on the soccer field and prayed for her arthritic hands, which she said were much better after praying. I then led her friends, Cynthia and Eugenia, to the Lord and stayed with them, worshiping together. They were very happy. Then, I ministered to another woman, who was in depression from an attack of the enemy. She had presented something to a university that she felt the Lord told her to do, but the school rejected it. We encouraged her by explaining how spiritual warfare works. We told her she would be matured and strengthened by this experience, and later I saw her dancing during worship.

We were praying for, teaching, and training people against warfare attacks. I then prayed for Patrick, a sweet man who wanted more of Jesus.

Our team prayed for a young boy who had never walked before. He was quite demonized, as you could see by his eyes, and we were still ministering to him as he walked around the stadium for the first time, like a newborn colt. His mother was being prayed for at the other end of the field. As she was being delivered from demons, the young boy's body was simultaneously being healed to a greater degree. I went back and forth, praying for both. There was a strong generational connection between the mother and her son that was being broken off. Every time I prayed over him and rebuked the demons, he would contort and double over, then continue walking. It was amazing. A whole team followed him, taking turns praying over him.

My life-changing moment came when I saw a very large, dejected-looking woman being escorted onto the field by several of her friends, far away from where I was. I was so relieved to see other members of our team praying over her—I sure didn't feel ready for her and forgot about it as the music began. It was extremely hot, and I stood in the little sliver of light pole shade. My eyes were closed in worship, Don had left, and when I opened my eyes, guess who was right next to me? The large woman I had seen across the field! I was so happy she had already been ministered to! We can call this lady "L."

I greeted L, and she gave me a struggling face. I asked her what was wrong, and she told me her legs were numb. I figured I could give a little prayer. Keeping my eyes open, as we were taught, I placed my hands over but not touching her legs and immediately sensed my hands were in the wrong spot, so I placed them over her stomach. I saw something move, like a lump in her stomach. I asked her what that was, and she said it was "the demon." I said, "No." She said, "Yes." We went back and forth a few times. I asked her who told her this was a demon, and her answer was, "the witch doctor."

Oh! I then told her I would go get another team member. I looked for Don but never found him, nor did I find anyone from our team. I went back, knowing the power of God and the authority I had in Jesus, and by then had a righteous anger within me. I asked L if she wanted this demon, since I didn't want to be in a spiritual battle if she did, and she said, "No." So I commanded the demon to leave and told it that L did not want it. I watched as the lump continued up her stomach toward her throat. I kept repeating that it must go and was not welcome, wondering if she might throw up or if I might be attacked. Surprisingly, it came out with the tiniest puff out of her lips. She then said that her legs had circulation and were nice and warm. What an experience that was, and all her friends rejoiced.

Afterward, Don went to talk to L and her friends, admonishing them to continue praying for her healing. He had them laughing— Don is so good at that.

I prayed for Doris, whom Don had sent me to. She was unemployed and was weeping. I gave her love and affirmation. She knew Don had sent me to her, and as I prayed for her, she began to fall in the Spirit, but I caught her.

During the ministry time, I brought another woman to Jesus. She told me she had wanted to accept Jesus so many times, but something always blocked her. How exciting that she finally came to the Lord!

We met Brother Jeremy, a priest who invited us to bless his church. We went, and what a sweet spirit he had. I will never forget how he, in turn, prayed over us. Our team gathered in a circle with Brother Jeremy in his flowing gray robe at the center. As he prayed, he extended his arms and blessed us while twirling, his robe billowing out. This deeply blessed us—a picture I'll never forget. We then left Soweto at 5 p.m., returning to our hotel with no problems.

Words from God to me at the end of this day:

This shall be a sign: you shall go in the wilderness calling the people to Me, and I will place a burning in their hearts, and I shall place them in a place for My good. I will, therefore, move amongst My people in a new way, and the people will be filled with joy. I will delight all those who come near them, and great shall be their prosperity among the nations. I will bring peace and a longing for My heart.

They will bring My gospel to the needy and hungry, and because of My anointing, all their needs will be met. They shall be overflowing with the abundance of My goodness and will multiply themselves for Me. In My Name forevermore.

Words from God specifically for me:

You will be called out and set apart for Me, as I have done all your life, and I will lead and guide you. You will not be ashamed, and others will see it is good, and it is Me. You will not be frightened or timid anymore, and I will cause those who rise against you to fall far away from you. So don't be anxious or afraid when this happens, for you will know it is I. I smile on you now and am pleased and will grow and grow in you with such strength and might and glory that you will think it is a mighty wind coming over you. But you will know it is not you. You will never be afraid again. I will lift you up, and you shall speak great things!

Words from God for our son, Aaron:

Great is the prosperity of Aaron, both spiritually and financially, and he shall be called a great nation to those amongst him. He will speak with great power those things taught to him, both to the rich and poor, and they will listen to him. I will be proud of him and value him as Mine. He will serve Me all the days of his life with great compassion and diligence and will be tireless.

Port Elizabeth

We flew to our last conference location in Port Elizabeth, where our hosts, Brian and Betty Ledger, greeted us with corsages, lots of love, and great sensitivity to our needs. When I first entered their home and stepped into the living room, the presence of God was thick in the atmosphere. I said, "This is where you pray." Brian was a prayerful man who had been part of a group that prayed for a man who was raised from the dead.

We had lunch with Brian and Betty's friends from their Anglican church. Lunch included soup from a pot that never seemed to run low. I believe we experienced soup multiplication that day, as the level of soup in the pot kept staying the same. They said this happens all the time.

In the afternoon, we went to a Methodist church in a township where the people entered the church single file in a procession, tapping their walking sticks and singing in Xhosa. The pastor, David Veka, had attended a John Wimber Vineyard conference and was so renewed in his spirit that his people were too—all sparkly-eyed with broad smiles. They sang "God is So Good" in Xhosa, and then in English. The Holy Spirit was so evident. The acapella singing reminded me of my Russian Molokan background.

One of our members was so touched that he gave his onyx ring to Pastor David as a symbol of brotherhood. A relationship developed between their church and ours as sister churches.

When we went to the altar to receive people for prayer as the ministry team, Pastor David came before me and fell to his knees for prayer. This deeply moved me, and I quickly set my emotions aside to anoint this most humble, holy man, hear from God on his behalf, and pray for him. Oh, what a joy to be considered useful for God's kingdom work.

At the end of the service, the congregation marched out the same way they came in—tapping their walking sticks, single file, singing in Xhosa "Onward Christian Soldiers." They came and left in the most reverent way of honoring the Lord.

In Southern California, we come to church with flip-flops on and a doughnut hanging out of our mouths. It was a great maturing experience to see how other cultures worship. I came thinking I was bringing them something—how prideful of me!

May 1, 1988. In the evening, we visited a church that had an orchestra, a choir, and preaching, yet the entire atmosphere was not very moving. We sang songs, and then our pastors gave their testimonies and afterward called on the Holy Spirit, but the people were not very responsive. So, we sang more, and eventually, some of the people came forward and were slain in the Spirit, though it seemed they were programmed for it.

I prayed for a woman, who had a broken heart, and then for Angela, who had a broken leg. The Lord showed me knitting needles working, a sign He uses to show me He is healing bones. One young woman confessed sexual sin with her boyfriend, and we prayed for her through repentance and about the guilt she carried. I also blessed a young man who wanted to be a pastor.

It was a very fruitful evening.

May 2, 1988. As I was praying for a woman with recurring headaches, the Lord revealed the word *caffeine* to her, and she understood what it meant right away. We prayed together for her to overcome her caffeine problem. She was also having marriage issues, and we prayed about her negative thoughts toward her husband.

I prayed for refreshment and renewal for a church leader and another woman who needed renewal and redemption of her time.

During the conference, we were again part of the ministry team praying for people. Pastor Gary Weins, from Colorado, called people forward with one leg shorter than the other. I saw a leg grow again in three short, even movements. I prayed for a woman who had a palpitating heart. As I prayed, her hand moved—I'm not sure what that was—and her face contorted. Then the palpitation stopped. It's always good to pray with your eyes open.

I joined Leslie to pray for a woman with pain in her ear and chest; both pains left! One man had a dead eye caused by an infection. We prayed, but nothing happened, so we prayed against dashed hope. He then asked about the baptism of the Holy Spirit, which usually includes speaking in tongues, but again nothing happened. We encouraged him to keep seeking.

I, along with another woman, ministered to a lady with cataracts. I could see them clouding her eyes, and as we prayed, her cataracts began disappearing. She said they were better, but I knew she needed more prayer. Leslie and I prayed more, but then Leslie left to pray for someone else—so many people needed prayer. I continued praying for the woman. She opened her eyes, amazed, and said, "Oooo, better." The cloudiness in her eyes was gone!

I also saw in the Spirit, fire on her lower back and received the word *strain*. I asked her if she had back problems, and she said "yes," then I asked if she felt heat, and she responded, "yes." I told her God was healing her.

While praying for the woman with cataracts, I heard a call for prayer for infertility healing. I knew I wanted to go to the stage for prayer for myself.

On the stage, the pastor knelt before me—an honorable gesture—but then placed both hands on my lower stomach and prayed. I had very mixed emotions, aware that a strange man was touching my lower abdomen while feeling the presence of God in my body at the same time. It didn't seem right to me. (You need to know I teach *Healing Prayer Etiquette,* and this is *not* how to do it!)

I felt very hot and actually felt my ovaries flip. The pastor then grabbed my face and spoke to the discouragement and bitterness I had against God—bitterness I never knew I had! That night, I awoke with my mind wanting to go back to old thought patterns of doubt, but instead, an explosion of light filled my body and brain, stopping the old thoughts.

Because of these physical manifestations, I allowed myself to hope again, though I had given up on giving birth to a child of my own.

My spirit was expectant, but each month that passed without results sent me spiraling into despair again. I knew God loved me and had a purpose for my life in ministering to others. However, 23 years of trying for a baby, the miscarriages, and becoming hopeful again were very hard to bear. I even had anger toward the pastor who prayed for me.

During this time, I saw legs grow, tumors leave, cataracts disappear, and people delivered. It was a wild time of moving in the gifts of God.

Everywhere Jesus went, He functioned as a healer, and that's what we were doing:

Now Jesus performed many other miraculous signs in the presence of the disciples, which are not recorded in this book. But these are recorded so that you may believe that Jesus is the Christ, the Son of God, and that by believing you may have life in his name (John 20:30-31 NET).

We went to Pastor Neville's church, friends of the Anaheim Vineyard, and after worship, our team began praying for some pastors and leaders. Don was led to pray for a certain couple, and the husband fell in the Spirit onto the floor. This experience is often called being "slain in the Spirit," which is usually a very peaceful experience, with someone there to catch the person.

Later, we all went to the front of the sanctuary to pray over the church, and someone brought the man up with us. The husband woke, and we continued to pray for and bless both him and his wife, anointing them with oil. They knelt, weeping.

Many leaders were on the floor, and we prayed over each of them. Pastor Neville brought out a basin of water, and he and his wife, Ruth, washed our pastor's feet. Ruth even dried their feet with her hair. We walked around anointing the pews and doorposts with oil. The atmosphere was so heavy with the Spirit, we wondered how much more we could take! The power of God is so strong—oh, how human we are. In heaven, we will be able to take it all.

Afterward, we went to Neville's house for a *braai* (BBQ) with chicken, lamb chops, and all the trimmings. Delicious. A woman gave me a haircut, and then I prayed for her, releasing her from many abusive things done to her. Sometimes, we ministered as opportunities arose.

We took a day trip to Jeffreys Bay, nicknamed J-Bay, famous among surfers. J-Bay is a surf capital due to the right-hand point break at Supertubes Beach, which seems to go on forever. The town is situated about 46 miles from Port Elizabeth.[64]

Interestingly, I had struggled with pain and tightness in my neck before we went to South Africa, but while we were there, I never had pain. I asked God, "O God, are we to move here?" but deep down, I knew we were not called to do that.

On our last day, we took a bus ride to Addo Elephant National Park. We saw one elephant, but I was nodding off the entire time—I was so tired. The next day, we flew home, and our lives have never been the same!

God's Miracles

1. Words, visions, and scriptures confirmed our mission trip with the Anaheim Vineyard to South Africa.
2. The enemy's attempt to scare us before leaving, with our tenant's son murdering a woman.
3. Money coming in we didn't need—abundant provision.
4. Being seated next to four South African women at a Bar Mitzvah and receiving an invitation from Hazel to stay with her while there.
5. Don's desire to see blind eyes healed and being included in prayer for a blind woman who began to see.
6. Helping a young man get an engagement diamond—Don bargained for him, and I got one too!
7. Receiving a "mantle" from John Wimber—our lives have never been the same!
8. Seeing a boy walk for the first time.
9. Praying for "L" and delivering her from a demon.

10. Brother Jeremy's twirling prayer of blessing over us in Soweto.

11. Experiencing the thick presence of God in our hosts' living room.

12. Witnessing the never-ending pot of soup, even though many filled their bowls.

13. Watching cataracts heal before my very eyes.

14. Visiting Pastor Neville's church, where the leaders displayed a genuine, humble reverence for God.

25

Australia

In September 1964, just a month after Don and I were married, my eldest sister and her family moved to Bunbury, Australia, following a word my brother-in-law felt he received to leave "Sinful LA." They married when she was just 17, and he was several years older. She was my very sweet older sister, and it was very hard to have her leave with their three children.

About eight or nine Russian Molokan families were all going to Western Australia to start a new life. Today, there are many Russian Molokan churches and families living in Australia.

Their departure was huge and made the front page of the *Los Angeles Times*. Hundreds, if not thousands, of Russian Molokan people were there to see them off, singing spiritual songs in Russian and dressed in their traditional church attire. The women wore long dresses with lace head coverings, and the men wore their Russian shirts tied with a *poise* (a tie with tassels).

My sister came home to visit only about two or three times after moving to Australia, and it's sad for me to have only occasional phone conversations with her.

In 1979, Aaron was four years old when we went to visit my sister, whom I hadn't seen in 15 years. She and her husband lived in Bunbury, which was about a three-hour drive from Perth, the main city in Western Australia. Bunbury looks and feels like San Diego in many ways, and it is also situated near the ocean.

This trip involved an 18-hour flight to Sydney, where we stayed for a few days to get over our jet lag. I came up with the great idea of wrapping 18 little toys and snacks and putting them into a drawstring bag for Aaron to open a gift every hour. A God idea, I'm sure, as he would get excited every hour, and the little treat would keep him occupied.

In Sydney, we took a few tours, but being jet-lagged, we had to take naps at all hours. It was hard traveling with a four-year-old who would wake up at two or three in the morning; keeping him quiet was quite the task!

We then flew to Adelaide, which took about two hours, and visited with Russian friends who met us at the airport. After that, we had a three-hour flight to Perth, where we rented a car and drove for three more hours to my sister and brother-in-law's house.

Don and I always wanted to take the Nul Abar Train ride across Australia—a three-day ride from Sydney to Perth. This train would stop at small towns along the way to deliver mail, groceries, and supplies, but we never had the opportunity to do so.

We stayed with my sister and brother-in-law for five weeks. To pay for our keep, we wallpapered several rooms for them. We drove to Albany, a point on the southern tip of Western Australia, known for its wild ocean waves. Don purchased an ivory whale tooth necklace for me.

My brother-in-law offered showed us a ten-acre station with a lake, hoping we might purchase it and move to Australia. We did consider buying the property and wondered how we might use the land. Don came up with the bright idea of repairing the fence, as the kangaroos—or "roos"—frequently plowed right through it.

We thought we could raise sheep and all that goes along with that. We learned about water witching with a dowsing rod, a method farmers used to find where wells should be placed. This practice, originating in Germany and used since the 1500s, involves divination. We laughed and realized this was not the plan for our lives.

We didn't do much other than visit my family. Aaron enjoyed playing with his cousin and the dogs. My sister's husband even had a load of sand dumped in front of their house—an enormous private sandpile for the kids.

Aaron had to go to the hospital while we were there because he had been bouncing on his knees for fun with his cousin! The floors were hard, and he did it so much that he woke up screaming in the night. Aaron was tested for rheumatoid arthritis, but that's not what he had. We got a free stay at the hospital through this ordeal—kind of an "across the pond" handshake.

Vineyard Ministry Trip

December 8, 1989. A word from God: "I am sending you places others dare not tread. Like walking on hot coals compared to others who burn their feet and can't get across, you and Don just fly across. I will show you many more things—you will see in Australia."

Shortly after receiving these words from God, I learned we would be joining the team from Anaheim Vineyard traveling to Australia in March. I prayed that evening and had a vision. In it, I saw the three of us—Don, Aaron, and me—traveling by jet to South Africa, Australia, and Russia, with the sense that these trips would be repeated. Then, I saw a jet departing from the Anaheim Vineyard Church.

Even though Aaron did not go to South Africa and Russia, I believe he was part of us—that's my take on seeing him in these visions.

Continuing this vision, I saw Jesus, the three of us, and large closed doors that I've seen before. Behind us were the people going on this trip. Jesus then opened the doors, and I saw many people in agony; they were crying and needed us.

March 2, 1990. Our team arrived in Sydney, Australia, very jet-lagged, but it wasn't yet time to check into our rooms. We decided to go to a matinee at the Sydney Opera House. For us, it was nighttime back in the U.S. We all bought the cheapest tickets, sat on the top row, and proceeded to fall asleep, poking each other as we snored! It was so funny but quite disturbing to others.

(Sidenote: While writing this paragraph of this book, I went downstairs to watch the news, and a picture of the Sydney Opera House appeared on TV. It is the Opera House's 50th anniversary! Little, mighty glimpses of God as He holds my elbow while I write.)

We enjoyed the show, even though we slept through most of it, and looked forward to the conference we were attending with the Anaheim Vineyard.

Don and I were part of the Prayer Team for a three-day conference on Spiritual Warfare, where we had many opportunities to pray for people and experience deliverances and miracles.

At the conference, John Wimber gave a prophetic word: "The Lord is giving thousands to those who have never had children." God has given Don and me many spiritual children throughout our lives, Amen! What an encouraging word—this watered our souls.

Our team was headed to Perth next for a second Spiritual Warfare conference. Upon arriving in Perth, we took a bus to our hotel. On the way, one of our team members discovered he had lost his wallet, which held all his cash and credit cards. I began praying earnestly, listening for God to tell me where it could be. As I prayed, I had a picture of his wallet sliding from his pocket to the side of the seat where he had sat on the bus. We called the bus company, told them where to look, and there it was!

Right away, one of our hosts let us know that there were 13 witchcraft covens praying against us. However, we were secure in knowing that God was with us and would protect us. Of course, the conference was on Spiritual Warfare!

The LORD is my light and my salvation; whom shall I fear? the LORD is the strength of my life; of whom shall I be afraid? When the wicked, even mine enemies and my foes, came upon me to eat up my flesh, they stumbled and fell. Though an host should encamp against me, my heart shall not fear: though war should rise against me, in this will I be confident (Psalm 27:1-3 KJV).

At the conference, while we were sitting in the huge convention hall worshiping, I saw in the Spirit a gigantic angel filling the room. From that picture, I just knew we would experience God in mighty ways.

I remember praying with a missionary couple who lived with the Aboriginal people. They needed prayer because their church had "left them behind." We didn't know what that meant initially. Apparently, their support had stopped, and they were stranded in Australia with no money to get home. I got their permission to let the conference leaders know about their situation since we could not handle it except through prayer. After praying, I led them to the conference leadership for further help.

I also prayed for a woman with a tumor. In a vision, I saw the tumor dissolving and disappearing. I stopped praying because I knew the healing was finished. I told her to see a doctor to confirm her healing. Sometimes people feel their healing taking place or feel warmth in the area. She felt warmth.

One afternoon, when Don and I were on the ministry team, we approached a short, elderly man near the stage and asked what he would like prayer for. He said, "I'm the next speaker." "Oh," I responded. So, we prayed for John White, the speaker. This man had written 25 books, served as a medical missionary, a professor of psychiatry, a church planter, and was a leader in the Vineyard Church.

John White presented a talk on humility and had us stand if we wanted to receive humility. Who wants to stand for that? But we did. He said, "None of you will ever be the same after this." I've read one of his books, *Parents in Pain,* and what a humble man he is for living through the grief and heartbreak of having a son who committed murder and was serving a life sentence. His son found Jesus in prison and was happy ministering to other inmates.

One of the speakers spoke about total surrender and gave a call for martyrdom. Wow—I've never been part of that call before. People streamed down the aisles to the altar in this large convention hall, surrendering completely. What a learning experience this trip was.

Don and I drove to my sister's house, three hours away, before the end of the conference. We spent two days visiting and stayed overnight. It was so hard on Don and me to stay with my sister for such a short time—we were so close, yet we needed to stay with our team.

We arrived home from Australia around midnight to much spiritual warfare. Our attorney was waiting for us in the driveway. Aaron, at 14, had taken our pickup truck down the street and crashed it head-on into a neighbor's car, fracturing his knee. Of course, it was the neighbor we would least want this to happen to! After prayer, Aaron's patella was completely healed, baffling the orthopedic surgeon.

The enemy tries to do everything to discourage tired ministers—this time, Don and me—but watching God's works and seeing the humility and devotion of others far surpassed the struggles we came home to.

Praises of God in This Chapter

1. The 18 tiny gifts to keep four-year-old Aaron occupied—a God idea.

2. My sweet brother-in-law showed Don and me property to buy so we could live in Australia and offered to dedicate our son, Aaron.

3. Visions from God helped us decide to travel for missions. These visions gave encouraging and insightful revelations.

4. The Sydney Opera House's 50th anniversary appearing on the news the same day I wrote about it in this chapter.

5. The wallet that was lost and then found after praying and receiving a revelation from God about its whereabouts.

6. Meeting the missionary couple to the Aborigines and connecting them to help.

7. The privilege of seeing a tumor dissolve.
8. Praying with one of the conference speakers.
9. Being able to visit with my sister.

26

Switzerland 1997

"Watch Me."

~ God

January 20, 1997

Eleven of us left for Berne, Switzerland, with our pastor, Craig Lockwood, leading our team from the Anaheim Vineyard. Together, we made up the Small Ministry Team, and this was our first International Healing Prayer Ministry trip. We had been asked to do a seminar in Berne at the Basilia Vineyard, which was a very exciting invitation for all of us.

Our trip began with a short layover in Toronto, Canada, where we visited what was then called the Toronto Airport Vineyard, a church that was experiencing revival at that time. Our team was prayed over with great power. I was slain in the Spirit, having a very relaxing time on the floor, able to receive from the Lord. While in this state of repose, I felt fire falling on and within me. In a vision, I saw and felt a swirling fireball go into me. All of this felt warm and not frightening.

I also saw my hands lifted, with fire coming out of them toward our team. Usually, this represents healing. I saw my mouth full of words, spilling out. God spoke, saying, "Watch Me," representing what He would do on this trip. I saw, in my mind's eye, a picture of what I believed to be God's forearm moving over the people. "Have fun" and "Take a risk" were words for Don—God knows he is a risk-taker. What a powerful preparation for what was yet to come through us on this trip.

Rosemary Speer was our hostess when we arrived in Berne, Switzerland. She had been brought to Jesus by Francis Schaeffer, her next-door neighbor. He was famous for writing the book *How Should We Then Live*[65] and co-founded the L'Abri community with his wife, Edith.

Sometimes we learn great, simple, and powerful lessons along the way of our lives, and Rosemary impressed me with her "tabernacle." As she showed Don and me around her home, there was a desk in the corner of her living room—a simple student classroom desk—with

Rosemary Speer, our hostess sitting in her "tabernacle"

her study books and Bibles stacked around it. This is where she prays, reads her Bible, and worships God. Rosemary invited me to sit in her "tabernacle," as she called it. I accepted her invitation, and as I sat at her desk, I felt the heaviness of the Holy Spirit in a mighty way.

Just as Rosemary had her tabernacle, I spent many hours praying in our master retreat. When a real estate broker was assessing our home, he stopped by our master retreat and said, "What's that?" I said it was the Holy Spirit. He felt the tangible presence of God in the atmosphere. Where we spend our lives in devotion to God, He wants to be there.

There were about 300 people on the first night of the seminar. Our team wasn't introduced until 9 p.m., causing us to be behind in the line-up of presentations we had prepared for the weekend. I was asked to give up my speaking time the next day so another person could speak, which meant I was no longer one of the speakers. That news brought me a lot of disappointment, as speaking was what I had looked forward to on this trip. I needed an attitude adjustment, thinking to myself: we pay our own way, I don't ask for money, and I came all this way—a lot of self-pity and griping.

The next day, a few of us didn't need to be at the seminar in the morning, so we went shopping and then came back for the ministry time.

The people of this church didn't have a regular meeting place, so each week, people were notified where church would be held. I loved how, in the middle of the service, after worship, there was a "fika" break—a coffee break with fellowship.

Several members of the congregation lived commune-style, and we were warmly invited to their large home for meals.

Don had been suffering from what is called surfer's ear, an inflammation of the cartilage on the tip of his ear—it was very inflamed and painful. A dermatologist who attended this church offered for us to come to her office, and she gave Don a cortisone injection into his ear.

Our pastor received an invitation to do a conference in Zermatt and asked Don, Ann, and me if we would go to put on a two-day conference there, as people were requesting a few of our team members. We left the next morning.

The Matterhorn, a mountain of the Alps,
overlooking the Swiss town of Zermatt

Zermatt—January 20, 1997

Many years ago, I prayed, "Lord, send me to those who feel You don't hear them anymore, those who feel that You have forgotten them."

Don, Ann Bowman, and I were sent out without proper prayer—on a wing and a prayer—which means without much chance of success. I truly believe being "prayed up" is necessary, but I also know we *should "be prepared in season and out of season" (2 Timothy 4:2).*

We arrived outside the city center of Zermatt by train, where our hosts picked us up. Cars were not allowed downtown, so our host parked, and from there we took a golf cart to our hotel. Maintaining the beauty, integrity, and character of this small, famous town was very important, and the only vehicles allowed were golf cart-style flatbeds. Edith Biner and Kobi Julen, the leaders of the seminar, greeted us and took us to lunch, where we discussed the details of what we would do over the next few days.

Zermatt is known for its wonderful skiing in the Alps, but we also heard it is a dark place where people come to commit suicide. We were told that because of superstition and the draw of the mountain, people feared it. We realized the atmosphere needed more of Jesus. We prayed to change the name of the mountain from the Matterhorn to *Berg-Gottes*—the Mountain of God.

For assuredly, I say to you, whoever says to this mountain, "Be removed and be cast into the sea," and does not doubt in his heart, but believes that those things he says will be done, he will have whatever he says" (Mark 11:23 NKJV).

On the way to our accommodations, God impressed upon me the words *Hungry Hamlet,* showing me that the group of people coming to our seminar was hungry for more of the Lord.

We were taken to the Alex Hotel and treated very nicely. Lunch was brought to our room before each seminar.

I was in prayer most of the night, and the next morning I awoke with more words for the people here in Zermatt:

> I will bring My resurrection life to you. There are some of you who have been spiritually dead. Some of you will be spiritually raised from the dead. Some of you have felt forgotten by the Lord. My message to you is that He remembers you! This forgotten feeling has been reinforced by people who pretended you do not exist.

I prayed:

Release the captives, Lord! Set them free from the strongman who holds them! Release the hold the enemy has on their mouths and their words. Their ideas have been shut up inside of them; let their dreams and hopes well up within them once again. Fan the flames that have died low; blow on them afresh by Your Holy Spirit. Let the fire be rekindled in them. Let them know You are with them.

Come, Lord, to this hidden valley. Let Your light shine as bright in the valley as the mountain is majestic. Let there be no comparison. Let Your people make a difference in the valley. They walk around as tiny lights in this valley. Now, Lord, magnify the power of that light so that others will know from whom they come.

Wake the people who have gone into spiritual slumber who have said, "It's too hard!" Scripture says:

Therefore He says: "Awake, you who sleep, arise from the dead, and Christ will give you light" (Ephesians 5:14 NKJV).

Let them realize it's You who will do this, as Scripture says:

You will not need to fight in this battle. Stand firm, hold your position, and see the salvation of the LORD on your behalf, O

Judah and Jerusalem. Do not be afraid and do not be dismayed. Tomorrow go out against them, and the LORD will be with you (2 Chronicles 20:17 ESV).

For this is truly the day they have waited for. But they thought You forgot them, Lord. Forgive them, Lord. Bring the enemy of Your people to their knees and release Your people. Restore the place of hope they had in You to hold on to the promises You gave them, for You surely have given some of them promises.

Let them become brave enough to hope again. Open the ears of these people to hear for the first time what their oppressors are really saying. Pop the plugs out of the ears of the oppressed. Let the oppressed truly hear and see the love and freedom being offered to them.

I felt all these words and pictures were given to me by the Lord. When He gives me these things, they are guaranteed to work when applied because they are from Him.

We ministered to about 60 people in a Catholic Church, with the priest in his robes watching from the back. Ann and I spoke on healing topics, and Don gave prophetic words. We divided the people into thirds, with Don, Ann, and I each leading a group. Then we selected a person who needed prayer and demonstrated deep inner healing prayer.

During general ministry times, we had words for people. One word was for backs that needed healing. Our translator was one of the people who received healing for her back. Don brought many to Jesus.

One young pregnant woman came for prayer for her son but ended up receiving prayer regarding her relationship with her mother, who had told her, "You are no better than an animal." She was always performing for her mother, wanting to be liked. Her son had a breathing disorder, and they both lived with her family, although she and her son were not liked by them. This young woman received salvation, and understanding came regarding healthy boundaries with her mother.

After an evening seminar, one of the men asked us to go to his home to pray for his wife, who had cancer, and for their marriage problems. Their house was carved into the top of a mountain, so Don and I trekked with poles up that mountain very late at night with a translator to minister to them. It was a very heavy time of deliverance between the two of them regarding their relationship. I'm not sure if there had been involvement with the occult, but it was an intense prayer session.

We got to bed very late. The woman attended our morning seminar the next day and was very happy.

Years later, we received a letter from this woman and her husband (translated into English):

Dear Don, Dear Hanya,

Thank you, a lot, for the lovely greetings and the blessings for the new year.

God has sent you to us as His wonderful messengers. He has lit a fire of His Spirit/Holy Ghost in us that can't be extinguished. Hallelujah. Regardless of the resistance from the Catholic Church, we walk with our heads held high. We walk in the 'victory crowd' (an old Christian term) through Jesus, our King. The time of my sickness was a big blessing for the whole family. We experienced what only He can give—true healing. In our weakness, He is strong. We also learned to be near Him (in His presence) and to expect everything from Him. Jesus made our marital relationship completely new. Praise the Lord!

Again and again, we experience miracles, and we are fascinated by our God. We are so thankful for His grace. Otherwise, we wouldn't have a chance. In the name of Jesus, we bless you and wish you God's mighty blessings, bonded through Jesus.

Lovely greetings to you . . .

On our last day in Zermatt, Don got to ski the Matterhorn, known for its majestic greatness and beauty. Shaped like a pyramid, it is situated between Switzerland and Italy. We went up the mountain in a cable car, and the snow was pinkish-red that day. This phenomenon occurs when dust storms from the Sahara in Africa make their way over the mountain from Italy to the Swiss side of the Matterhorn. Saharan dust storms are the largest on Earth, and when moistened, the dust turns red, giving the snow a pinkish-reddish hue—sometimes called "blood rain."

Our hostess, Edith Biner, left us with these parting words: "Your personalities impacted us."

We traveled back to Berne by train, joining our team for the conclusion of the seminar. We were entertained by what only Switzerland can offer—a yodeling demonstration. If you say these words fast enough: "I love the old lady, and the old lady loves me too!"—you're yodeling!

An exciting thing that happened in Berne was that Gordon, one of our team members—a handsome 42-year-old, single man—and Cendrene, our translator, a young, beautiful woman in her 20s, had eyes for each other. You can guess what happened next: yes, they fell in love. She came to the United States to visit Gordon, and while visiting, they had dinner with Don and me, announcing they were getting married. They asked us what we thought. We knew this was a done deal and discussed all the ramifications of their age difference, but it didn't seem to matter to either of them. They married, and the last I knew, they had two children.

Here are a few stories of inner healing prayer from our ministry in Switzerland:

We prayed for a woman who had two children in their 20s. The enemy was targeting her, using her children to trigger her emotions all the time. We prayed over the issues her children had, breaking any demonic hold the enemy was using to get to her. She also said, "Death is my friend." We look for key phrases like these that open the door for the enemy to have a continual "heyday" with someone. We asked her to reject those words. She needed not to want death to be her friend, to "make dead" the death wish and to proclaim instead that she wanted to live. We used this opportunity to question her if she wanted to live. We brought clarity to her words and beliefs.

Next, a middle-aged woman came with a very pale and lifeless countenance, looking as though she might have a spirit of death on her. She had sleeping issues that needed therapy and medication. Growing up, her father and mother fought every day; her father beat her and was a womanizer, which brought great sadness to her as a child. She said, "I hate the way parents live." She never married or had children. Our words are powerful! She remembered her mother tying a rag around her neck as though to strangle her, and her attitude about being strangled was, "It doesn't matter, do it if you want." Her mother did this several times, making her feel helpless, and in time, she gave in to destructive beliefs. She felt she didn't have anyone to help her. She seemed to succumb to the power her mother had over her and surprised herself with the negative attitude she had as she told us her story. We had her renounce her death wish. We helped her realize that not all parents are bad and ministered to her pain.

Another woman was abused by a priest, her mother, and her aunt, repeatedly. She was paddled so hard that she could not speak and closed off. Some of the words she spoke to us were: "They really put me in chains, I was squashed, it narrowed me and hindered me in my future." She had anxiety but never told anybody, and she had a death wish. We came and gave her a voice to be able to tell what happened to her for the very first time. We ministered love to her, giving her permission to speak, and for the first time, she felt validated.

Blessings While in Switzerland

1. Our first official Small Ministry Team International Conference.
2. Sitting in Rosemary's "tabernacle"—a simple, unobtrusive place filled with the Holy Spirit.
3. Being invited to travel to Zermatt to do a conference for 60 people after feeling discouraged when my speaking time was taken away.
4. God speaking to me in a prophetic way for the people of Zermatt.
5. Successful ministry at the conference in Zermatt, both individually and through holding a corporate healing time.
6. The miracle of the late-night mountain climb, where we prayed for a couple's marriage to be restored and for the wife to be healed of cancer.

7. Receiving a letter of thanks and blessing from the couple we prayed for on the mountain.

8. Removing death wishes from several people, salvations, and healing.

9. Giving a voice to a woman who had lost it.

27

Don's Illness

You have decided the length of our lives.
You know how many months we will live,
and we are not given a minute longer.

Job 14:5

January 1997

Upon arriving home from our trip to Switzerland, Don developed an infection called osteomyelitis in his ankle. As we were leaving the airport after our flight home, I noticed Don was limping while carrying our luggage. I asked him why, and he just said his foot hurt. We came home, and his foot became very red and swollen, worsening as the days went on.

We had an appointment to see a doctor, but Don was misdiagnosed. The doctor said, "If it was osteomyelitis, you wouldn't be sitting up like this." I told him that Don's mother had a high pain tolerance, and I thought Don did too. We went home with an appointment to return that Friday.

Our pastor, Craig Lockwood, called us, asking if we would take his place in ministering to 20 Korean pastors visiting from Korea on that Friday; we were honored to be asked. Don said he would like to minister to these pastors, but I felt we might need to go back to the doctor. He chose ministry, delaying care for another five days, and by this time, Don was using a cane to walk.

When we saw the doctor again, Don was immediately hospitalized; he did, in fact, have osteomyelitis—an infection in the bone. Don underwent three back-to-back surgeries on his ankle under general anesthesia, every other day. After the third surgery, Don had a very hard time waking up and told the doctor, "No more!" He was in the hospital, isolated, for 11 days, and his poor foot had major openings on each side of his ankle.

Don returned home on a Sunday with a PICC line installed so that the antibiotics could be delivered directly to his heart. A nurse set him up when we got home, but the IV pack later failed in the night.

The next day, we went to the rehab center for his therapy to soak and debride the wounds—a very painful procedure. While I was setting up the rest of Don's appointments with the receptionist, I noticed the cup of water Don was holding was tipping over. I shouted to the therapist to help Don. We ran over to him in the waiting room, where he was passed out, and I began to pray: "Don, it's not your time! I command the demons from Zermatt to go in the name of Jesus. I pour the blood of Jesus on you." All those things just came to my mind, and I prayed them out loud. Immediately, Don's eyes opened. He later told me he was going through the tunnel on his way to heaven, and people were waiting for him. He also said, "It was so peaceful. Why did you bring me back?"

The young therapist was kneeling there as I prayed, and when Don woke up, I turned to him and said, "Did you hear what I prayed?" He said, "Yes," very stirred, and I told him we would talk about it tomorrow. The therapist was a Christian who attended Calvary Chapel but had never seen anything like this before. I believe

Don came back from dying. The ambulance arrived and took him to the ER.

When Don had been released from the hospital to go home, the day before, his doctor was giving me instructions for his medications, including his blood pressure medication. I told him that Don had already taken it that day, but the doctor insisted he had not, so I gave him another dose later that day, overmedicating him. After therapy, when he was taken to the Emergency Room, they told me his blood pressure was 25!

Don's surgeon was our neighbor, Fred, who lived down the street from us, and I believe Don's foot—and his life—were spared by the surgeon's perseverance.

He was on IV super drugs for about four months, barely able to walk, as they had to break his bone to flush it with antibiotics during the surgeries. The infectious disease doctor never found an entry point for the infection.

It was a long, hard illness, but with all things, the Bible promises joy. Our friend Ann Bowman, a Greek professor, came and wrote thank-you cards for me. Our friend Marilyn called to say she heard from God that "This was not unto death," which confirmed the exact word that God gave to me. That's how God works on our behalf, loving us and bringing us comfort. Our contractor came to take the trash bins out for me, and a neighbor brought a full kettle of "everything soup"—ground beef with every vegetable you can think of, including a jalapeño pepper. I ate that for breakfast, lunch, and dinner every day. What a comfort that was to my very weary body, soul, and spirit.

We hadn't been to church in four months, and The Anaheim Vineyard wanted to bring church to us one evening. We gave permission for only 12 people to come, as Don was extremely sensitive to noise, but 17 came. Pastor Monty Whittaker gave a sermon, and his wife Brandi, along with her guitar and some intercessors—people who pray fervently—walked all through the house singing and praying. What joy and love were brought to us in our isolation.

I learned that life can change in an instant, and the peace of our simple daily life had a deep joy. The biggest things were caring for Don, bringing him downstairs for the day, choosing what we wanted to eat, and maybe renting a Blockbuster movie. Everyone helped with our rental business.

The Lord had spoken to me that we would go to the desert by the end of May. We were invited to a Vineyard marriage retreat in Palm Desert the last week of May with our friends, Pastors Kevin and Suzanne Springer. I believed that Don would be healed enough by then to travel.

Our friends from Edinburgh, Scotland, Eric and Isabel Noble, came to stay in our Pier Colony condominium and traveled with us to the retreat. The most amazing thing is that Eric and Isabel led a marriage group at their church, and Isabel would often say to me that they always needed to work on their marriage.

During the seminar, we filled out many pages of questions, and then a chart was given to us with 30 boxes. Each of us was placed in a box according to our answers and how we compared to our spouse. Eric and Isabel found themselves as far apart as you could get, and would you believe it—Don and I were in the same box? How could that be?

The Springers then invited us to come to the desert and learn to golf, with three days of easy golf lessons by Moe Norman, an autistic man who developed a simple strike method. We accepted their invitation, and after three days of lessons, I, who had never golfed, was able to hit a ball straight and far. Don had been an "A" racquetball player, but we knew that was no longer possible considering the effects of his illness. Now, at 82 years old, Don golfs twice a week. What a blessing it has been for him to continue exercising in such a fun way.

Don has experienced a few more near-death experiences, but God had plans for my man and our life together.

A Bit about Marriage

"And the two shall become one flesh'; so then they are no longer two, but one flesh" (Mark 10:8 NKJV).

I have a funny little story about marriage—it may not have been funny when it happened, but it is now. I was turning 40, and Don wanted to buy me a mink coat. My mother-in-law, Vera, heard about it and insisted on paying half, saying, "All women turning 40 need a mink coat." Remember, she was in fashion design. The man who was helping me try them on became very flirtatious, even in front of Don, and I resisted it—I think this was just the way it was done in those specialty stores. He said in front of Don, angrily, "You two are joined at the hip." Yep! He said it.

John Mirk, active in the late 14th and early 15th centuries, included this rendition of Genesis 2:24 and Mark 10:8 in his sermon collection entitled *Festial*: "For this a man shall leave father and mother and draw to her as a part of himself, and she shall love him and he her, truly together, and they shall be two in one flesh."[66] I love this and believe this is how Don and I love one another, which was proven by being in the same "box" at the marriage seminar in Palm Desert.

As you know from our dating stories, we both prayed about who God would have us marry, so our marriage has always been based on our Christian beliefs.

A person standing alone can be attacked and defeated, but two can stand back-to-back and conquer. Three are even better, for a triple-braided cord is not easily broken" (Ecclesiastes 4:12).

Our marriage, with God in the center, is the three cords woven and intertwined together, which allow us to stand strong against the winds that have surely blown throughout our lives. Jesus is our connecting cord, making our marriage stronger than we could ever do ourselves.

When young ones are looking for their lifetime partner, I advise them not to be unequally yoked, as the Bible teaches in 2 Corinthians 6:14 NKJV, *"Do not be unequally yoked together with unbelievers."* There is strength in two people walking together with the same convictions.

I encourage young couples to find similarities in beliefs and lifestyles so that the differences in comfort and communication are narrowed down to make life a bit more compatible. I have found, through counseling others, that many spouses who have married outside this principle are lonely in their marriages. They are unable to share in the spiritual joys they discover in their relationship with Jesus. Don and I have vital conversations about God, work, and just life all the time. This brings me great joy and satisfaction.

We have had experience with Asian culture over the years, as you will see—traveling to several Asian countries and even attending a mostly Asian church for four years. This gave us the opportunity to minister to many mixed-race couples. I am not racially biased. Many major issues in their marriages had to do with cultural differences, which can be found in any cross-cultural marriage. Nothing bad, but there is a reality to overcoming the differences. Here are a few examples:

A pregnant Caucasian wife married to an Asian man was crying as her live-in mother-in-law insisted she eat these "awful foods" that were making her sick, while scrutinizing everything she did every day. They could not afford an apartment of their own. There was also the young Caucasian woman who married a first-born Asian man and, as tradition dictated, lived in her mother-in-law's home, saying to me, "I just want white food once in a while."

While dating, it is important to visit the other's family to experience their style of living, cultural ways, and habits, as this is how your future spouse was raised. Meeting at college, your environment is on equal footing, but when you are with their family, it's good to see the interactions that take place between them. You may be surprised at the changes you see in your partner, and you must realize your future children will be part of your new blended family. All of this must be considered when deciding on your future marriage plans.

It is very important, when considering who you will marry, not to base your decision solely on feelings. Be equally yoked, communicate your ideas and dreams, and share your backgrounds to face the challenges that may come with the drama and trauma of each other's pasts.

I heard it once said that after you marry, it's not only two people sleeping in your bed but six—you, your spouse, his mother and father, and your mother and father.

Seeing God in Don's Illness

1. The words from God and prayers of deliverance that opened Don's eyes as he was on his way to heaven prematurely.

2. Witnessing to the young therapist who saw the miracle of Don coming back to life after therapy.

3. Having our neighbor Fred, who was also a surgeon, care for Don.

4. The friends who came to help, encourage, and feed me.

5. Loving friends who brought the church to our home, blessing and cleansing it of sickness, grief, and pain.

6. Going to the desert in May, just as God had told me, with dear friends from Scotland, where Don and I learned about our marriage (we were in the same box).

7. Both of us learning how to golf in three days—a gift from friends—giving Don a new sport more fitting for his lifelong injury.

8. Sharing with young people looking for their lifetime partners what Don and I have learned as we've worked together for 60 years to create a loving and enduring marriage.

28

The Magnificent Three
England, Scotland, Germany

Friends come and friends go, but a
true friend sticks by you like family.

Proverbs 18:24 MSG

England—September 1996

Don and I were invited to visit Eric and Isabel Noble in Manchester, England, in 1996, and then Scotland in 1998. You read about these friends whom we entertained in our Pier Colony condominium and almost missed meeting, but who became dear to us and lifelong friends.

In 1996, we flew to England and were invited to stay with Paul and Anne Wood, wonderful people of God. Paul picked us up at the airport, and that evening they had a home group meeting at their house. I knew Don had words from God for the group, but he did not say anything. Then the leader said that Don and I would be leading the group that night. We were jet-lagged, but Don had a chance to share the words God had given him for these people, and we imparted gifts of teaching, healing, worship, and much more. We shared a box of See's chocolates that were gone in a moment. It was a powerful night.

The next day, Anne took Don and me to tour Hampton Court, where King Henry VIII and all his wives lived.

Don had previously stayed at an older woman's home, named Betty, with a group of men when they were on a ministry trip to Bulgaria, England, and Scotland. She left them with an invitation to visit her again, and we took her up on that.

Betty picked us up from the Woods' home and drove us a few hours to her 200-year-old stone house, with a river flowing through her property. The yard had beautiful flower gardens and vegetable gardens with a hothouse, where she picked fresh vegetables for our dinners.

She was a lovely woman in every way. Seeing her sitting in her rocking chair by the fireplace in her kitchen and watching her cook on her Aga cooker was amazing. Aga cookers were a popular and innovative way to cook from the 1920s through the 1960s. This made me want to live just like her.

She was delighted to have us and treated us like royalty. During dinner one evening, we began discussing healing, since that is what we mostly helped people with, and she confided that she missed her husband who had passed away. She told us she visited with her deceased husband every evening, that he would appear at her dining room window and they would visit. We told her that this was not her husband but a demon spirit—a spirit not from Jesus—that picked up the characteristics of her husband. We told her we needed to pray with her, and that she would need to say goodbye to her husband.

We prayed with Betty, and she said goodbye to her husband. Evenings were such a lonely time for her, so we talked about how she could change her routine and begin depending on Jesus as her husband, as it says in Isaiah 54:5a: *"For your Creator will be your husband."*

Don and I apparently had a purpose for this visit—to deliver Betty from her loneliness. She was a beautiful woman, and we praise God for having brought us here.

We encountered another older gentleman who missed his deceased wife, with whom he visited every evening. We were called to cleanse his house of spirits that were noisy in the attic and kitchen.

We then visited Eric and Isabel, who were living in Manchester— what beautiful hosts they were. They drove us to Edinburgh, Scotland, where we shopped and did some sightseeing. Their daughter, Audrey, and her husband had us for dinner.

We visited the Manchester Vineyard and enjoyed several meals with Pastor Martyn Smith and his wife, Linda. They later came to the USA and stayed in our Pier Colony hospitality condominium. We showed them around and invited them to our house. What fun it is to be part of the body of Christ!

Scotland and Germany – July 1998

Eric and Isabel had moved from Manchester, England, to Scotland, near Edinburgh, and invited us to join them for a bed-and-breakfast trip along the eastern coast of Scotland. Once Don had recovered more from his osteomyelitis, we went with great joy! We left three weeks after Aaron and Sam's wedding. Eric put together the entire trip. They were trusted, loving, mature friends, and were exactly what we needed at this time of our lives.

Scotland is a beautiful country. We visited castles, stayed in castles, and had dinner in a castle. The bed-and-breakfast places were all very quaint; it was so nice to come home to a warm meal and bed after a long day of driving and sightseeing.

One night, we stayed in a very old hotel in Edinburgh. I was having a hard time sleeping, even though we wore ourselves out each day sightseeing. I began to pray, and in a vision, I saw a gigantic floor-to-ceiling ugly demonic being. These buildings are hundreds of years old—this thing had lived there for a very long time. I shook Don to tell him, but he just told me to pray, so I did until I saw it dissolve into a small pool of liquid and disappear. I was then able to sleep. Thank you, Lord, for the spiritual gift of being able to see in the spiritual realm and for understanding the authority we have in Christ.

Behold, I give you the authority to trample on serpents and scorpions, and over all the power of the enemy, and nothing shall by any means hurt you (Luke 10:19 NKJV).

We went to church in Aberdeen one Sunday and were invited to say a few words at their evening service. The Spirit of God was very powerful, and you could tell this was a praying church—the Lord was there.

I saw a vision of the Lord at the front of the church, and He said, "I delight in my people." Later, I saw a large, powerful waterfall in the same place, and a face appeared in the waterfall and said, "I am the water of life." When I see something as powerful as that, I know God is ready to do something big!

Later, I saw the water from the waterfall flowing out the front door and sweeping the young ones off their feet along with it. Their feet stuck up in the air, and they had such surprised, happy looks on their faces.

After worship, I prayed for a woman whose doctor had declared she could never dance again, as she had a fractured knee, and she loved to dance in the Spirit. As I prayed, I saw in the Spirit knitting needles sewing the fracture back together and told her I believed she was better. She said the pain was gone, and by the end of the evening, she was dancing to the worship music. Praise the Lord! I know now that when I see knitting needles in action, the Lord is healing bones. At least that is a true principle for how God works through me.

We continued sightseeing along the east coast, and it was wonderful! I collected little goat statues since goats were such a happy part of my childhood. I found a Lenox black-and-white porcelain china goat in Edinburgh.

While writing this chapter, I asked Don what he remembered from Scotland, and he said, "When you order fish and chips, they put it on a piece of paper and put it in your hand." He is usually the history guy!

Eric and Isabel have both gone to be with the Lord. What a rich relationship we had as brothers and sisters in Christ. It is rare for friends to come into your life to enrich and comfort you as they did in ours. Isabel and I shared the same birthday—February 27—so I think of her every year.

Germany

We returned to Eric and Isabel's home, then flew to Germany for about five days to visit with other friends we had met through hosting at our Pier Colony condominium.

We stayed with Wolly and Marianne Peuster, who threw a surprise birthday party for Don. Many pastors and their wives were invited. We had a joyous time eating dinner, and afterward, Don and I had the opportunity to minister encouraging words to everyone.

One Sunday evening during this visit, we were invited to speak in Heidelberg at a Lutheran church young adult service. There, I gave my *Healing of Shame* message, and Don decided he would do a corporate healing of shame ministry time. We had never done it corporately before. It was quite a success, with somber responses, tears, and gut-wrenching personal testimonies.

I motioned to the pastor's wife for the guitarist to begin playing when I felt the ministry time was ending, but instead, she came up to the microphone and began singing beautifully in tongues—a spiritual language received through the baptism of the Holy Spirit. When the service ended, I went up to her and told her how beautiful it was and asked if she did that often. She responded, "I have never done it before." It didn't seem strange to anyone, and it was a beautiful moment.

We stayed with Jorg and Dr. Sabine Dohnicht, a godly couple who worshiped with their guitar after dinner each night. Our time with them was short, as they both needed to work. They also had a special apartment outfitted for visitors devoted to ministry, just as we had done with our Pier Colony condominium. When we experience a taste of loving, giving hospitality, it inspires us to offer it to others as well.

We visited with Siegfried and Gudrun Koble, whose backyard overlooked the Black Forest. We hiked through the beautiful green hills. I especially remember the dinner we had with their family when we first arrived at their home. They served a native dish of Switzerland called Raclette. A special cooking device on the table melted Raclette cheese in small individual trays, which we poured over bread, potatoes, or meats. What a treat that was!

A few months after we returned home from Scotland and Germany, Aaron and Sam's son, Coby, was born on November 30. What a joy! When the nurses brought him to us for the first time, they said it was amazing to see how much he looked like his father. I helped Sam and Aaron for the next few weeks. It was so fun to celebrate Christmas with them and great-grandmother Vera. Aaron read *The Littlest Angel* to all of us, and he was so proud to do it![67] Don's Uncle Nick, Auntie Donna Shubin, Uncle Jack, and his friend Sandy came for a BBQ in the afternoon.

God's Deeds in This Chapter

1. What we do today counts for our tomorrow. Through our hospitality ministry, we met many wonderful friends who returned the favor when we needed rest and refreshment—they came to our rescue.

2. Opportunities were given to us to minister to others, even while on vacation, which brought help to others and great satisfaction to our souls.

3. The deliverance of a woman from the visitations of her dead husband.

4. Using my spiritual gifts to conquer demonic forces that I encountered in the old Edinburgh hotel.

5. The healing of a woman's knee in Aberdeen, enabling her to dance again.

6. The pastor's wife sang in her spiritual language for the very first time in front of the congregation.

7. Don's surprise birthday party was given by our friends in Germany, and we discovered Raclette cheese with friends.

29

Sweden and Denmark 1998

In January, before our trip to Sweden and Denmark, I had been very ill with the flu and couldn't get rid of a chest cough that had lingered for quite a while. Our trip was coming up in March.

Around this time, I had been praying for God to do whatever it would take to mature our son, Aaron, but I added, "Lord, have mercy, protect him, watch over him, and keep him safe."

In February of that year, Aaron told us he was going to Mexico with his fraternity to build something. Instead, he drove with a friend to Nebraska, through the Rockies, in winter, in his little red Chevy S10 pickup truck to see Sam. On the way home, he slid on black ice off the freeway, totaling his truck. He called at 10 p.m. on a Sunday night after Don and I had put in a full day at the church, telling us he was at the hospital in Nebraska. Praise the Lord, Aaron and his friend were okay. We flew them home the next day, minus his truck.

During this time, Don's 84-year-old mother had emergency surgery and was staying with us to recuperate. This is a picture of the warfare that was happening in the few months before our ministry trip.

I received many words in my quiet time with the Lord as I prayed about our upcoming trip:

- I heard from the Lord, "I will bring you great success on this trip. They will respond."

- In a picture, I saw Jesus going before us and saw our footprints over Denmark and Sweden. This word picture was confirmed by two others.
- Another picture I saw in my mind's eye was a heart that had been struck with an arrow, and as the arrow was pulled out, it broke, leaving the shaft.
- I saw a broken leg in a cast, fractured just under the knee. I would be looking for someone with that ailment.

One woman who was praying for our team saw a red carpet roll out and said that this trip would be pivotal.

Craig Lockwood was the pastor of our Healing Prayer Teams at the Anaheim Vineyard. We were invited to Stockholm by Hans Sundburg, who was the Vineyard Director over Sweden, the Nordic countries, and Russia. He was also an Associate Professor in Systematic Theology at the Scandinavian School of Theology.

Healing Prayer Conference – March 18-30, 1998

We went on the 12-day ministry trip to Sweden to do conferences on healing prayer in Stockholm, Malmo, Copenhagen, and Denmark, as well as to speak and minister at church services, leaders' meetings, and home groups. Pastor Craig Lockwood, Ann Bowman, and I were the conference speakers.

March 20-21, 1998 – Conference at Vineyard Christian Fellowship, Malmo. Calle and Ulla Erlandson, the pastors of the Malmo Vineyard, welcomed us at the bus station, and we went to the Savoy Hotel for lunch. Later that day, we went to their home for dinner, where we met our hosts.

On Friday evening, Craig spoke on *Origins,* and our team did a skit on how *not* to create a safe environment when praying for people. We gave very funny examples.

The seminars given were *How We Become Emotionally Broken People, The Power of the Cross,* and *Confession,* with a clinic on confession in the afternoon. People filled out a form about something they needed to confess and met in pairs to hear and bless one another.

On Saturday evening, I spoke on *Steps to Forgiveness.* Don and another woman led the ministry time by asking for forgiveness on behalf of specific sins done by mothers and fathers. This exercise always brings many wounds to the surface, allowing people to forgive their parents.

There is a Danish concept called *Janteloven,* the Law of Jante, a code of conduct from a fictional man in a novel. The term is multifaceted, but it basically means that you should never call attention to yourself. You should not promote yourself as being someone special, and you should not let anyone else be special either. You should not say, "I'm good at . . ." or "I'm gifted at . . ." It's a form of false humility that stifles honesty in relationships and the free development of evangelism and giftedness in ministry.

One of our team members said that he had lived with this *Janteloven* attitude all his life, though he never had a name for it. He publicly repented of it and invited the conferees to join him in renouncing its hold on their lives. The crowd loudly joined him in this as Pastor Craig led everyone in prayers rejecting this attitude that many joked about but also had.

I got the words "sweet smell of success" for the group—that people were going after the success of the world. God says, "Give it up!" We are to go for success in the things of God. Two young men came to me for prayer. One had tingling in his hands for the "sweet smell of success" word. They had a calling on their lives but were not moving in this calling. I prayed for them.

For those at the conference called to the nations, "God was beckoning them and had crowns for them." I felt heat in my chest as this word was given to me.

I brought a girl from the New Age movement to the Lord. There was a woman with a broken leg in a cast, fractured in two places. I remembered that I would be looking for someone with a fractured leg, and I prayed for her.

After worship, Calle, the pastor, felt God leading him to ask for testimonies from the conference. He called the congregation to join him in renouncing *Janteloven*, and the Holy Spirit came in great power—so much so that they spent the rest of the service in ministry and extended worship. The position of senior pastor of a church can call upon God with great power and authority.

Ministry words and pictures I had for people:

- "You have been crying out for peace for a long time, and He is here like a dove to give you the gift of life. Come, those who have never accepted Jesus; He says, 'Welcome.'"

- There is a mind that is "grinding and grinding." This place is for you also. (A vague word to me, but it had significance for someone.)

- There are at least two hearts that are broken and crying. Jesus wants to gather the tears of your heart and take them to Himself.

- There is a picture of a heart with hands worshiping out of it. God wants you to have a deeper inner worship and life of service.
- There is a release of rain in this room. Angels are outside dancing and twirling.
- "I will bring great mercy upon these people and see that their purposes are fulfilled."

It was obvious that there was a new liberty in the church. There was empowerment and refreshing, deeper emotional healing, and the people prayed for us.

Denmark

Later that Sunday morning, we traveled by ferry from Malmo, Sweden, to Copenhagen, Denmark. Pastor Fleming Pederson, who was planting a church in central Copenhagen, met us when we docked. We had pizza at Pastor Fleming's home, took a walk with his wife, Anne, and realized that Sunday was not a special day in Copenhagen. There are many unchurched people in Copenhagen, and only one percent attend church. It was a very dark atmosphere spiritually, making it challenging to minister here. I saw in the spirit something like a large block—a heavy weight—hovering low over the city and the country and saw a Christian trying to crawl out from under it. The translation of this vision was that it was a very hard place for a Christian to live and minister.

We were privileged to be the speakers for Fleming's first public services. Our pastor, Craig Lockwood, spoke on *Paraclete*, referring to the Holy Spirit as our helper, and spoke about how we are to come alongside the weaknesses of others and help them along. We give an "emotional hug" to people by listening with concern, bringing warmth to their hearts.

"Comfort the fainthearted, uphold the weak, be patient with all" (1 *Thessalonians 5:14b NKJV*).

Don had a word for the church. He saw the church as a shop freshly opened for business. The business was presenting Jesus to the people of Copenhagen, but the shop needed merchants to attend to the customers, and in some cases, to go into the streets to find new customers. Don led an altar call then and there, calling people forward who were choosing this church as their home church and affirming their commitment to this new ministry with Fleming as their pastor.

Following the altar call, Don led the ministry time and encouraged those who had words of knowledge to share them. That led to prayer for most people present who had a variety of needs—some needed physical healing, others sought healing for depression, and still others had deeper inner healing issues that had surfaced during the conference.

A woman with pain in her heart came to me for prayer. I had a picture of how her heart was connected to her mind. She said her heart would only hurt when she worked too hard. As we prayed, I also saw a picture in my mind's eye—a spiritual image of tears coming out of her heart, and Jesus was catching them. I shared my picture with her, and it resonated. I had her name the tears—hopelessness, fear, and other words. She also told me she had pain in her knees and down her legs to her feet, which she identified as fear. I placed my hands around her knees without touching them and got the impression that there were bands just under my hands.

I stood up and asked her if she had been involved in occult activity. She said yes and that she had been prayed for about her involvement, but these attacks continued. I asked her what occult connections were still there; she said her mother and sister were still involved. We were in an area steeped in New Age activities. I began to pray to break any connection, and in doing so, I saw in the spirit a hook in each of her shoulders. I prayed to cut the soul ties (connections) between her and her mother and sister. I then asked the Lord to protect her, stooped down, put my hands on the bands I had seen, and came against any demonic activity from her mother's and sister's occult influences. I saw the bands break and then asked her if her legs felt better—she said yes.

This woman was not a bad person; she was an intercessor—a person who prayed for others—but was walking with her head down. I then found out that she had been raped at a young age, and we prayed for healing from that trauma. I encouraged her to let the pastor know what had taken place in case any of her symptoms returned after we left.

Next, we saw a woman totally freed from arthritic pain in her back; another person found release from demonic oppression related to past New Age connections, and others found emotional healing.

We were not without warfare. One man was very disruptive throughout the ministry time, but God used one of our team members to stay with him for the rest of the evening.

One man said, "I have this tiny little heart, and when I show it to anyone, they shoot it." We are such delicate creatures and need to be handled with care.

Some words from the Lord given to me for Pastor Fleming and his wife, Anne:

- "I will build this church; you worry and won't wait."
- "Fleming, I love and cherish you. You see, my plans are better. I am sending you helpers."
- "New Beginnings," "Alive." The Lord was confirming that Fleming and Anne were joined in unity. "Joy, joy, joy in the land."

Stockholm

March 24, 1998. Our team traveled by train back to Stockholm, where we enjoyed a lovely lunch with pastry cups, whipped cream, and cloudberries for dessert at Hans and Lotta Sundburg's home. Afterward, we had a meeting and prayed for the upcoming week of ministry.

Don and I were then taken to our host's home, and people began arriving for a home group that she hosted that night. We spoke about our passion for the Lord, challenged them to do the same, and ministered words of knowledge to this community. Don anointed each one with oil, and I followed, praying prophetically for each person.

Some of the ministry time focused on group members who were dealing with personal challenges, such as sadness about family or questioning life purpose during a job transition. I saw in the Spirit a crown on the leaders' heads and told the people that they were to bless and honor their leaders. Don and I then prayed over them.

I had a picture of two women singing and dancing. One woman told me she dreamed of this at night! She looked very sad before this word, but after we prayed, she was beaming. This picture was validation from God for something she loved doing.

We continued receiving words that night at this home group. I received a word that there was a calling on two or three men's lives, but they weren't moving on it. They were hiding from their God-given calling. These men responded and allowed prayer into this area of their lives.

We saw a lot of fruit coming from these words given to us. This home group was so welcoming. We had a wonderful Swedish waffle meal with fresh mushroom soup, and before the night ended, they prayed for us.

Norrkoping

March 26, 1998. Don and I were driven to a church in Norrkoping, Sweden, for an evening conference with about 40 people packed into a small room.

I spoke on forgiveness, and we both ministered. Don shared a word that it was time for the women to be recognized as co-laborers with the men. He called forward the women who felt God was gifting them in prophecy and intercession; the pastor later added deliverance. Don asked each man present to come to the microphone to bless and pray for the women.

The power of God fell as the women, who were deeply touched, responded to the Lord's presence. They received affirmation and were empowered for ministry, all to the great delight of Pastor Andreas and his wife. What a powerful and fruitful evening.

March 27, 1998. During the prior week, our team had spread out to minister at various home groups in the evenings and speak and minister at a couple of leaders' meetings. During the day, we had individual prayer appointments with people seeking healing prayer.

Today marked the beginning of our ministry out of the Stockholm Vineyard. We enjoyed Coq au Vin and rice for lunch, after which Don and I prayed for a couple. We went to Hans and Lotta Sundberg's home for coffee and a special cream cake with jam, where we strategized about ministry and had a nice visit. That evening we attended the regular weekly renewal service, where in recent months the focus had been on physical healing.

Pastor Craig spoke to about 120 people and led a group ministry time, inviting the Holy Spirit to reveal and remove negative labels people might be wearing due to the lies they had believed. The labels could have been words others had named them or words we named ourselves outside the truth of God, such as "loser," "stupid," and the like.

March 28, 1998. A vision the Lord gave me before the evening conference was of the Holy Spirit entering the conference, and I heard the words, *"I am here to do mighty works."* My impression was that He, God, would let the works be as gold and silver, implying they would be precious.

I saw the Lord turning over the leaves of our lives and looking underneath. I received these words and shared them with the group: *"Let Him; it will set you free. Don't be afraid! The Holy Spirit is going deep into your heart to cleanse you. It's good for you."*

Many people from the New Age sector sent others to come and learn from us. They had to sit through worship, where I am sure they were touched, and many responded and received prayer.

A woman Don and I prayed for earlier in the week shared that her dental fillings from years past had caused a toxic reaction, leaving her highly sensitive to electrical currents. Her sensitivity was so high that just being around all the lights and equipment in the church caused unbearable pain. God brought substantial healing during the prayer time, and she was even able to attend the conference that day!

Another woman I ministered to was the child of missionaries to Africa. Her father left for six months when she was not even a year old, and her mother struggled with his absence. In a childhood memory, she remembered being in a crib in a small, dark kitchen, lonely and just wanting her mother to sit next to her. She experienced childhood grief, feelings of wanting to disappear, and many other emotions. We let her speak her feelings, prayed truth into her, and had her take it all to the cross of Jesus, the ending place of all sin and hardship. There is always peace for those who surrender themselves to Jesus. Anytime we go deep, we allow as much time as needed for people to express every detail of their experience and to be specific about their feelings. Children living with a depressed person can sometimes internalize those emotions and grow up wondering why they feel depressed themselves.

March 29, 1998. We were in our final conference sessions in Stockholm. Craig spoke on *Healing of Shame* and then led the group through a time of finding healing for undealt-with shame. I gave my *Steps to Forgiveness* teaching, followed by a ministry time.

During our time in Stockholm, we were served a special lunch, Reindeer Pie. I thought you'd like to try it:

REINDEER PIE

1 lb. Ground Reindeer, Deer, or Elk

1 Tbsp. Butter

1 Onion, chopped

3/4 cup canned Mushrooms

2 Tbsp. Crème Fraiche

1/3–1/2 cup Blue Cheese

2 Tbsp. Black Currant Jelly

Instructions

Preheat the oven to 350°.

Fry the meat, onions, and mushrooms in the butter. Add the crème fraiche and let the mixture boil for a couple of minutes, stirring occasionally. Place the meat mixture into a buttered casserole dish and cook for about half an hour. Remove the casserole from the oven and immediately mix in the blue cheese (we like 1/3 cup) and jelly. Serve with mashed potatoes.

Shhh! My secret—I use ground beef.

March 30, 1998. We left Sweden early Monday morning and arrived home Monday evening.

March 31, 1998. Talk about warfare! In preparation for this trip, we had many challenges, and we came home to even more.

The next day, we discovered that our office had been emptied by a man who once owned the building but then rented from us. He moved out of his rented space while we were away, taking all the furniture we had offered to purchase from him along with our computer, which held all of our business records. He refused to return the computer to us but eventually did.

April 1, 1998. Aaron tells us he is getting married and having a baby!

A woman recently asked me, "I've heard people use the word warfare, but I don't know what that is." Warfare often involves seemingly ordinary, natural occurrences happening unexpectedly, all at once, overwhelming a person. These often come at strategic times of ministry to confuse and weaken you. Warfare touches important things—our health, family, and business matters.

The solution is powerful prayer, along with others interceding on our behalf. I have found that praying specifically is essential to receiving powerful answers.

God Sightings in Sweden and Denmark

1. We had many opportunities to impart what God has given to us in mighty ways, healing both physical ailments and emotional wounds.

2. We witnessed the spiritual condition of Denmark and saw in the Spirit a hovering, hard rock-like disc over the country, calling for specific prayer and authority.

3. God showed His love to us through the care and hospitality of the Nordic people. We enjoyed fabulous food, including Reindeer Pie.

30

Sweden 1999

I can do all things through Christ who strengthens me.

Philippians 4:13 NKJV

April 5-20, 1999

The previous year was quite eventful, with our son Aaron's marriage to Sam, the birth of our new grandchild Coby, our ministry trip to Sweden and Denmark, and a visit to friends in Scotland and Germany. Don's mother, Vera, was undergoing major dental work, and I spent many days and hours with her, which was very hard on both of us. She was determined to keep her teeth so that "she could chew," and I agreed with her.

Don and I were invited to Sweden a second time, to lead an Anaheim Vineyard team of 12 to Stockholm, Malmo, Orebro, and Goteborg. This would be a continuation of our first trip, the previous year, as well as adding Orebro and Goteborg. Since our trip the year before, three people from Sweden visited the Anaheim Vineyard to learn about and be trained in healing prayer. They returned to Sweden and began training teams of their own, which meant we had trained people waiting to join us for ministry abroad.

A vision someone had for our trip was, "I see lightning shooting across the ocean, igniting the flame of your passion into the hearts of the people."

Prayers we prayed before leaving on this trip:

- That we would bring blessings to the people we would be encountering. "Lord, you've gone before them, and you've prepared the way."
- For the Spirit of truth to set the captives free.
- Unity of purpose in the Spirit for our team, to be examples of the New Testament church to the communities we visit, and that the people would be amazed at the love among our team members.
- An anointing over our team's eyes and ears to see and hear the secrets of the Lord's heart.
- For the Lord to show our team God's heart for the places they would go and for the people they would encounter.
- For the Lord to take the team out of the natural realm into the supernatural through the Spirit.
- That the joy of the Lord would be the team's strength and give them joy and expectation as to what He would do.
- That the power of the Lord's name and blood would be with us should we come against spirits connected to euthanasia, sexual sin, suicide, and abortion
- For the scales on people's eyes to fall off and that they would see the true ugliness of their sin, realizing how offensive it is to God's heart.
- For the Lord to give people a passion for life.
- For people to break free from nicotine addiction and regain control of their lives.

- For the power of God's Word to set the people free.
- For the empowerment of each team member.
- For the people to be filled and to receive the truth and knowledge of the Lord Jesus Christ.
- For protection of the food and water consumed on the trip.
- For protection for the team's families and businesses, as well as for healing, health, and wholeness in each family member.
- For traveling mercies for each team member.
- For wisdom and discernment of the Lord's guidance, direction, grace, and mercy through the Holy Spirit.
- That the Holy Spirit would create and execute the agenda of the meetings.
- For great and lasting fruit and a harvest.
- That there would be a tremendous revelation given to all the team members.

We not only covered ourselves in prayer beforehand, but while abroad, members of our team called in real-time prayer needs to prayer warriors back in the U.S. All this to say, we prayed!

Stockholm

Don and I stayed with Eva Evingard and her daughter, Johanna, in Stockholm—what a beautiful home. Eva gave us her own room, saying, "Since it's winter, the house is cold." The other room must have been freezing. I've learned from being in Nordic countries that when it's winter, it's winter, and I love how they always have bright fresh flowers to bring spring beauty into the dark, damp atmosphere of their homes during the winter season.

April 7, 1999. Our team met with house group leaders, and we taught on *Healing Prayer Teams as a Resource*. In the afternoon, we went to Old Town, did some shopping, and then prayed for people in teams. These sessions lasted at least an hour, sometimes up to two hours.

April 8, 1999. Our team of 12 gave individual prayer sessions all afternoon, and in the evening, I taught *Vision and Values for Prayer Teams* to pastors, leaders, and healing prayer team members. We then had ministry time.

April 9, 1999. We prayed all afternoon for people, and in the evening, Ann gave a teaching, ending with a time of response.

April 10, 1999. This was a teaching day. We taught *The Fruit of Painful Situations, The Decision Tree, Prayer Structure, Creating a Safe Environment,* and *Personal Freedom Through Confession and Cleansing.* That evening, I taught *Healing of Shame* to about 300 people, with translation, as it was an open evening for many who did not understand English.

After speaking about *Healing of Shame,* there was a long line of young men who were crying like babies from things that had happened to them in childhood. What a joy it was to minister to them and see God going to the deep places yet to be healed.

April 12, 1999. A sightseeing day in Uppsala. I could not go and needed to rest the entire day because of exhaustion and only got ready when the team arrived for dinner.

April 13, 1999. We then divided our team: Ann led half the team to Malmo and Copenhagen, where we had gone last year. Don and I led the other half of the team to Orebro and Goteborg.

Orebro

Don and I were on our way to Goteborg with our six-member team, and on the way, we stopped in a city called Orebro, where we did a one-day seminar with Pastor Anders Hagstrom, who was planting a new church. The people organizing this event advertised it as "Vineyard Healing Team" and put flyers in the New Age Center. We were told that many New Age people would be there. We met with the church elders regarding the evening service.

I was told by one of my team members to change my message to a salvation message but chose to stay with the one I had on *"Healing of Pain."*

This seminar was held in a coffee house, and when I began teaching, I heard loud music and asked the people in the kitchen to turn it down. They told me it was coming from next door, a dance studio doing salsa dancing. This was my background music for much of the evening.

I did include a salvation message at the end, with an altar call for salvation and healing. Several New Age people came forward wanting to know about the gospel. Some of the team members spoke with them, and the seeds of life with Jesus were planted. Others came for healing of their bodies and emotional conditions, and God was present for them in wonderful ways. I was also told that this group of people wouldn't come to the front for an altar call—it was more normal for them to be sent to the back—but this proved untrue, as many came forward at my invitation. We will never know how deep this time of ministry went, but the small church that was forming would continue the work.

Our team who traveled by van from Stockholm to Orebro for this night of ministry headed back to the Stockholm Arlanda airport for a flight to Goteborg.

Goteborg

April 15, 1999. Our hosts were Goran and Anne Mae Falthammer, and we stayed in their very large, unique three-story home. The top floor was rented out like an apartment to a couple, the second floor was divided into apartment-like spaces for their high school-age children, and the parents lived on the first floor. We stayed on the basement floor next to their prayer chapel. The chapel was a room set aside for prayer and resting in the Lord, with a fireplace, candles, and bean bag chairs. It was a very relaxing atmosphere to connect with God.

The tenants on the top floor invited Don and me to dinner one evening. It was fun for the husband, who was going to be in a barista competition, to practice his skills on us. He had special coffee for the competition, which cost $100 per pound. Although we weren't allowed to drink it, he showed us the beans. He went on to win the competition, and when we asked how it went, he said all the competitors were pretty much on the same skill level, but when he served the judges, he also served the competitors. This act set him apart as the winner. We developed quite a relationship with this couple, and they allowed us to pray with them for various issues in their lives. They, in time, came and stayed with us at Pier Colony.

April 16, 1999. We had afternoon prayer teams today and held a conference in the evening. There were 75 pastors, leaders, counselors, and people interested in learning about healing prayer. I spoke about *Salvation and The Power of the Cross* and all the elements that are available to us from Jesus' death, such as the cross being the ending place of all sin, a place of rest, cleansing, protection, new beginnings, etc.

I was so weak from exhaustion, and my health was wavering so much that I needed the worship leader's stool to sit on for this evening's teaching.

Our host seemed to feel sorry for me at the end of the evening when I did an altar call. I called people forward who had never understood salvation and the power and benefits that come from Jesus' death and resurrection. These were pastors and Christian counselors who should know all of this, and I thought to myself, in my insecurities, "They know all this, who am I to tell them?" My host later told me that he prayed, "Please give her one, Lord" (meaning at least one person to come forward). Well, about 30 came forward, and I needed to ask for their prayer team's help. It was a wonderful move of God that night. It was not about me, my knowledge, or the state of my health. Don was a great encouragement during the altar time.

April 17, 1999. I spoke on *The Fruit of Painful Situations* and *The Decision Tree*. My teammates then taught *Team Structure* and *Creating a Safe Environment for Healing Prayer*. Later, I taught *Healing Through Forgiveness* with a clinic where they could practice forgiveness. In the evening, I spoke about *Healing of Shame*.

The response to what we came to impart was wonderful. At first, some of the leaders made sure to let us know that they already had a prayer/counseling model that they had all been trained in. We taught and demonstrated the training we came to present. When they saw how the Holy Spirit did the healing in such a short period of time, they were amazed. They realized the technique we showed them could integrate well with what they used.

As we got to know Hans Sundberg, the Vineyard Director of the Nordic Countries and Russia, the thought crossed my mind that since I am Russian and can speak a bit of the Russian language, maybe this was a road to minister in Russia. However, this never happened.

Prayer Stories from This Trip

One woman, whose father was a transvestite, said she carried so much shame connected with his condition that she felt like she had no father. Her friends made fun of her father because he was "like a clown," and she knew what he was. We prayed demonic strongholds off of her regarding her father and the shame involved.

This next testimony is about a young man who was a house group leader and a worship leader, who willingly engaged in sexual encounters while in leadership. He shared his story:

> I've always had high thoughts about myself and how a Christian should live, but I've never lived up to it myself. I lost my virginity when I was 20 years old, and after that, I had several sexual relationships. For about one year, I almost left God and lived just as I wanted to, but I was in emotional pain all the time because I knew I lived in sin and that I could never run away from God.
>
> When we met last Thursday, I had to deal with my previous sexual relationships. After the prayer session, I felt really good, and the first thing I realized when I left was how quiet everything was. I thought it was just the neighborhood, but when I got home, I felt the same quiet there as well. All the noise didn't bother me as it used to, and I felt like a new creation. I felt light and happy; a great peace surrounded me.
>
> Two hours after the prayer, the person we had prayed about called me. I had not heard from her in a month! We talked as friends and got along really well. I now have hope for the future.

Every night for the last four years, memories of my previous sexual relationships have given me pain, and the memories have haunted me. But last Thursday, when I was going to bed, I felt pure, and the memories just weren't there. I felt pure and free, and I had never slept that well before. My thoughts about the girl we prayed about weren't mixed with my other relationships, and I wasn't comparing her with them. It felt really good. Now I can move on in my life. I can start all over again and not look back at bad memories.

I want you to know that this situation has been so hard on me that I have been sitting in the kitchen at my home with a knife to my wrist, trying to find the courage to take my own life. As you can see, I didn't find it! I just want to thank you for your help and tell you how much this has meant to me.

One woman, who had been atrociously abused as a baby by her father, couldn't believe she could openly talk about the details of her abuse with us, nor that we encouraged her to get it out. Her mother knew about the abuse, but her father had threatened her mother's life. She and her brother were raised in children's homes. A few days after our prayer session, she described what she had thought the church was like. Using her hands to represent an open Bible, she mimicked mumbling words as if reading it, then slammed it shut. She believed people who went to church were pious and couldn't imagine there were people who actually cared and wouldn't be offended to hear real life. She was amazed that we could do this type of ministry in a church. Laughing with unbelievable joy, she said:

"This is the most important and fantastic thing in my story. I reached out my hands and touched the feet of Jesus while he was hanging on the cross, and his blood came into me and washed me clean. I want to tell you that it feels like it's not until now my life has really begun, and I want to live the rest of it the way God decides."

What an honor and privilege it is to touch lives such as these.

Our business ran very well this time, and Don's health was fine. Altitude seemed to affect our bodies. Don's foot, from the osteomyelitis infection and surgeries, swelled from the long plane rides, so we had to watch him carefully.

This was a whirlwind tour and a highlight for me, as Don and I were privileged to lead this great team. I was stretched in my teaching and leadership skills, and it was a very profitable trip. We give God all the glory.

As a result of your ministry, they will give glory to God. For your generosity to them and to all believers will prove that you are obedient to the Good News of Christ. And they will pray for you with deep affection because of the overflowing grace God has given to you (2 Corinthians 9:13-14).

God's Blessings on This Trip

1. Don and I were given the privilege of leading this team of 12 to Stockholm, Orebro, and Goteborg.
2. Traveling with people who prayed fervently and even called in our requests to the U.S.
3. The sacrifice of Eva in Stockholm when she gave us her own room.
4. Learning about bringing a springtime atmosphere into dark, cold days with colorful bouquets, which I do to this day.
5. Being able to minister to the New Age community, bringing the salvation and healing message to them.

6. Staying in a house with a private chapel, which encouraged me to have a room dedicated for my devotional life.

7. Realizing that, even without credentials and as a woman, I could teach and minister to people whom I perceived as more accomplished than myself. Everyone comes with their own issues and problems and needs a safe place to respond to them, no matter their position.

8. The cost of being stretched beyond myself in travel, teaching, and ministry, and the satisfaction of it all.

9. The precious people who responded, either at the altar or in private sessions, with transparency, and watching God work and heal their lives.

31

Switzerland 2001

Happiness is a perfume you cannot pour on others
without getting a few drops on yourself.[68]

~ *Ralph Waldo Emerson*

Women in the Marketplace Conference
September 28 - October 4, 2001

My friends Ann Bowman and Janet Moen, who were world travelers and missionaries with Campus Crusade for Christ, led a group of women to Emmetten, Switzerland, for a Global Women's Conference on *Ministering in the Marketplace*. This conference was organized by Campus Crusade for Christ International, now known as CRU. Ann was one of the speakers, and she asked me to be her roommate. By this time, we had done a lot of ministry together.

We left for Switzerland—Ann, Janet, the other women, and I. It was a rare event for me to travel without my husband, Don, who is known for, as he says, "carrying my purse." Boy, did I miss him! Our airplane landed, and we scrambled to get onto a train, which was about five feet above the ground. People grabbed our arms, pulling us onto the train, and it took a village to get all our baggage in. I was 56 years old at the time.

Emmetten has the most beautiful scenery, and it made me think of the song from *The Sound of Music*, "The hills are alive with the sound of music."[69] Oh, the awe-inspiring beauty.

There were many women at the conference from all parts of the world, even Mongolia. We were there as a ministry team to provide private deep inner healing prayer sessions for women who wanted it. It was very special to hear these women speak about their different cultural situations and unique needs. Having a translator added an extra layer of complexity to the sessions, making it challenging to fully connect, but we managed.

These are a few stories from our time in ministry:

Egypt

A lady from Egypt had a mother who was dying of cancer and was afraid she would also get the same cancer her mother had. Together, we traced this fear back to her fear of death. She had seen her father die when she was 12 years old, which left her feeling scared and insecure. We prayed about her father's death, helping her deal with her fears and trauma, and then had her bring closure to her relationship with her father by saying goodbye to him. We also prayed over her fear of cancer and dying, breaking any generational line of cancer from her mother to herself, and extended the prayer to cover her daughters as well. We ended by taking everything that was revealed during prayer to the cross of Jesus, who died for our fears, hurts, and failures. This was all done with a translator; it was tedious and took a very long time.

Iran

A Jewish businesswoman from Iran, who was responsible for a staff of five people, came to the conference very lonely. She was shaking uncontrollably, and when we asked her about it, she told us she had previously had cancer, and the shaking had developed after her chemotherapy treatment. This woman had deep-seated anger, which caused people to shy away from her. She told us this anger was a generational trait that came through her mother. She had been a revolutionary since her teens, and her best friend betrayed her to the police, resulting in her spending seven years in prison.

Our team walked her through the emotions she had regarding her friend. During this process, she shared the words and emotions she wished she could have spoken to her old friend who betrayed her:

"I'm like you—wicked. I didn't expect this of you. You shocked me, and now I don't have confidence in anyone, not even myself! I can't trust anyone. I love them, but I can't trust them deeply. You only came to show them (the police) to me. I don't know how I feel. I get angry. I would like to forget. I want a new heart without the suffering."

I prayed with her about her anger, and in a vision, I saw a seed of the generational anger, plus a tree and its roots all being uprooted. I shared this vision with her, and then she forgave her friend. When I asked her to take all her anger, sorrow, and pain to the cross, I reminded her of the loneliness she had mentioned, and she took that to Jesus too, leaving all her pain with Him—a safe place and the reason He died for us. God healed her in such a beautiful way.

"I, I am he who blots out your transgressions for my own sake, and I will not remember your sins" (Isaiah 43:25a ESV).

On our last night, we had a special Spirit-filled speaker from Austria. All the women arrived wearing their countries' traditional attire, and we enjoyed worship and dancing performances representing several nations.

After the conference, Ann and I traveled to Germany to visit her friends, where a private ministry opportunity awaited us. A woman had been praying for her husband for many, many years, and he was finally open to receiving prayer. God took us all the way to Germany for this one prayer and salvation opportunity. Jesus does that—He goes after the one.

"What man of you, having a hundred sheep, if he loses one of them, does not leave the ninety-nine in the wilderness, and go after the one which is lost until he finds it?" (Luke 15:4 NKJV).

The best way to find happiness is to give it.

Blessings of God

1. Being privileged to pray with women from many countries.
2. Enjoying the cultural diversity of the women in traditional dress, worshiping, and dancing.
3. The privilege of flying to Germany to minister to one man.

32

El Salvador: "The Savior"

"Heal the sick, cleanse the lepers, raise the dead, cast out demons. Freely you have received, freely give."

Matthew 10:8 NKJV

"And it will be, when you have taken the city, that you shall set the city on fire. According to the commandment of the LORD you shall do. See, I have commanded you."

Joshua 8:8 NKJV

February 10-20, 2017

Our friends Jared and Kelly Mueller and their two sons, Ezra and Benjamin, gave up everything on June 19, 2014, to become missionaries to El Salvador in Central America. They were sent by our church, Hope Chapel, in Huntington Beach, California. This was a bold, brave, and courageous move.

Before Jared and Kelly got this call, I remember Don and I sitting across from them at a dinner hosted by our pastors, Paul and Ainsley Harmon. I kept looking at Jared and Kelly and finally told them that whatever they were up to, we were behind them and said, "I believe in you." At this time, they didn't even know what it was that God was calling them to.

It wasn't long until Jared and Kelly received clarity on what God was calling them to do—they would be missionaries to El Salvador.

El Salvador was known as one of the murder capitals of the world. In 2022, the President of El Salvador arrested tens of thousands of suspected gang members. He built a prison that could hold 40,000 inmates, surrounded by 37 guard towers. The problem was that the government not only arrested gang members but also journalists and ordinary Salvadorans, including many teenagers.[70]

The United States even gave a warning for its citizens not to travel to El Salvador. Kelly told me that gang members kill each other often.

We were told that there are vigilantes who break into homes at night to scare the living daylights out of young ones hanging around with known gang members, hoping this would prevent them from continuing any association with the gangs. Vigilantes are not law enforcement but regular people who gather on their own to enforce the law themselves, thinking the elected law officials are inadequate to do the job.

I remember one thing Jared and Kelly had on their hearts for El Salvador when they first arrived was to start youth camps. Many of the youth were being recruited into gangs, but if the young ones were active church members, the gangs would often leave them alone. The camps were a success—they grew each year and were eventually given to the nationals and are ongoing.

It was announced at our church that there would be a ten-day mission trip to visit, encourage, and minister with the Muellers in El Salvador. I began to pray about Don and me going on this trip. As I prayed, I received the word "Go." It's interesting that our missions team is called the 'Go Team.'

The year before our church announced this trip, on October 25, 2016, I awoke seeing the words "Clarion call" over my head—this is one way I hear from God. "Lord, what is a Clarion?" I looked it up and found: "A Clarion is a medieval horn and means loud and clear."[71] "It means a call to something that is hard to ignore, and a strong request for something to happen."[72]

Again, during one of our church services, before the announcement of this trip to El Salvador, I was praying and had a vision of wheat swaying in a field. Then I saw the word "ripe," meaning this field was ripe for a harvest.

Looking much further back, a few years in my journal, on October 22, 2014 (notice all the Octobers), I heard God say: "I am bringing you up and out, to the fields of harvest," and then I saw sheaves of wheat swaying and waving, beckoning for me to come. Then I heard, "Go to the nations I am sending you to."

In Joel 3:13a (NKJV), it says, *"Put in the sickle, for the harvest is ripe."* We would be going to be harvesters of wheat.

Jesus said to His disciples,

"The harvest truly is plentiful, but the laborers are few" (Matthew 9:37 NKJV).

This harvest was not literal wheat but precious souls ready for salvation. With all these visions and words from God, without a specific direction, I was ready and expectant to find out where to go.

In an entry in my journal in 2014, I wrote, "Jared is plowing and watering, you will just pluck the grains off with your fingers. Easy! Fun and rewarding."

After hearing about this mission trip, I received yet another confirmation for going by hearing the song "This Land is Your Land."[73]

Any time we talk about "taking a land," we mean bringing the atmosphere of the Holy Spirit to replace any other spirit that dwells there. This is best done with those who own the land or have been given authority over it. Since we were being invited by the Muellers, who had taken the land of El Salvador by living there, we went under their Spiritual covering and the authority given to us by their invitation.

The Lord spoke to Joshua about taking the Promised Land,

"Every place that the sole of your foot will tread upon I have given you" (Joshua 1:3a NKJV).

"And it will be, when you have taken the city, that you shall set the city on fire. According to the commandment of the Lord you shall do. See, I have commanded you" (Joshua 8:8 NKJV).

The book *Taking Our Cities for God—How to Break Spiritual Strongholds,*[25] some of which was written at our Pier Colony condominium by John Dawson, is one I would highly recommend for fighting the spiritual battles that are in cities. It's interesting that part of that book was written in Huntington Beach, my city—a city that I have fought for in prayer.

Both Don and I received our confirmation to go on this trip, and by the inspiration of God, we were being prepared for it many years before.

The team was led by Wayne Palica, our Missions Director at the time, and our pastor, Paul Harmon. The team met at our house once a month for dinner and prayer in preparation for this trip, bringing unity and strength to the group. We organized prayer where each of us was assigned a day to pray and fast. Dr. Moots Ikuhara, the team doctor, led the medical part of this trip.

The Bible talks about praying together. Moses did not go alone to fight battles, and in our case, to take the land. It says in *Matthew 18:19b* (NKJV):

"If two of you agree on earth concerning anything that they ask, it will be done for them by My Father in heaven."

In Exodus 17:11-12 (NKJV), it says that Moses took Aaron and Hur up to the top of the hill and interceded before the Lord in prayer:

"And so it was, when Moses held up his hand, that Israel prevailed; and when he let down his hand, Amalek prevailed. But Moses' hands became heavy . . . And Aaron and Hur supported his hands, one on one side, and the other on the other side; and his hands were steady until the going down of the sun."

When his friends held his hands up, they were winning the battle, and when his hands came down, they were losing. Notice that they did this together.

A promise from James 5:16b (NKJV) says, *"The effective, fervent prayer of a righteous man avails much."* We would not go to this dangerous country without the powerful intercession of prayer for fruit, protection, and the Lord's perfect will to be accomplished. Our success would only be achieved under these truths.

Wayne asked me to speak at one of the churches before we left for El Salvador. As I prayed about it, I had a vision of a white flag with a blue crest.

When I read a journal entry of mine from February 2013, as I prayed for El Salvador, I saw the same flag with the same blue crest. Isn't God wonderful in confirming this to me? During the trip, I saw this flag flying over the largest Christian Baptist church in El Salvador. The church took up whole blocks of the city. I asked Jared about the church, and he said it's known for sending a vast number of people out to plant churches, and he wanted to visit them to see how they do that.

A flag is sometimes called a banner. One of the names of God is Jehovah Nissi—Lord My Banner (Hebrew). The Banner of God is a symbol of God's presence. Generals in battle usually carry a flag with an emblem so soldiers know and feel confident when they see it. Marching bands are led by a flag bearer. The Olympics also open with each country carrying its flag.

I believe the vision of this flag, with the precise blue emblem that the Lord showed me several times, gave me confidence that I was there to speak the Lord's words and do His works. The Lord would be with us on this trip, and it would be powerful.

Our group was instructed not to wear the colors red or blue or anything that might say 'Los Angeles,' 'L.A.,' the number 18, 'MS,' or the number 13, as these all represented gang names and symbols.

We left on Saturday, February 11, and when our team arrived in El Salvador, we stayed at the Hotel Santa Elena, a lovely small boutique hotel. I needed to refresh myself, and after stepping out of the restroom, I missed a very small step. My ankle did a mighty fold, and I sprained it, falling onto the stone floor. I was grounded for the afternoon, and there was no ice at the hotel. Thankfully, the team doctor rubbed medical cream on it and wrapped it for me. I limped for several days in pain—not quite a good start, especially since we came to pray for people to be healed.

That night we walked to dinner from the hotel. With my ankle, it was a bit of a journey. Afterward, we attended the 'Operation Solid Life' class at the Muellers' church.

Upon experiencing the culture of El Salvador, I expected a mini version of our Mexico trips. El Salvador had an unexpected softness, sweetness, and gentleness, which was beautiful to behold. The food was different, with a more mellow flavor than Mexican food. All of this was quite delightful.

The next day, Don and I realized we did not have our carry-on baggage, which contained wrapped gifts, my Bible, and other necessary items. It had been left at the airport in the hustle and bustle of gathering everyone's luggage. Kelly and Don drove to the airport, but flights had ended for the day. No one was supposed to be stationed at the kiosks, but two men were there. When Don asked if they had our baggage, they showed him a bag. Don said, "Yes, that's ours." It was a miracle the two men had stayed the extra ten minutes; otherwise, no one would have been there. As Kelly and Don walked away, they looked back, but the men were gone. Where did they disappear to, and who were they?

After this ordeal and before ministry began, we enjoyed a fun day at the beach and did some artisan shopping.

San Jose Arriba

We traveled to the city of San Jose Arriba, where Pastor Paul preached a message.

On one day of ministry, I prayed for many people, and I saw miracles in the lives of everyone I prayed for. Glory to God.

The people in San Jose Arriba had heard of Christ, but when we asked if they had Him in their hearts, most did not. We had the privilege of explaining the plan of salvation to them, and almost all received Jesus. It was as easy as buttering bread to explain salvation, followed by their eager "Yes."

Later that day, Don was asked to join the pastor to go into a 'hovel,' or a shed, where you would think an animal might live. A man lay on a pallet, very disheveled, hungry, and sick unto death. They prayed for him, delivered him, and he was healed. Don really felt the presence of God. The next day, we saw the man again—he was clean, nicely dressed, and coherent. He even wanted to serve with us. What a miracle! What a joy and reward to be part of that day.

Then there was Ines. Jared shared, "On our second day in San Jose Arriba, we had the honor of serving and praying for Ines, who was 102 years young. Now almost completely blind and very frail, she was served in a much-needed way in the very poor community of San Jose Arriba. When asked if she knew Jesus, most people said yes but didn't have a personal relationship with Him. This was not the case with Ines. As Hanya and I asked her our normal question, 'Do you know what Jesus has done for you to receive eternal life?' This very

Hanya and Ines (102 years old)

frail lady lit up and began to declare how He had saved her and recounted the numerous blessings He had given her. What a joy it was to serve this wonderful saint, born over a century ago!"

That day, I prayed and saw God heal headaches by the dozens, as well as shoulder pain, feet, diabetes, knees, eyes, protection for families, and so much more. Everyone was getting healed. The first person I prayed for was a man, and I had a translator, which added another layer of confusion. When I asked him what I could pray for, he said his prostate! Well, I was a bit taken aback but could not show it. I wanted to laugh, but it was not funny!

When we prayed for a woman's headache, it moved from one side to the other. I prayed against the generational sins in her family line, and it was gone!

One woman had been paralyzed with pain on one side of her face, ear, and head for 14 years. I felt led to ask a few questions regarding her ex-husband, who I discovered still aggravated her. I prayed for separation from his words against her, and against hexes, vexes, and curses made against her. The pain she had endured for 14 years was completely gone.

Many, many, many people were experiencing headaches, so we prayed. Jared said, "They don't drink enough water." The people are poor, the water is not safe to drink, and they cannot afford bottled water.

The saddest situation was when a man came and sat down in front of me with sores all over his body. I was convinced they were hives and asked him what happened. When he told me they were rat bites, I was horrified. They were in his house, and it took everything I had in me not to recoil from him. As we said before, we were in a very poor area, and we were told we needed to wear closed-toe shoes.

Jared approached me to tell me everyone was lining up in the prayer line, even those who only wanted the free glasses. He instructed me to go up to those people, give them a quick prayer, and lead them to the line for glasses. As I began to lay hands on the foreheads of those in line, the Lord began giving me specific words of knowledge for each one—there were about 40 people. I was receiving so many words from God that I called Jared back to translate for me. What an honor to have been used in such a way.

Being led by all the words and pictures from God regarding going on this trip and obeying Him by going to El Salvador, I was rewarded well with the joy of seeing the fruits of God's Spirit on behalf of the people. All praise to God.

Santa Ana

In Santa Ana, the church called Nuevo Amanecer, or 'Day Spring,' called the local police station to have officers present for the medical clinic our team had set up because our doctors had drugs on site. The Police Chief, Eliseo Samuel, was a Christian, and most of the officers under him received medical care, while many or all received prayer from our team, and several received Christ. Eliseo told Jared Mueller, "Under this uniform, we are human beings."

It was discovered on our last ministry day in Santa Ana that one of the medicine vials of a widely-prescribed drug, which was always about three-quarters full, was now empty at the end of the last day. Unbeknownst to us, God had been replenishing it this whole time. I have seen this happen on our travels in different ways—the miracle of multiplication, right before our eyes.

That afternoon, we prayed for people in teams. Many of the people had very Catholic beliefs, so they all said they knew Jesus. Our part was to ensure they had a true knowledge of salvation.

Jared brought me the mother of a church member to be prayed for. She babbled non-stop, and after prayer, she was delivered from whatever her ailment was.

One woman needed prayer for infertility, and I gave her Isaiah 54, which begins with, *"Rejoice, O barren one who does not bear;*

break forth and shout aloud" I then encouraged her through my own infertility experiences. This scripture was given to me by my mother when she was at our house; she just opened the Bible and randomly pointed to this scripture. I have memorized many verses from this chapter, and they have sustained me with hope throughout much of my life.

I was to teach that evening, and I was very exhausted from the many days of ministry. That afternoon, I saw the white flag with a blue crest that I had seen in a vision several times, and I knew it was a confirmation that I was supposed to be there to teach and minister.

The God of Israel gives strength and power to His people. Blessed be God! (Psalm 68:35b AMP).

I had absolutely no anxiety—the calmest I have ever been in front of an audience! The ministry time was powerful, with Jared translating for me, and I know for sure one man was healed. I divided the congregation into groups to pray for their nation, and many received prayer from one another and from our team members.

Our team had four days of powerful medical and prayer ministry. The medical clinic served 713 people during our trip. It was such a blur of traveling to different cities to set up the medical clinic, providing prayer, and giving away reading glasses that some only wanted as a fashion statement.

The next day, Jared took us to look at a possible church plant facility, which became Hope Chapel San Salvador for a season.

On our last day, we went to church, where Jared graduated students from Operation Solid Life (OSL), and then we were invited to Jared and Kelly's for dinner and farewells. Pablo Pena, the country's national Foursquare president, came and presented gifts to us with many thanks.

Since then, the Muellers have planted Hope Chapel San Salvador and have been in the country for about ten years. Jared is also now on the Regional Coordinator team with Foursquare Ministries International (FMI) for Foursquare Central America.

Miracles of God in El Salvador

1. The privilege of knowing the Muellers and being part of their calling in El Salvador by serving in many ways.

2. Phenomenal words and pictures about El Salvador were given to me by God before knowing the Muellers would become missionaries there.

3. Confirmations God brought regarding our church's ministry trip to El Salvador—Don and I were supposed to go.

4. Gathering and praying as a team and seeing these prayers answered.

5. Being surprised by the words from God coming out of my mouth on behalf of the 40 people waiting for glasses.

6. The healing and deliverance of the man living in the shed, allowing him to get off his pallet and wanting to serve with us.

7. The favor with the police department guarding us, as well as being able to minister to each one of them.

8. The multiplication of a well-known medicine—this one vial lasted throughout the trip, only running out when we were done.

9. Praise to God for the many healings and salvations.

33

China and Hong Kong
40th Anniversary Trip

September 25 - October 15, 2004

Even though I am not highlighting many of our vacation trips in this book, some were exceptional for different reasons, and you will soon see why this one was special. As our 40th wedding anniversary was coming up, we decided we needed to take a special trip. Don wanted to go to China, but I was reluctant, thinking it was too third-world, and I felt I couldn't relate to the Chinese people because I didn't know any. Don persisted, and I am glad he did.

Anytime I go anywhere, I believe in the scripture that says, "Everywhere I place my feet, I am bringing Jesus to that place."

How beautiful upon the mountains are the feet of him who brings good news, who proclaims peace, who brings glad tidings of good things, who proclaims salvation, who says to Zion, "Your God reigns!" (Isaiah 52:7 NKJV).

I prayed this often as we traveled, expecting God to hear and respond. It is amazing that exactly one year later, in October 2005, we were again in East Asia, but that time to serve God.

We chose a wonderful tour company, and there were only 16 people in our travel group. This meant we had a smaller van in each of the six cities we visited: Beijing, Shanghai, Suzhou, Xian,

Chongqing, Guilin, and Hong Kong. When traveling to countries like China, you find that the people who go are usually seasoned travelers, which meant there was no extraordinary drama in our group—unlike, for instance, a cruise with party-goers. Our group was great. One woman even had her oxygen tank but went everywhere—that was an amazing learning experience.

For a bit of history, I will list the dynasties and nationalities of China. I wasn't going to bore you with too many historical details, but my dear friend Sherry encouraged me to add historic insights to this chapter, as she has never been to China. When I say "dear friend," I mean the kind who, when I mentioned I was having major back surgery, said she'd fly out and be with me for ten days. She did, sitting right next to me, and when I got up to do anything, she was there, helping Don with my care and cooking with him.

Dynasties of China

Han Dynasty (BC 206 - AD 220): During this first dynasty, silk robes came into fashion. They were simply made but very expensive and became a symbol of status. The first recorded name for China in the West was 'Cerae,' after the Roman word for silk, *Ceres*.[74]

Tang Dynasty (618 - 907 AD): This dynasty was the most prosperous and cosmopolitan in Chinese history. Buddhism arrived and gained many adherents during this time. The Tang capital (now Xian) was then the largest and greatest city in the world. Women were more liberated, and plump, full-figured ladies were considered most attractive. The dress for ladies was quite provocative, including wide, long sleeves and the use of elaborate hairpins.[75]

Ming Dynasty (1368 - 1644 AD): They embraced the teachings of Confucius after 100 years of Mongolian rule. Ming society was very conservative, and clothes, especially for ladies, were very long and covered as much skin as possible to protect a lady's modesty. Embroidery was widely used in fashions for the more affluent.[76]

Qing (Manchu) Dynasty (1644 - 1912 AD): The last dynasty of China. The Qing was a time of merging cultures, between Han people and Manchu, Europeans and Easterners. Changing attitudes and customs were seen in clothing, particularly the famous *qipao* (chee-pow), or *cheongsam* as it is known in Cantonese. Tailored to accentuate a woman's figure, the *qipao* was a radical change from the traditional dress of the time. Yellow could only be worn by the emperor and his family. During the Qing, while Han women still bound their feet, the ruling-class Manchu women did not. This dynasty was known for working with jade carving, painting, and porcelain, and for the development of *jingxi* (Peking Opera).[77]

The Nationalities of China

Han: Of the 56 different nationalities in China, Han Chinese are predominant and make up 91.51% of China's population.[78]

Hui: While sharing the same language and characteristics with Han people, Hui are Muslim and live mostly in Ningxia, an autonomous region in north China.[79]

Hani: Of Tibetan descent, they live mostly in the mountains of Yunnan Province.[80]

Bai: Most Bai people live in Yunnan Province and believe they are descendants of the butterfly.[81]

Bouyei: People who hail from Guizhou Province and are known for making most of the Batik cloth sold throughout China.[82]

Yi: People who live in northern Yunnan and western Sichuan Provinces, known for their great hunting skills.[83]

Uyghurs (wee-ger): A majority of Uyghurs live in the Xinjiang Autonomous Region in the extreme northwest of China. They are of Muslim Turkic descent.[84]

Mongolian: The descendants of Genghis Khan, Mongolians traditionally led nomadic lives, traveling across the Asian steppe in search of grazing fields for their horses and livestock.[85]

Beijing

Beijing was our first city to visit, and we stayed at The Peninsula Palace Hotel. We visited The Forbidden City, which is now called the Palace Museum and occupies the central part of Beijing. This was the Imperial Palace of the Ming and Qing dynasties. The construction of this grand city began in 1406, and 24 emperors ruled the whole country from here for 500 years.[86]

As we were walking into The Forbidden City, I looked to my left and saw a Starbucks Coffee shop, of all things! Of course, the architecture was made to blend into the environment.

We toured The Summer Palace on the water, which had 3,000 halls and pavilions, an important tourist site. The people in China are very active and retire in their late forties or fifties. Most care for their grandchildren as their children support them financially. Often the adult children need to work in a far-away town, leaving their children with their grandparents. You see elderly people playing unusual instruments, singing, dancing, exercising, and playing games. We saw much beauty, but I am sure the poorest areas were shielded from us.

While we were in Beijing, Don and I walked some of the Great Wall of China—what a sight to behold. It took more than two millennia for the Great Wall to be completed, beginning in the seventh century BC. Many dukes constructed the wall during their warring periods around their territories for self-defense. The wall snakes through the country and was built with local resources, changing in height, width, and building materials. This is just a bit of its history.[87]

We visited the Hutong in Beijing, which are ancient narrow streets, by pedicab, learning about life in the city during the reign of Kublai Khan. China has these Hutong neighborhoods in the thousands. We visited a local home where we were served tea, and I was especially impressed—and appalled—by the overwhelming sound of loud chirping in the courtyard. Unlike us in the U.S., where we have birds in birdcages, they have green pet crickets up to eight inches long! What a shock! We attended the Beijing Opera and were delighted by the costumes and dance performances, and they demonstrated the elaborate makeup and face-painting techniques of the performers.

Shanghai

When I think of Shanghai, our next city, I envision a city of myriads of tall buildings. Shanghai is a cosmopolitan center of business and commerce. We stayed at the Marriott Hotel and enjoyed an amazing acrobatic show after dinner one evening. We visited the famous Bund, Shanghai's most iconic sight and the city's most famous mile. The Bund is a waterfront area and a protected historical district lined with business buildings, banks, and hotels, like the structures seen along the Thames in London or the Seine in Paris.

We visited the Jade Buddha Temple, founded in 1882, with two jade Buddha statues imported to Shanghai from Myanmar. At first, I hesitated to go inside the temple, fearing I might "catch" the evil spirits, but I felt strength and peace, knowing the Holy Spirit lived inside of me. I was really impacted watching the people worship and bow down to these very ugly, impressionistic god statues. Some of the gods were gold, some black, some had snakes, and others had dark, scowling faces. One woman and her two-year-old child were bowing down together—this brought a new realization of how lost the world is.

Suzhou

On to Suzhou with its beautiful water gardens. I especially enjoyed the Silk Factory tour, where we purchased silk bedding at a bargain and carried it all over China. We saw the process of silk making, which is made by the larvae of silkworms being fed mulberry leaves. After they have molted several times, they spin a cocoon. Once the cocoon is formed, it is dropped into a pot of boiling water, effectively killing the pupae (the inactive form before becoming an adult). The silk filament is extracted by brushing the cocoon. It takes about 2,500 silkworms to spin a pound of raw silk. Each cocoon contains about a mile of silk filament. It was interesting to watch. The first use of silk in China was for wrapping a child for burial.

Back to Shanghai, then we flew to Yichang and boarded the cruise boat named *Victoria Prince* for our three-day Yangtze River adventure. The Three Gorges Dam project was under construction and was necessary to bring electricity to the country as well as to increase the Yangtze River's shipping capacity. This was a very controversial mega-project. The dam allowed for safety by reducing the potential for flooding, which was a common occurrence. In 1931, floods on the river caused the deaths of up to 4 million people. We were schooled in the tremendous effort it took to move about 1.4 million villagers, who had lived for centuries on the banks of the river, to higher ground or even to the city. Ancestral homes were demolished, communities and families dispersed. The dam's construction would cause the lower parts of the mountains to be flooded with water once the dam was completed. There was fear that if the Three Gorges River was bombed during a war, the vast amount of water released would overrun the entire city of Shanghai.[88]

I was amazed that the phone I had with me, which was the size of a small loaf of bread, connected to the U.S. as clear as a bell. I was talking to family and friends with no problem at all, despite the very tall mountains around me.

As we traveled down the river, we were shown the "hanging coffins." People would wrap their dead and put them in crevices or caves, or hang them along the mountain. The higher they were hung, the closer they would be to heaven.

Within the Yangtze River there were rivers that flowed from it with their own names. We left our little cruise ship to travel down one of the tributaries in smaller boats. Such unending beauty. One boat was called a pea boat, piloted by six paddlers, each one having their part in the process. It was funny to see the paddlers in short shorts and sport coats. They were told they needed to dress up, as before they weren't wearing much down below. They sang to us, and other men came up to us in the water to sell us souvenirs.

Along the way, we stopped and climbed a 12-story pagoda, Shibaozhai (*Sher-bao-jai*), built leaning against a natural rock and made of wood without nails. We climbed steps at first, then ladders that became narrower and narrower. I finally gave up on the last ladder, realizing that if I fell, it was a long way down, and I was a very long way from home.

Chongqing

Our boat arrived in Chongqing, and we were taken by bus on an excursion to Buddhist sites. The next day, we went to the museum of The Flying Tigers, a group of American pilots who volunteered to help the Chinese in World War II to fight against the Japanese invasion of China, before Pearl Harbor was attacked.

Xi'an (Shee-Ahn)

We stayed at the Shangri-La Golden Flower Hotel. Xi'an is world-renowned for the underground mausoleum of the First Qin Emperor and his life-sized terracotta legion of warriors and horses, over 2,000 years old. The statues and carriages were in exquisite condition. Each warrior was carved by an artist creating the face of another man next to him, replicating each other's faces as they worked. Thus, all the workers were represented in the faces of this gigantic army.

This city is more than 3,000 years old. For 1,000 years, the city was the capital for 13 dynasties, and 73 emperors ruled here. The predominant religion of Xi'an is Taoism, a Chinese religion. There are 27 Taoist temples, 200 Taoist priests, and 50,000 followers. Eighty thousand people have followed Christianity here for the past 1,300 years.[89]

We enjoyed dinner that evening, followed by a fountain and music show that represented the Tang Dynasty. The singing and costumes were colorful and enjoyable, and the dinner was a dumpling banquet.

Guilin

Upon arriving at the Sheraton Guilin Hotel, the scenery was quite unlike anything I had ever seen before. The mountains all had sharp peaks or high, narrowly rounded ones and were beautiful to behold—think Chinese ink paintings. These sights are permanent pictures I took in my mind and will never forget.

We had lunch in the hotel and were pleasantly surprised to hear people speaking Russian, which is always fun for me as I understand quite a bit of the language. It turned out that an entourage of security for President Vladimir Putin was there, securing the hotel and area for his arrival in the next few days. We ended up speaking with many of them, and it was exciting to have almost been with President Putin.

We took a tour on a boat down the Li River, and lunch was cooked for us. I failed to mention that I have seafood allergies—meaning all things from the ocean—so even the pan having shrimp or seafood in it before my chicken dish would most likely cause a reaction. I carried my protocol of Prednisone and a Z-Pak and had to go through three courses of this protocol on our 21-day trip; this lunch was one of those times. I always had a granola bar with me in case the food was questionable, which was pretty much all the time.

One of the souvenirs of interest you could buy was a delicacy: pickled snake, presented in a pretty labeled jar with red paper over the top. I doubt you could enter the U.S. with that.

Interacting with employees was always such a treat since they all wanted to learn English or learn about the United States. We visited Guilin's caves, much like Carlsbad Caverns in New Mexico, and went to a cloisonné factory. From there, we went to a tea farm where we were given the woven traditional Chinese hat and experienced a tea ceremony.

Upon being seated in our touring van to go to the airport, the tour director made an announcement that she had received a very important phone call. She emphasized that the van had been cleaned to an extraordinary length, as there were some very important people on it. Not to brag, but could the name Galitzen—being Russian and with the Russian President coming—have anything to do with it? Have any of you ever heard of Prince Galitzen? I'm sure we were checked out as part of the security preparation for President Vladimir Putin's arrival—or am I getting a big head?

Hong Kong

My first impression of Hong Kong upon arriving from our flight was the myriads of very tall, plain condominium buildings that housed the 7.6 million people.[90]

Hong Kong is not called "third world"; it is now considered one of the "newly industrialized countries," especially in relation to the Four Asian Tigers, which include Hong Kong, Singapore, Taiwan, and South Korea, due to their economic development.[91]

"In 1839, Britain invaded China. . . . Britain, as one of its first acts of the war, was to occupy Hong Kong, an island off the coast of southeast China. In 1841, China ceded the island to the British, and in 1842, the Treaty of Nanking was signed, formally ending the First Opium War and the first Anglo-Chinese conflict. In 1898, Britain was granted an additional 99 years of rule over Hong Kong.

On July 1, 1997, Hong Kong was handed over to China . . . formulating a new policy based upon the concept of 'one country, two systems,' thus preserving Hong Kong's role as a principal capitalist center in Asia."[92] With this transition, Hongkongers became Chinese citizens, a status they continue to hold today.

We visited Stanley Market, where we could purchase clothing at very good prices. I remember getting some cashmere sweaters for $30, though the quality wasn't as soft as if we had paid more for higher-quality cashmere.

The tailors in Hong Kong are the best, so we went to the recommended tailoring shop where we chose fabric for two suits for Don. He was measured, and we returned the next day for a fitting; the suits were later delivered to where we were staying, the Kowloon Shangri-La Hotel.

I enjoyed seeing so many people living on their boats at the Aberdeen Harbor in the Aberdeen floating village. The harbor is known to contain 600 "junks" (floating homes) and is home to 6,000 people. Imagine how you would do life living on a boat. Many people living on these junks are well-known for being fishermen, turning their houseboats into floating restaurants where they serve their fresh catch in the evenings.

Hong Kong was a whirlwind of a tour. China was an incredible adventure, and you will see what comes of the scripture I prayed throughout our trip:

"I have given you every place where the sole of your foot will tread" *(Joshua 1:3a BSB).*

Glimpses of God in China

1. The woman in our tour group who did this incredible journey with her oxygen tank, teaching me that obstacles don't mean inaction.

2. Learning the richness of Chinese culture and seeing God open doors into this community in the years to come.

3. Being with Russian security who were preparing for President Putin's visit to Guilin, and the royal treatment we received in the van by our tour guide on our way to the airport.

4. Praying the specific scripture, Joshua 1:3, claiming the land everywhere we went.

34

East Asia

*"I have given you every place where
the sole of your foot will tread."*

Joshua 1:3a BSB

October 21-31, 2005

If you notice the date and the above scripture, you will see that this trip is exactly one year after our fantastic 40th wedding anniversary trip to China. I truly believe that praying this scripture throughout China opened the door for us to go into East Asia once again with the specific purpose of serving God.

In declaring this scripture, *"I have given you every place where the sole of your foot will tread"* (Joshua 1:3a BSB), I believe a supernatural thing happens in the heavens, which causes the spoken Word to come forth. The written Word is called *logos* (Greek), which means "word" and is the actual printed Word in the Bible. As we voice the words of scripture, declaring them aloud, we—with the authority of the Holy Spirit given to us—cause this printed Word to become a *rhema* (Greek) word, bringing it to life, an action of our utterance.

Our belief and trust in God the Father, Jesus Christ, and the Holy Spirit bring us the confidence to declare the written Word, which results in many miracles. Why not? It's already declared in the written Word, so it is God's truth. We're just bringing it into action, calling it forth, making it spring to life, and causing miracles that have been procured for us by the shed blood of Jesus Christ. I believe we fail to appropriate the gifts of healing and miracles already made available to us, and we are guilty of a lack of stewardship of the Lord's sacrifice for us on the cross when we do not claim the Lord's goodness to the fullest.

Don and I met Janet Moen when we attended the Vineyard Church in Anaheim, California. She came to join and observe our prayer teams and to learn from us. Don and I were first coordinators of the Healing Prayer Teams and later became overseers of many teams. Funny story—at first, I didn't know who Janet really was. Janet is an ordained pastor, chaplain, and missionary, and is the Director of International Impact, Inc., her missionary organization. She spent time in the Philippines, and she also speaks Thai. Janet asked me how she could help our teams, so I put her in charge of snacks for about 20 people. The joke was on me! I just didn't know who the new people were who came to learn and be part of our prayer teams.

Little did we know, it was through Janet, her influence, and her connections that Don and I were privileged and blessed to travel with her to East Asia, and later to Thailand.

Janet Moen, and Colleen Sullivan, Don, and I took this trip to East Asia to minister to missionaries, especially those planted on university campuses through a very large, well-known Christian organization I cannot mention. We went to this country to prayer walk university campuses, and I believe we visited six of them. We went to look for opportunities to minister to people by listening, caring, and praying.

We went to one vibrant, luxurious, upscale city of commerce and business, filled with young people—a lot of people—most of whom needed to hear the Word of God. We went to a museum, and I had placed myself at a comfortable distance from the glass to observe a historic sight, but this city was so dense with people that even in the museum, people were crowding my space. A woman immediately placed herself directly in front of me, which, as an American, made me extremely uncomfortable, and I was offended by her aggressiveness, as I considered that space mine. I still had a lot to learn about cultural differences.

As this was a country that did not appreciate Christianity, we needed to decide on code words to use on our trip. We decided on "G" for God, "rap" for prayer, and "FT" for family time, meaning church. If we were praying in public, we kept our eyes open and gestured with our hands as we prayed so it would look like we were conversing with one another.

Sweet Colleen, who traveled with us, recently passed away after a heroic battle with cancer in her early fifties, and I want to give a tribute to this wonderful young woman. Colleen had always wanted to be married, but alas, it was not to be so. She was a vibrant woman devoted to serving God.

I hired Colleen to help me downsize my home office, and what a wonderful time we had. One day, she wrote down beautiful attributes she saw in me. I still have the original sheet in my desk to this day, keeping it there so that I can be reminded of her beautiful thoughts about me. I treasure this sheet, even more so now after her passing, and would encourage all of us to be mindful of loving others in tangible ways. She is still ministering to me after she is no longer here, through her beautiful words.

Our schedule for our six days there consisted of teaching and training the nationals (with translation) and expats (those from other countries) who were serving with a Christian organization. We taught them how to pray, followed by practical training in groups. I remember having ten nationals in a circle and praying for one young woman through a painful experience when all of the nationals began sobbing regarding their own issues. I thought they were in sympathy with the woman I was praying for, but the Lord was revealing painful issues in all of them. They caught on quickly and were going through their own hurtful problems, so as I was ministering to one, ten were being healed. This prayer time was being translated, making the work twice as long and taking twice the amount of energy. Many of the women's problems revolved around their devotion to their parents. There was a pull between staying loyal to their parents and serving God.

Family loyalty and obligation are deeply rooted within East Asian culture. Firstborn children are expected to support parents, grandparents, and other family members who might need help, whether with caretaking or finances. Parents expect to be supported by their firstborn. If their son or daughter doesn't have a "real" job and is supported by others as a missionary, this is not understood and is considered offensive to these parents.

Doing prayer training for these leaders was like being given keys to unlock the hearts of young men and women tormented by shame, unspoken hurt, or guilt. We came to provide God's healing reparation in ways that no man could.

Amidst all the training, we visited campuses in the morning, met with the missionary students there, and had prayer appointments in the afternoons. There were many healings, but I did not journal them because we were working very hard.

We put on a *Healing of Hearts Conference* where Janet taught the four styles of prayer: conversational prayer, prayer walking, using prayer as we read the Word, and a prayer method used in spiritual warfare. She taught *Hearing from God* and how to set up a team for individual healing sessions.

In the evening, I taught *Healing Prayer* and *Healing of Shame,* which is God's way of working tenderly to heal a person from self-hatred or lack of forgiveness toward others and themselves. To my surprise, the room was packed. Even though this was an optional seminar, more than half of the leaders came to this session. It was a beautiful time when the Spirit of the Lord's presence was in our midst. Each person walked through forgiveness with Jesus as He helped them release years of bitterness, self-hatred, and unforgiveness. The tears and somber hearts of these people were a precious sight to behold. Janet told me she specifically remembered when I asked the group to bow their heads, ask the Lord for forgiveness, and also forgive those who had hurt them. There was a sense of the Holy Spirit hovering over these precious men and women. It was a very powerful evening.

Don thrived as he gave his talk on *Financial Investments: Being a Good Steward* and was then available for small group discussions. Of course, only men attended, and if you know Don, his energy soared as he enthusiastically challenged those attending the seminar to wisely invest!

As we followed the lead of this worldwide mission organization, we were privileged to be included in the confidential leadership meetings. Most of the key leaders in this Asian country were between 19 and 25 years old.

On my evening to speak, I had friendly competition. Attendees could choose between me and a noted speaker, Os Guinness, who was speaking on the same evening. He was born in China, where his parents were medical missionaries. Os, as he is called, has written or edited more than 30 books and received his education at the University of London and higher education from Oriel College, Oxford. He is also the great-great-great-grandson of Arthur Guinness, the Dublin brewer. So, who would they come to hear? Ha! I did have a nice group, though, and it was a very powerful evening. On another day I spoke, I had to compete with the students' schedules, as it was their designated day to get hot water for their tea and to wash their clothes—a necessary part of daily living.

We were planning to attend a house church, but the logistics were so complicated that we could not. It took an hour for everyone to arrive, as they needed to be discreet. Only one or two could arrive at a time, and then another one or two, and so on. Neighbors weren't always kind to Christians and could turn them in, as some houses were targeted and watched.

There were two stories that stood out to me after our time in East Asia for various reasons.

The Story of Apple Butter. We visited a married couple in East Asia from the U.S. who were in great need. The woman was extremely homesick and needed prayer. The Lord gave me the words "apple butter," and when I asked her if that meant anything to her, she burst into tears. God knew this would speak to her and wanted her to know that He understood what she was going through. I believe her husband needed to hear her deep sobs to take her needs very seriously and consider the possibility of returning home.

Apple butter is not something I ever eat, buy, or serve, so I was surprised to receive that word for her. I knew beyond a shadow of a doubt that God was speaking through me. Apple butter was her favorite thing from home, and she missed it dearly. The significance of hearing this from God meant so much more than the apple butter itself—it was simple but profoundly powerful. I love hearing from God.

A Snapshot into the Life of an East Asian Taxi Driver. Before traveling to East Asia, our leader Janet decided to keep our group small, believing that four was the perfect number for this trip: Janet, Colleen, Don, and I. This allowed us to be in one taxi and appear like typical tourists, avoiding being discovered as Christian missionaries.

One day, our taxi driver told us that he owned his taxi in partnership with another man, as cars were extremely expensive. Each partner had 12 hours to use their shared taxi. You would often see a taxi along the side of the road with its hood or trunk open, signifying that it was out of service. Drivers had to make repairs along the side of the road during their 12-hour shifts.

The driver's seat was barricaded with a clear divider to protect the driver from disease and theft. Some road facts I learned along the way: the traffic lights were four minutes long, and at the yellow light, cars zoomed through the intersection. Traffic was so congested that many policemen were stationed at intersections. They didn't need to drive around; they were always ready to untangle the many traffic jams.

Reflection. I believe this trip was the gateway to another mission trip to Chiang Mai, Thailand, soon thereafter.

Where Is God in This Chapter?

1. One year later, after walking the land in East Asia and claiming it for God on an anniversary trip, we returned by invitation.

2. A *logos* (written word) became a *rhema* (spoken word) by proclaiming it, giving it utterance, and bringing it forth. God did this for Don and me through Joshua 1:3.

3. We were allowed into strategic meetings with leaders.

4. Hearing the word "apple butter" brought forth the anguish of a missionary woman's homesickness, allowing her husband to see that a return home was necessary.

35

Thailand

The LORD is close to the brokenhearted
and saves those who are crushed in spirit.

Psalm 34:18 NIV

2005-2008

Once the door was opened for Don and me to start traveling to Asia, we began going on missionary trips to Thailand. These trips were through an invitation from Janet Moen and her ministry as Director of International Impact, Inc., in California. Janet has been a very dear friend to both Don and me for a long time. As mentioned earlier, Janet is a pastor, chaplain, and was a missionary with Campus Crusade for Christ (CRU) to the Philippines for five years and to Thailand for another five years. She also speaks the Thai language.

Don and I met Janet in 1993 when we were coordinators and then overseers of the Healing Prayer Teams at the Vineyard Church in Anaheim, California. We ran a healing prayer group every Sunday afternoon for quite a while, where Janet came to learn healing prayer and became a member of our teams. Janet was sent by another friend, Ann Bowman, who was also with Campus Crusade for Christ. Ann studied at Dallas Theological Seminary and helped edit *The Woman's Study Bible*. She and I traveled together several times and taught our *Healing Prayer* seminars.

I didn't know much about these women when I first met them, and if you remember from my East Asia chapter, I put Janet in charge of snacks when she asked what she could help me with. Little did I know she was a qualified, seasoned missionary, pastor, and chaplain. She reminded me of that some years later, and it makes me chuckle as I think about it now. I was impressed with Janet when she told me she never had the desire to marry, which is very different from any other women missionaries I have known. Most missionary women would always have prayer for a husband as a prayer request. Well, Janet told me she never had a need to marry until she turned 55 when she told God, "Okay, I would like a husband now."

While many of us are waiting for answers to our requests to God, we passionately keep doing what is before us and keep moving forward. As part of Janet's training to become a chaplain, she took a course in Ohio, where she met Bob, a widower of one year, who was also studying to become a chaplain. They were married within a year of Janet telling God she was ready to marry. Many younger missionary women wouldn't allow themselves to rise to a higher position of leadership, keeping themselves available for a marriage opportunity—this was not the case for Janet.

Don and I took three trips to Thailand with Janet and her International Impact missionary organization. This is my best attempt at recalling the dates.

Hua-Hin, Thailand: Missionary Conference

January-February 2005. On December 26, 2004, just before our trip, there was an extremely powerful earthquake with a magnitude of 9.1 off the coast of the Indonesian island of Sumatra in the Indian Ocean. This earthquake generated a devastating tsunami, stated to be

100 feet high, and 230,000 people were reported dead. According to the CDC (Centers for Disease Control and Prevention), most of those who died were buried or cremated without being identified.[93]

The popular tourist resort area of Phuket was badly hit. The tsunami struck the west coast of Phuket Island, flooding and causing damage to almost all the major beaches. This tsunami lasted seven hours and reached across the Indian Ocean, devastating coastal areas of Indonesia, Sri Lanka, India, Maldives, Thailand, and as far away as East Africa. It became questionable whether we would be going on this mission trip, but it was eventually decided that Hua-Hin, the city we would be going to, was far enough away from the devastation. We arrived at the Regent Cha-Am Hotel, where we would be helping with a missionary conference. The attendees were missionaries from East Asian countries through Janet's connections.

Before we began to serve as prayer team members at this conference, two members of our team traveled to Phuket to be part of the rescue operations. They ended up being part of a team identifying bodies through dental records and returned carrying a very dark spirit of death on them. We gave them immediate healing prayer for all the trauma they encountered doing this work.

We ministered to many attendees of this conference, having 50-minute appointments for deep inner healing prayer. Our team of 12, that included new friends to us, prayed for many people. Someone even booked me for seven prayer sessions one afternoon that went into the evening. This was after I told my friend I would only go on this trip if I had no more than four prayer sessions scheduled per day. We must always keep a good attitude for 'Plan B.'

A horrific story—one of our team members, a man traveling without his wife, told me while riding in the van that he would marry me if he was not already married. Don was in the van too! Uh-oh, red alert—"Who is this guy?" I asked my leader. It seems unhealed people can come on missionary trips too.

With my seafood allergies, I ate Spaghetti Bolognese and salad every night to be safe, and I loved it. We were in Thailand for the Chinese New Year celebrations and enjoyed all the costumes and colorful displays of sweets and special foods in the marketplace.

Chiang Mai, Thailand: School of Leadership Conference

July 8-18, 2005. Janet invited us again to Thailand only a month after returning home from the Chinese New Year conference we had just attended. Janet had received an email from Catherine, the prayer leader for the mission organization holding the conference, who had already seen God work through prayer teams sponsored by Janet's International Impact mission organization. Catherine had a great influence in the country within her mission agency. The email invited us to teach about prayer and to pray for those who wished to receive it. Catherine gave us great freedom in choosing the topics and timeframes for our seminars—this was quite an honor.

This trip was to minister to the needs of about 150 key leaders from nearby Asian countries at a School of Leadership Conference in the Holiday Garden Hotel in Chiang Mai, Thailand. Chiang Mai is the largest city in mountainous northern Thailand, known for its beautiful ancient temples. Our team was Janet Moen, Mary McBride, Don, and me. It was a new thing to bring Healing Teams to this training conference.

We arrived in Thailand eager and ready to serve. Among the four of us, we ministered to 28 people in total, praying with each person for one hour, and we did this every afternoon for five days. Most of these sessions needed translation, and several men asked especially for Mr. Don, remembering him from our previous trip. It was hard to operate in the freedom of the Spirit at times as most of the leadership we prayed for was under great legalism due to the structure involved in their style of ministry.

I had the opportunity to teach about *Forgiveness*—many responded to the ministry time with their heads down on the tables in deep contemplation. Don and I role-played father and mother, representing their parents, asking for forgiveness on their parents' behalf for specific things done to them. There were many tears.

The average age of this conference was mid-twenties, and it was rewarding to be raising up future pastors and leaders. We became pastors to them, listening to many conflicts.

On our days off, we enjoyed traveling to the floating gardens by speedboat through the narrow canals with dirty water splashing all over us. The weather was hot and humid, and it was such a treat to have dinner as a team at the end of each day. We discovered durian, a tropical fruit that looks deadly. The large, round fruits are covered with massive thorns that stick out four inches or more. When you cut open the tough skin of a durian (with a machete), there is a hideous-looking pulp that has the consistency of thick pudding. The odor of durian smells like garbage, dirty dishwater, and spoiled cantaloupe. It's gross—and the scent is so nauseating that hotels in Thailand don't allow the popular fruit on their premises. What looked ugly and smelled revolting turned out to be both sweet and pungent. God made durian. Would it surprise you to see that there is something good in that hidden, stinky situation that God allows us to go through?

Chiang Mai, Thailand: Empress Chiang Mai Hotel

January 23-February 4, 2008. By now, these trips to Thailand had become a regular invitation. We took a team of friends from NewSong Church in Irvine, California, to Chiang Mai, Thailand, to minister to full-time missionary workers. Our team was Steve and Elizabeth Lu, Jenny and Simon Yeh, and two more women. This team was from Sola Dei, formerly called MORE, a Friday night gathering from NewSong Church where Don and I taught and trained on deep inner healing prayer.

Janet Moen and others would be joining our group when we arrived at the conference hotel, together we comprised a team associated with International Impact, Inc.

When we arrived in Thailand, jet-lagged and tired, we discovered that our breakfast was not included as part of our hotel stay. Some of our team members were on tight budgets, so Don and I felt that we needed to cover the cost of their breakfast in the morning and were ready to do that. When we got to our room and turned the lights on, there was a big electrical explosion, and the lights went out. We needed to change rooms, and because of that inconvenience, we were all given free breakfasts. I think God had something to do with that, along with Don's negotiating.

Our prayer teams came experienced in all types of prayer, and we led many people through inner healing prayers while we were there. We helped bring healing to dry areas, physical and emotional trauma caused by financial hardship, separation from their families, rejection by their families for following Christ, marital struggles, and challenges with their leadership. There were many heavy needs, and it was rewarding to minister to these full-time missionaries.

By this third trip to Thailand, we had built trust with the leadership of this organization as well as the missionaries as they flocked to us. One young man was ministered to by Don the first year, then came to introduce his fiancée on our second visit, and together they brought their baby girl to us for a blessing on our third trip. We had to leave like celebrities, having to hide away with everyone chasing us.

We enjoyed ourselves after hard days of ministering and took in a lot of heaviness from those we prayed for. We rode elephants, went to the elephants' art show where they were trained to paint with their trunks, and did some shopping, of course. It was great to experience casual river rafting, nice dinners, and floating on boats to the flower market where we bought food.

Here are six stories, written by various team members, that come from among the 70 staff members we prayed for on this trip. In cases of neglect and abuse, we asked permission to take their situation to their superiors. Those who came for prayer were met by God. Those who were willing allowed God to heal their wounds—some recent, some deep, and some wounds they didn't even know existed.

Chronic Depression and Loneliness. When we began our prayer for a lady named JJ, I saw a vision of a girl standing on the other side of a fence watching other children play. In the vision, JJ felt lonely and isolated. We asked JJ what her pressing need was, and it was to deal with her chronic depression, loneliness, and rebellion. She wasn't getting along with her teammates and felt that her teammates were not listening to her ideas. We determined that the root of the little girl's rebellion came from her mother, who married a man her grandmother did not approve of. Unfortunately, this rebellion also led her grandmother to not like JJ because she looked like her father.

JJ felt rejected and alone as her parents sent her and her sister to live with their grandmother.

We helped JJ by praying for her, guiding her to forgive her parents. She needed to forgive them for leaving her alone when she was three years old while they worked, which is common in their culture. We walked her through forgiving her grandmother as well. We also asked Jesus to meet JJ, and she sensed Jesus' embrace and love for her!

Tomboy. A young woman took a course on shame and sexual abuse. Afterwards, she came to our prayer session stating these courses had triggered a childhood memory of her own molestation. As she began to remember the tragedy, the woman realized that she didn't like men looking at her and that she was purposely dressing and acting like a tomboy.

While praying for her, as she remembered the incident, she could sense the presence of the man who abused her. After confronting him and speaking out what she needed to say to him, she then forgave the abuser. The prayer team members explained to this young woman that forgiveness is not about forgetting or justifying what the abuser did to her. Forgiveness is a choice not to seek revenge but to let God judge, releasing the perpetrator to Jesus to be the righteous judge. After she forgave her perpetrator, the team led her to a time of confession and prayer of repentance for not choosing to be the woman of God that He created her to be, and instead hiding behind the facade of being a tomboy. After her confession and repentance, the team blessed and cleansed her of any feelings of dirtiness and anointed her with oil.

Loneliness from Abandonment. A young woman came to her prayer appointment wondering why it was so hard for her to be part of social groups, thus blocking others from coming near to her. She felt lonely and unable to enter into relationships.

We discovered that, as a young girl, the woman's mother had left her and her father for a year and a half.

We prayed with the young woman through this traumatic time in her past, where she was able, with many tears, to talk about the feelings associated with her abandonment and what this had done to her as a little girl. She forgave her mother.

Jesus, in a picture in her mind, came to her, held her, and removed her from the room where she had been abandoned. The picture was so vivid that she even knew the room where the abandonment had happened. She then took all this time of trauma, the loss of her mom, and the sad memories of what occurred in that room, as well as herself, to the cross. After this, she was peaceful.

Parental Emotional Abuse. I had a wonderful experience with a young woman who wanted deep healing. God showed this young woman that everyone is worth loving and that His love is freely given; you do not have to prove your worth.

This woman was not loved and treated harshly by one of her parents, even through adulthood. This caused her much self-doubt, feelings of unworthiness, sadness, and the inability to love others and to receive love. While she was truly a beautiful woman, she did not feel loved.

God met this woman in an amazing way! All I had to do was hold her and allow her to be cradled and cuddled while she cried and cried, representing Jesus' wrap-around presence and love for her.

Finally, she believed that she was worthy of His love, with no strings attached. When I saw her eyes, I could see that there was now true love inside of her—Jesus—and she seemed to have received deep healing where she had not been loved. I saw that she had a look of wonderment, hope, possibilities, and worthiness. It made my heart melt. I think it softened me and allowed me to receive more love from God while she was being healed! How gentle and loving God is! I am so blessed to have experienced this miracle!

Never Good Enough. One young Chinese girl we prayed for came from a performance-based family, especially her father, who worked very hard to support them. When they could finally spend time together, the only thing he asked her was about her schoolwork: "Did you improve your grades?" In her parents' eyes, she felt she was never good enough. She believed they cared more about her grades than about her as their daughter.

For her family, "losing face" among their friends and relatives was unacceptable. We walked her through healing prayer and forgiveness. While praying, she let go of the bondage between her and her parents, and as she paused, she let Jesus minister to her in her imagination by letting Him take her to the beach where they played together. This picture came from her; we did not suggest it. She just wanted to have fun and expressed her joy at being with Jesus.

After praying with her, she said this was the first time she had really felt freedom in her spirit. She did not worry about meeting her parents' expectations anymore because she finally realized that God does not love her for her good grades—God loves her!

Sailboat Vision. While a team of us asked a woman a series of questions, I had a picture that quickly flashed through my mind of a small sailboat with the sails open, gliding through calm waters. In the distance was a buoy with a bell and a steady blinking light on top. The water was calm, the weather was clear, and in the distance, there was land. As I drew this picture on a piece of paper, I had no idea what this might mean or pertain to as we proceeded. When the opportunity arose, I passed this drawing to my prayer team leader, and she gave me a nod to share it with the woman.

As I finished explaining the picture to her, she quickly related to it, and it allowed her to reveal very deep things that she needed healing from. God uses signs and wonders, and the gifts of the Spirit, to bring clarity, healing, and understanding to people. At the end of the session, the woman was extremely free. We praised God for His wisdom and guidance and were amazed at how sweetly God worked in her life.

By this time, people from many nations attending this conference saw what we were doing, and they began to bring their teams to minister in Thailand as well. I remember a specific Korean team that came while we were there, and we decided we were not needed in Thailand anymore. Amen!

God's Miracles

1. I praise God for the opportunity to minister as leadership for our Healing Prayer teams, which allowed me to meet such special people like Janet, who then took us to explore Thailand. You never know what God will do in your life.

2. When Janet said to God, "Okay, I would like a husband now." The simple faith of a woman in her fifties who served God faithfully all her life—and then asked God this question that was answered.

3. Free breakfasts for all of us when Don and I needed to change rooms because of faulty electricity upon late arrival, fulfilling the need for team members who did not come prepared for that added expense.

4. The two women who came to serve at the conference and were then led to Phuket to serve after the devastation of the tsunami, identifying bodies just three weeks after the disaster. I am sure there are extra rewards in heaven for these two.

5. The favor and trust that grew for Don and me as we returned to Thailand time and time again, each time given more to do—a biblical principle (Matthew 25:29).

6. When other people at this conference, from Korea, saw us ministering and began to bring their teams to do the same—they caught the vision.

36

Cypress

Limassol, September 2006

Don and I went on a ministry trip with Elias Malki, a Lebanese man, to the country of Cypress with our pastor, Steve Purdue, from Church of the Coastland in Huntington Beach, California.

Elias was an amazing man of God! His grandfather was beheaded for the gospel of Christ. Elias had such faith for healing that God would give him details about people who were watching him on television, and they would get saved and healed. A woman once stood up and laid her hands on the television as she watched Elias share about her personal situation with cancer, and she was healed!

MEGO (Middle East Gospel Outreach), Elias' organization, has a retreat center located in the mountains above Limassol, a city on the southern coast of Cypress, where 40 pastors and leaders from Egypt, Iraq, Palestine, Israel, and Syria came to stay for a conference we were attending.

I was given the opportunity to teach with Elias about forgiveness and was embarrassed when he loudly pointed out that I didn't need my notes—that the message was in me. The Iraqi pastors there were going through a terrible time, needing to keep their wives and daughters protected in their country during Saddam Hussein's leadership and the national unrest, so we prayed with them.

Don and I stayed just down the hill in a small, shall I say modest, motel. Think army blankets and a water hose in the shower that constantly spewed water, flooding the bathroom. It did, however, have a nice, small restaurant. This was the only local and convenient place for us to stay.

Elias was a powerful man in the Spirit, yet we would find him in the kitchen chopping cabbage for our dinner.

On one of our day trips, Elias was unable to join us because he had Israeli stamps on his passport, and there was a certain bridge he could not cross into Jordan if they saw those stamps. On another free day, we drove into a nearby city and visited a church where the Apostle Paul had preached.

We were scheduled to go on to Israel, where I was possibly going to speak to women, but a war broke out and it became unsafe. Instead, we took a flight in the middle of the night to England. We were picked up from the airport and taken directly to the church where Elias was going to preach. After the service, we went to lunch. Traveling with Elias was a bit crazy at times.

One time, Elias came to speak at my church in California, and as he walked humbly down the aisle to the pulpit, I saw in the Spirit the heavy anointing he carried—it was very kingly.

Elias was considered the Billy Graham of the Middle East or like the Apostle Paul. As we walked down the street with him, people would honk their horns, wave, or stop us as we walked. He had a television program, and once, when we traveled to Israel with him, we watched his program in a private home in Bethlehem.

You might be interested in reading a book he wrote called *Ambassador of a Higher Power*.[94] What an anointed man of God he was.

Privileged to Serve God

1. I was given the honor of speaking to Elias' select pastors and leaders from Egypt, Iraq, Palestine, Israel, and Syria.
2. Watching Elias in the kitchen humbly chopping cabbage for our dinner after having done ministry all morning.
3. God showed me Elias' powerful anointing as he walked to the pulpit.
4. Seeing the honor and respect Elias had with people.

37

Finishing Well

But I'm Not Done Yet!

~ Hanya Galitzen

"Return home and tell how much God has done for you." So the man went away and told all over town how much Jesus had done for him.

Luke 8:39 NIV

It ought to be the business of every day to prepare for our last day.[95]

~ Matthew Henry

Don and I often talk about wanting to finish well in this life, and I have shared in this book the many ways we have sought to hear God and follow His leading. On this earth, we realize we are ambassadors for Christ while far from our heavenly home since, *our citizenship is in Heaven (Philippians 3:20 NKJV), and we are sojourners and pilgrims (1 Peter 2:11 NKJV), or temporary residents and foreigners (1 Peter 2:11 NLT).*

Don and I have lived a big life, and writing this book was an edict given to me by God to leave a legacy for our children, grandchildren, and anyone else who will be reading it. This book is an expression of a voice that has been buried deep within me, and I can now sigh a breath of satisfaction knowing it is well with my soul in its completion. Even though this is "My Story," as you have read, it's Don's too.

The trip to South Africa in 1988 lit a fire in me that has never gone out; without having heard from God and obeying Him to go to a scary place (scary for me), this passion to serve God may not have happened to further the Kingdom through an ordinary servant like me. Being immersed in healings and miracles taking place right before me and through me changed me forever. I had given the Lord free rein to take me to many places I would not have gone if I hadn't given Him full control of my life. I took seriously the word spoken to Moses, then to Joshua, that "everywhere I set my foot" I take for Jesus. Don too would, I am sure, say the same thing.

The LORD spake unto Joshua the son of Nun, Moses' minister, saying, "Every place that the sole of your foot shall tread upon, that have I given unto you, as I said unto Moses" (Joshua 1:1b, 3 KJV).

The deep joy and satisfaction of doing God's will is something money can never buy and results in an abundant life. Even though I never received any part of my family inheritance promised to me by my father—"one acre for each of us children and two for Mama Hazel"—the City of Industry (family property) became more valuable as the years went by, but God had more for Don and me. Even though I was left out of my earthly family's monetary inheritance, I have received a better one!

"And we have a priceless inheritance—an inheritance that is kept in heaven for you, pure and undefiled, beyond the reach of change and decay" (1 Peter 1:4).

I am grateful for every hardship of refining the Lord Jesus has allowed in my life to purify me in bringing Him the glory due His name. I have tried to live as fragrance spilled out from the flask of my body for the cause of Christ.

Don and I have endured our sufferings, sickness, infertility—things common to mankind—and Don will still "carry my purse" (meaning helping me as I teach). We are enjoying our latter years, although our sufferings continue. Don just had a stroke two years ago, five days after taking the first dose of the COVID vaccine. It was a major stroke in the speech area of his brain, making it difficult for him to find the correct words from time to time. We are grateful he has no paralysis or slurring of speech and is still vitally involved in life, running our business, playing golf twice a week, being called to teach at Whittier College several times a year, and advising many people in many areas of life. The Lord has done great things, and I am grateful.

I once asked God what my life's road would look like and expected, as His daughter, that my loving Father would show me a very smooth, straight road before me, but instead, He showed me a road full of craggy rocks of various sizes, with hardly a space between. Thankfully, I saw angels on each side of me holding me up under my arms, and when I looked down, I saw Jesus at my feet placing each foot on each craggy rock exactly as it should be placed.

"For he will order his angels to protect you wherever you go. They will hold you up with their hands so you won't even hurt your foot on a stone" (Psalm 91:11-12).

"Righteousness will go before Him, and will make His footsteps into a way [in which to walk]" (Psalm 85:13 AMP).

The vision I received lined up with scriptures that have been given to us in the Bible as promises. I wonder if I had not known Psalm 91 beforehand, whether this vision would have spoken to me so perfectly.

I want to be in a place in my life where no matter what the surrounding circumstances are, I will continue the straight path I feel is ordained for me.

"Because strait is the gate, and narrow is the way which leadeth unto life, and few there be that find it" (Matthew 7:13-14 KJV).

Jesus is still placing my feet on the craggy rocks on the path of my life, where and how each foot needs to step. Knowing He is with me as He has shown me in this vision in such detail causes me to know I can trust Him even through the harder days. We are not in Heaven yet, and even though the battle has been won through Christ's suffering, death, and resurrection, we, as His children, will continue to experience victory through our problems as we choose to lean into Him.

I often ask myself, are Don and I church planters through our coffee house? Teachers? Evangelists? Givers? The Apostle Paul was a tentmaker, Jesus was a carpenter, and we are just ordinary people answering the call of God to make disciples of all nations, and, as John Wimber used to say, "Doing the stuff" of the Kingdom.[96]

"Therefore, since we are surrounded by such a huge crowd of witnesses to the life of faith, let us strip off every weight that slows us down" (Hebrews 12:1a).

Oswald Chambers said, "Once I press myself into action, I immediately begin to live. Anything less is merely existing."[97]

"For You, LORD, have made me glad through Your work; I will triumph in the works of Your hands. O LORD, how great are Your works!" (Psalm 92:4-5 NKJV)

The late Eugene H. Peterson in his book, *A Long Obedience in the Same Direction,* said, "Our attention spans have been conditioned by 30-second commercials."[98] How long does our interest last in a project, what does it take to snuff our passion? There is a saying, "Keep on keeping on." I hope to instill this in our children and grandchildren.

When I think about what legacy I want to leave to my son, Aaron, daughter-in-law Melissa, my grandsons, Coby, Brendon, and Dillon, and those who have crossed our paths, it would be leaving our spiritual heritage with them, showing them that we don't do things without looking to God for our answers.

Collections

In the natural realm, Don and I will pass some collections down to our children and grandchildren.

I was raised on a small ten-acre farm. We had goats that made me happy, and we laughed about them a lot. I have collected many miniature goats from around the world—one from Switzerland, a china goat from Scotland, and one from an antique shop—a unique collection for sure.

I have savings banks (piggy banks) collected from banks we visited around the world. Most have the names of the banks on them. One large savings bank, in the shape of a brown lion, came from China; one was a radio savings bank from Alaska; the savings banks from Germany were a little girl and boy named Penny and Marc, and I have many more.

We have 36 mounted and framed pins from NASA. We were given the opportunity to purchase these pins that represented completed projects regarding space shuttles, rockets, and other things related to space travel that only employees had access to.

We also have Don's mother's collection of 12 army officer decanters, which are quite impressive, displayed behind glass in our home. My mother-in-law, Vera, claimed to be a plain woman who once said she wanted to be buried in a pine box, so I was surprised to discover a fancy egg collection she had. When I asked her why she collected them, she wouldn't tell me. One day, I discovered she was born on an Easter morning, which reminded me that there are reasons why people do things. Don and I inherited the Bible that used to lie open in his family's Russian church when Don's grandfather, Michael Galitzen, was the preacher.

I have made scrapbooks of our life and of the many trips Don and I have taken. These scrapbooks contain not only pictures but also pertinent documents such as birth, graduation, and baptismal certificates and mementos.

Don's 80th Birthday

On October 2, 2022, Don turned 80, which was a great blessing to us. I was planning to give him a birthday party, but when the guest list came close to 90, I thought to myself, "Oh, I can't do this, it's too much for me." Paul from our church was also turning 80, as well as our friend Donna, and he suggested I host a party for all three of them. I thought having a party this way would be a smaller number of people, but to my surprise, the combined total came to 84.

The party was scheduled for Saturday, October 15, from 1 p.m. to 4 p.m. A major storm was predicted for the exact day and time of the party. I prayed earnestly—or shall I say desperately—for God to change the weather, remembering in the Bible that you can do that. While I prayed, I had a picture of what I believed to be Jesus pushing the clouds away with His hands, then turning and blowing more clouds away in another direction.

Don's 80th Birthday

People were to be bringing chairs and tables for the party at 11 a.m., and I already had made an alternative plan to put them in different rooms all over the house. However, after seeing this vision, I had gained enough faith to set up outdoors despite the prediction of a major rainstorm. The storm did not arrive at the scheduled time. The party ended at 5 p.m., and then the rain came with tremendous force. Isn't God faithful? He hears and answers our prayers!

"Ye have not, because ye ask not" (James 4:2b KJV).

Our 60th Wedding Anniversary

There are times we experience extraordinary joy and need to express it in various ways. We celebrated our 60th wedding anniversary on Friday, August 16, 2024, by going to lunch at a favorite local restaurant. We shared with our waiter what day it was for us, and he came back to show us the table number where we were seated—Table 60!

Later that evening, Don, sitting in his chair, looked out of the window and said there were fireworks near Warner Avenue. We could see them from our family room window; they continued for a time. We were watching the news, and the weather lady said to go outside and look at the moon, so I did. It was the brightest ever; it's called a "supermoon." God was celebrating our anniversary with us with a spectacular show! Always be looking for God—He is there.

The next day, we had a grand feast for our family and special friends at a nice restaurant. In the Russian tradition, when you are very thankful for something, you have a prayer and feast of thanksgiving to God; we call it a "blagodarnost." The day was a joyful commemoration filled with God's presence in celebration of our 60 years of marriage and devotion to one another.

"He rejoices over us with singing" (Zephaniah 3:17b NKJV).

Bye-Bye Clothes

These epic occasions caused Don and me to begin talking seriously about the last part of our lives, which, as people walking in wisdom as best as we can, cannot be ignored. An interesting and not-so-fun "finishing well" project was preparing for our burials. Our Russian "bye-bye clothes" and burial instructions will be ready with a simple phone call so our family doesn't have to organize this while grieving.

In January of 2023, as Don and I went to get measured for our burial clothing, we passed an accident on the highway where a body was covered with a tarp. The enemy was trying to scare me about death, but I declared that the spirit of death could not get a hold of us and that God already knew every day of our lives and every hair on our heads. We had a fun time with Phyllis, who was quite a lively, fun woman and would be doing all the preparation of our clothing. Don decided he wanted us to be buried in the same cemetery where our parents were buried.

I recently had a dream. I'm not a big dreamer of spiritual things, but this dream was of me on my deathbed with my daughter-in-law, Melissa, standing next to me. I didn't see myself as really sick in my dream and was joyfully telling Melissa, "It was quite a ride (life), wasn't it? And there's MORE!!" I was so excited to be going to heaven where there would be MORE!! I believe it was God's way of telling me that dying is not dreadful for a child of God. I also had the impression that my death was not imminent.

I have seen a few family members pass with the preparation of heaven coming down to earth for them. How exciting for them! Years ago, I went to visit Don's mother in a home down the hill from us, as I did most every day. Vera was nearing her last day on earth and was bedridden. As I walked into her room, she lifted her head a bit and had the most delightful look on her face. It was radiant, and she said, "Oh, you brought your friends!" Vera was looking beyond and behind me, at what I believe were angels.

One other amazing dying experience we had was when Don's cousin Manya was given an unexpected prognosis of only three weeks to live after experiencing some back pain. Her liver was failing fast, though she was not a drinker. We were allowed to visit her in her home, and I was apprehensive about what awaited us. What a surprise it was to enter her home and feel the peace and presence of the Holy Spirit.

What would we talk about, I thought. Don and I sat down at her bedside, and he began recalling their fun times as children. Stories upon stories, like jumping on Grandma's bed when they were supposed to be napping. They were laughing and giggling so hard. We asked if we could pray for her, then anointed her with oil and prayed.

We later heard from her daughter that a few days before her passing, Manya would raise her hands in praise, looking intently at a corner of the ceiling of her room. What was she looking at? Angels awaiting her? She was comfortable, peaceful, and quiet when she passed. I gave her eulogy.

"Gather up thy feet in the bed, see the waiting band of spirits! Angels waft thee away. Farewell, beloved one, thou art gone, thou wavest thine hand. Ah, now it is light."[99]

That is what the Scriptures mean when they say, "No eye has seen, no ear has heard, and no mind has imagined what God has prepared for those who love him" (1 Corinthians 2:9).

If you will remember, Don had a near-death experience and felt tremendous peace while going through the tunnel toward his heavenly reward. He told me that nothing mattered; his only thoughts were how happy he was as he was on his way to an entrance into brightness, guarded by two very tall beings waiting, holding garments for him.

Lessons from Our Biblical Forefathers

Our biblical forefathers have interesting stories about how they prepared for their departure from this world. Here are three examples—King David, Samuel, and Abraham:

King David's Final Charge. Before King David's death at about age 70, he gave instructions to his son Solomon:

As the time of King David's death approached, he gave this charge to his son Solomon: "I am going where everyone on earth must someday go. Take courage and be a man. Observe the requirements of the LORD your God, and follow all his ways. Keep the decrees, commands, regulations, and laws written in the Law of Moses so that you will be successful in all you do and wherever you go. If you do this, then the LORD will keep the promise he made to me. He told me, 'If your descendants live as they should and follow me faithfully with all their heart and soul, one of them will always sit on the throne of Israel'" (I Kings 2:1-4 NLT).

King David said:

"Praise be to the Lord, the God of Israel, who has allowed my eyes to see a successor on my throne today" (1 Kings 1:48 NIV).

After giving these final instructions to his son, "He uttered this as his last best wish and desire; and when he had uttered it, he sank back in his bed."[100] (Charles Spurgeon) It was his last prayer:

"Let the whole earth be filled with his glory; Amen, and Amen" (Psalm 72:19b NKJV).

What a peaceful way to die. David, who had committed adultery and murder and was not allowed to build the temple, was granted such a peaceful end.

Samuel's Farewell Address. *"Samuel said to all Israel, 'I have listened to everything you said to me and have set a king over you. Now you have a king as your leader. As for me, I am old and gray, and my sons are here with you. I have been your leader from my youth until this day'" (1 Samuel 12:1 NIV).*

Behold, the king walketh before you" (1 Samuel 12:2b KJV).

Samuel then gave his probable last public statement, reminding the people of all the great things God had done for them and warning them not to rebel against God, lest His hand come against them.

Abraham's Legacy. Abraham prepared well in his last days, ensuring Isaac was well endowed and protected from the siblings born of Abraham's concubines by sending them away, so they would not interfere with Isaac's life.

But Abraham gave everything he possessed to Isaac. While he was still living, he gave gifts to the sons he had by his concubines, but then sent them away to the country of the east, putting a good distance between them and his son Isaac . . . Abraham lived 175 years. Then he took his final breath. He died happy at a ripe old age, full of years, and was buried with his family . . . Abraham was buried next to his wife Sarah. After Abraham's death, God blessed his son Isaac (Genesis 25:5-11a MSG).

Abraham's son Isaac was blessed because of his father, *"I am the God of Abraham your father; don't fear a thing because I'm with you. I'll bless you and make your children flourish because of Abraham my servant"* (Genesis 26:24b MSG).

As Isaac was blessed because of his father Abraham, who obeyed his God, I pray our son, Aaron, his wife, Melissa, and all their children—those born naturally as well as those who lived with them—will be imparted with the goodness of God.

Aaron and Melissa

These days, we spend a lot of time mentoring Aaron and Melissa in the ways of our business and are beginning to pass down assets to decrease our value for the sake of future tax burdens on Aaron. This means lots of dinners at our home discussing their progress in their business endeavors. Melissa, especially, is so much like Don, and she says she wants to squeeze all the information out of him that she can. Aaron and Melissa work well as a couple, and we all love being together and praying regarding our business.

We're living in the midst of a prayer I prayed: "Lord, please allow Don and me to live long enough and be healthy enough to help Aaron and Melissa transition into our business, and for Don and me to be able to enjoy it." We're in it now. I told Don, "We are living right now, the answer to my prayers!"

Don and I recently had the time of our lives going on vacation with Aaron and Melissa, taking a cruise on the Columbia and Snake Rivers. What a refreshing time, taking in God's nature and realizing the love that exists between the four of us! A past mayor of Huntington Beach was on the same cruise, and his wife commented on our wonderful relationship with Aaron and Melissa. This trip came after a draining time having to remediate eight of our apartment units from mold, and we were all exhausted. The respect and honor from our children on this trip were water to our souls. Don and I never even lifted our luggage!

Caleb's Bold Faith

Caleb, another man of faith I greatly admire, earned his right as a leader in the tribe of Judah by his total dependence and obedience to God alone.

Caleb said: *"I wholly followed the Lord my God"* (Joshua 14:8b NKJV).

Moses said of Caleb: *"You have wholly followed the Lord my God"* (Joshua 14:9b NKJV).

God said of Caleb: *"But My servant Caleb, because he has a different spirit in him and has followed Me fully, I will bring into the land where he went, and his descendants (his seed) shall inherit it"* (Numbers 14:24 NKJV).

Everyone recognized that Caleb had the tenacity and strength above others to take the promised land. What was that "different spirit" Caleb possessed? God had a plan for the Israelites, but they became "as grasshoppers" when faced with the giants that awaited them in the promised land. Caleb, though, had his eyes fixed on the giant clusters of grapes, the flowing rivers, and all the beauty—not the giants in the land. He saw the promise.

Let us rid ourselves of our fears and procrastinations and let's not be like the others who feared the giants, hindering us from entering the promised land.

It was 45 years after he began serving God that Caleb still had extraordinary amounts of courage and devotion to God and said:

"Here I am this day, eighty-five years old. As yet, I am as strong this day as on the day that Moses sent me; just as my strength was then, so now is my strength for war. . . Now therefore, give me this mountain" (Joshua 14:10b-12 NKJV).

God blessed Caleb with added years, exceptional strength, and unusual vitality that allowed him to conquer a foreign kingdom and establish a lasting heritage for his descendants. God also blessed Caleb through Joshua by giving him Hebron for an inheritance. Look at Caleb's boldness as he proclaimed:

"Now therefore, give me this mountain" (Joshua 14:12a NKJV).

Hebron belongs to Caleb . . . still today, because he gave himself totally to God, the God of Israel (Joshua 14:13b-14 MSG).

What does this exceptional strength mean? As Don and I are aging, we have an effervescent spiritual life constantly flowing through us that only weakens when we disconnect from intimacy with our Lord and Savior. "You are not done," is a recent prophetic word given to Don and me, and we know there is no retirement for God's children.

Therefore, we do not lose heart. Even though our outward man is perishing, yet the inward man is being renewed day by day (2 Corinthians 4:16 NKJV).

"Growing older does not have to mean growing ineffective. With the power of God and the confidence of Caleb, we can overcome even giants"[101]

Stay in the race, go forth, and conquer the land He has given to you—your sphere of influence.

Therefore . . . be steadfast, immovable, always abounding in the work of the Lord, knowing that your toil is not in vain in the Lord (I Corinthians 15:58 NKJV).

As for me, my life has already been poured out as an offering to God. The time of my death is near. I have fought the good fight, I have finished the race, and I have remained faithful (2 Timothy 4:6-7).

I WANT TO BE A CALEB AND FINISH WELL.

You thrill me, LORD, with all you have done for me! I sing for joy because of what you have done (Psalm 92:4).

"When I come to die, give me Jesus. You may have all this world, but give me Jesus."[102]

Amen! Come, Lord Jesus! (Revelation 22:20b)

Afterword: The Way to Peace

If you have read the pages of this book and have never experienced a personal relationship with Jesus before, or perhaps you have been far from Him, I want to invite you to receive the free gift of salvation.

The gospel is as simple as this: God created you for a relationship with Himself. We were all designed to know and follow God intimately, but sin separated us from God, since God is holy, meaning without sin. So, although we were designed to know God, our sin blocks us from knowing Him. Two crucial factors about sin are that all have sinned, so no one is sinless except for God, and sin leads to death!

That is the hard truth, but God in His loving kindness did not leave it that way. He sent His son, Jesus, who is perfect and without sin, to come and pay the full payment of sin by dying on the cross so that all we would have to do is repent of sin and believe that Jesus paid for our sin—and that is how we are restored to a relationship with God. So, it is as simple as that to receive eternal life in knowing God.

Do you want to turn away from your sin and follow Jesus? Please pray this prayer:

"Dear Lord Jesus, I know that you love me by dying on the cross for my sins. I know I am a sinner. Forsaking my past, I open my heart today and receive you as my Lord and Savior. In Jesus' Name, Amen."

"For 'Everyone who calls on the name of the Lord will be saved'" (Romans 10:13).

"For God so loved the world that He gave His only begotten Son, that whoever believes in Him should not perish but have everlasting life" (John 3:16 NKJV).

"For all have sinned and fall short of the glory of God" (Romans 3:23 NKJV).

"He personally carried our sins in His body on the cross" (1 Peter 2:24s AMP).

"But as many as received Him, to them He gave the right to become children of God, to those who believe in His name" (John 1:12b NKJV).

Welcome to the family of God!

Notes

Endorsements

1. Peuster, Marianne, and Wolfgang Peuster. *God's Angel Comes for Breakfast: Discovering a Prophetic Lifestyle.* GGE Verlag, 2016.

Preface

2. Netanyahu, Bibi. *Bibi: My Story.* Threshold Editions, 2022.

Chapter 1: My Childhood

3. Gaither, Bill, and Gloria Gaither. "Something About That Name." The Ultimate Playlist - Gaither Homecoming, Spring House Music Group, 2016. Spotify, open.spotify.com/track/5U9EaWOLhoNAfaHlJlTM6a?si=1Kr8J3PA RX-EkXUfPZAUgg.

4. "Maxim Rudometkin." *Wikipedia*, 15 June 2024, en.wikipedia.org/wiki/Maxim_Rudometkin (There is no access to the book, but this page exists about its author)

Chapter 2: They Call Him "The Prince"

5. Henry, Matthew. *Matthew Henry's Commentary.* Bible Gateway, www.biblegateway.com/resources/matthew-henry/Gen.2.21-Gen.2.25. Accessed 1 August 2024.

6. Spurgeon, Charles. *Morning and Evening: King James Version.* Hendrickson Publishers, 2010.

Chapter 3: Ancestors

7. Travel.State.Gov. U.S. Department of State, travel.state.gov/content/travel/en/us-visas/immigrate.html. 22 July 2024.

8. "Lithuanian coat of arms." *Wikipedia*, 1 August 2024, commons.wikimedia.org/wiki/File:Lithuanian_coat_of_arms_Vytis._16th_century.png.

9. A. Alexandre, and Christine H. Galitzine. *The Princes Galitzine: Before 1917 . . . and Afterwards.* Washington D.C., Galitzine Books, 2002.

10. "House of Golitsyn." *Wikipedia*, 1 August 2024,
    en.wikipedia.org/wiki/House_of_Golitsyn.
11. "Golitsyn Family." *Britannica*, The Editors of Encyclopedia, 1
    August 2024, www.britannica.com/topic/Golitsyn-family.
12. "Grand Duchess Anna Petrovna of Russia." *Wikipedia*, 1 August
    2024,
    en.wikipedia.org/wiki/Grand_Duchess_Anna_Petrovna_of_Russia.
13. "House of Golitsyn." *Wikipedia*, 1 August 2024,
    en.wikipedia.org/wiki/House_of_Golitsyn.
14. "House of Golitsyn (World of Imperial Russian Glory)." *Alternative
    History*, 1 August 2024,
    althistory.fandom.com/wiki/House_of_Golitsyn_(World_of_Imperi
    al_Russian_Glory).
15. "House of Golitsyn." DBPedia, 1 August 2024,
    dbpedia.org/page/House_of_Golitsyn.
16. "Welcome to Gallitzin Borough." Gallitzinpa, 1 August 2024,
    www.gallitzinpa.com/index.php.
17. "Gallitzin State Park Guide." Glendale Valley Campground, 1
    August 2024, glendalevalleycampground.com/wp-
    content/uploads/2022/10/Gallitzin-State-Park-Guide.pdf.
18. "The Princes Galitzine." Galitzine Library, 1 August 2024,
    galitzinelibrary.com/index.php?id=31.
19. Davis, Adele. Let's Have Healthy Children. New American Library,
    1972.

Chapter 4: Infertility

20. "Patrick Steptoe." *Wikipedia*, 1 August 2024,
    en.wikipedia.org/wiki/Patrick_Steptoe.
21. Panchuck, Michelle. "What's the Word? – 'Woman.'" WKMS, 1
    August 2024, www.wkms.org/education/2019-01-31/whats-the-
    word-woman.
22. Spurgeon, Charles. *Morning and Evening: King James Version.*
    Hendrickson Publishers, 2010.
23. Good Reads. Quote by Stephen Hoeller.
    www.goodreads.com/quotes/398626-a-pearl-is-a-beautiful-thing-
    that-is-produced-by. 22 July 2024.

Chapter 6: A Call to Learn and Teach

23A. Henry, Matthew. *Matthew Henry's Commentary*. Bible Gateway, www.biblegateway.com/resources/matthew-henry/Isa.28.9-Isa.28.13 . Accessed 25 September 2024.

Chapter 7: So, You Want to Be a Landlord

24. "Bootlegging." *Britannica*, The Editors of Encyclopedia, www.britannica.com/topic/bootlegging.

Chapter 8: Pier Colony

25. Dawson, John. *Taking Our Cities for God: How to Break Spiritual Strongholds*. Charisma House, 2002.

Chapter 10: Hebron House: A Place of Refuge

26. Chambers, Oswald. *My Utmost for His Highest*. Grand Rapids, Our Daily Bread Publishing, 2012.

27. White, Paula. Paula White Ministries, December 2003, television broadcast. Sermon.

28. "Red Cross Emblem Symbolizes Neutrality, Impartiality." American Red Cross, 1 August 2024, www.redcross.org/about-us/news-and-events/news/2020/red-cross-emblem-symbolizes-neutrality-impartiality.html.

29. Muir, Alexander. "Whose Lips Will Plead." Thankyou Music/Adm. By worshiptogether.com songs.

Chapter 11: A Call to Healing Ministry

30. Spurgeon, Charles. *Morning and Evening: King James Version*. Hendrickson Publishers, 2010.

Chapter 13: Austin, Texas

31. "Word of Knowledge." *Wikipedia*, 1 August 2024, en.wikipedia.org/wiki/Word_of_Knowledge#:~:text=In%20Christia nity%2C%20the%20word%20of,gift%2C%20the%20word%20of%20 wisdom.

32. Oxford Languages. (n.d.). Lackadaisical. In Oxford Languages on Google. Retrieved July 25, 2024, from languages.oup.com/google-dictionary-en/.

33. "Dissociation and dissociative disorders." Mind, 1 August 2024, www.mind.org.uk/information-support/types-of-mental-health-problems/dissociation-and-dissociative-disorders/dissociative-disorders/.

Chapter 16: Sequim, Washington

34. Tomlin, Chris. "Good Good Father." The Ultimate Playlist, sixstepsrecords/ Sparrow Records, 2016. Spotify, open.spotify.com/track/1mWdyqs6Zvg8b1lKjDc8yB?si=vFmee3iAR 3OoskPtFxt5jQ&context=spotify%3Aalbum%3A2XOKt6AVcxdBs1 Za7AxGj2.

35. Henry, Matthew. *Matthew Henry's Commentary*. Bible Gateway, www.biblegateway.com/resources/matthew-henry/Joel.3.9-Joel.3.17, Accessed 1 August 2024.

Chapter 20: Mexico

36. "Zona Rosa." Wikipedia, 1 August 2024, en.wikipedia.org/wiki/Zona_Rosa.

37. "Five Things to Know About Acapulco's Famed La Quebrada Cliff Divers." *Travel Professional News*, 1 August 2024, travelprofessionalnews.com/five-things-to-know-about-acapulcos-famed-la-quebrada-cliff-divers/.

Chapter 21: Russia and Turkey Adventure

38. Leonid Brezhnev." *Google Arts & Culture*, 1 August 2024, artsandculture.google.com/entity/leonid-brezhnev/m0d8xy?hl=en.

39. "Cold War." *Britannica*, The Editors of Encyclopedia, 1 August 2024, www.britannica.com/event/Cold-War.

40. "Watergate Scandal." *Britannica*, The Editors of Encyclopedia, 1 August 2024, www.britannica.com/event/Watergate-Scandal.

41. "KGB." *Britannica*, The Editors of Encyclopedia, 1 August 2024, www.britannica.com/topic/KGB.

42. "Federal Security Service." *Wikipedia*, 1 August 2024, en.wikipedia.org/wiki/Federal_Security_Service#:~:text=The%20Fed eral%20Security%20Service%20of,into%20the%20FSB%20in%20199 5.

43. "Tartars." *Wikipedia*, 1 August 2024, en.wikipedia.org/wiki/Tatars#:~:text=Historically%2C%20the%20te rm%20Tatars%20.

44. Lermontov, Mikhail. *A Hero of Our Time*. Penguin Classics, 2001.

45. "Mikhail Lermontov." *Wikipedia*, 1 August 2024,
en.wikipedia.org/wiki/Mikhail_Lermontov.

46. "Azerbaijan." *Britannica*, The Editors of Encyclopedia, 1 August
2024, www.britannica.com/place/Azerbaijan.

47. "Baku." *Britannica*, The Editors of Encyclopedia, 1 August 2024,
www.britannica.com/place/Baku.

48. "2022 Report on International Religious Freedom: Azerbaijan." U.S.
Department of State, 1 August 2024, www.state.gov/reports/2022-
report-on-international-religious-freedom/azerbaijan/.

49. "Azerbaijani (Azeri)." UNESCO, 1 August 2024,
en.unesco.org/silkroad/silk-road-themes/languages-and-endanger-
languages/azerbaijani-azeri.

Chapter 23: Israel

50. "Megiddo." *Britannica*, The Editors of Encyclopedia, 2 August 2024,
www.britannica.com/place/Megiddo.

51. "Herod's Palace (Jerusalem)." *Wikipedia*, 2 August 2024,
en.wikipedia.org/wiki/Herod%27s_Palace_(Jerusalem).

52. "Masada." UNESCO, 2 August 2024,
whc.unesco.org/uploads/nominations/1040.pdf.

53. "The Tragic History of Love, Courage, and Loss: Masada A
UNESCO Heritage Site" UNESCO, 2 August 2024,
culturetrekking.com/the-tragic-history-of-love-courage-and-tragic-
loss-masada/.

54. "Solomon's Pools: Built by a prophet, restored by a sultan." *Daily
Sabah*, 2 August 2024, www.dailysabah.com/arts-
culture/2014/11/18/solomons-pools-built-by-a-prophet-restored-
by-a-sultan.

55. "What Happened in Caesarea in the Bible?" *Fellowship of Israel
Related Ministries*, 2 August 2024, firmisrael.org/learn/what-
happened-in-caesaria-in-the-
bible/#:~:text=The%20town%20was%20the%20setting,of%20the%2
0first%20gentile%20believers.

56. "Those Who Leap Over the Threshold." *Entrusted to the Dirt*, 2
August 2024, entrustedtothedirt.com/2020/09/17/those-who-leap-
over-the-threshold/.

57. "Kufi." *Wikipedia*, 2 August 2024, en.wikipedia.org/wiki/Kufi.

58. "Battle of Jericho." *Wikipedia*, 2 August 2024, en.wikipedia.org/wiki/Battle_of_Jericho#:~:text=According%20to% 20Joshua%206%3A1,shouting%20on%20the%20last%20day.

Chapter 24: South Africa

59. "Apartheid." *The Britannica Dictionary*. 2024.
60. "Crimes Against Humanity." United Nations, 2 August 2024, www.un.org/en/genocideprevention/crimes-against-humanity.shtml.
61. "P.W. Botha." *Wikipedia*, 2 August 2024, en.wikipedia.org/wiki/P._W._Botha.
62. "Soweto uprising." *Wikipedia*, 2 August 2024, en.wikipedia.org/wiki/Soweto_uprising.
63. "The Significance of 1976." Apartheid Museum, 2 August 2024, www.apartheidmuseum.org/exhibitions/the-significance-of-1976#:~:text=16%20 June%201976%20was%20never%20be%20the%20same%20again.
64. "Gqerberha." *Wikipedia*, 2 August 2024, en.m.wikipedia.org/wiki/Gqeberha.

Chapter 26: 1997 Switzerland: Berne and Zermatt

65. Schaeffer, Francis A. *How Should We Then Live? The Rise and Decline of Western Thought and Culture* (L'Abri 50th Anniversary Edition). Crossway, 2005.

Chapter 27: Don's Illness

66. Mirk, John. Mirk's Festial: *A Collection of Homilies; Volume 1*. Lagare Street Press, 2022.

Chapter 28: The Magnificent Three: England, Scotland, Germany

67. Tazwell, Charles. *Littlest Angel*. WorthyKids, 2006.

Chapter 31: Emmetten, Switzerland

68. Philosiblog. Quote by Ralph Waldo Emerson. philosiblog.com/2012/04/27/happiness-is-a-perfume-you-cannot-pour-on-others-without-getting-a-few-drops-on-yourself/. 2 August 2024.

69. Carr, Charmain, et al. "The Sound Of Music." The Sound of Music (Original Soundtrack Recording), Rodgers & Hammerstein Holdings, 1965. Spotify, open.spotify.com/track/1O6e8ewSwx8ijeMoVUrW5I?si=1pOK-uxhTxCbD4h4HrUZ5A&context=spotify%3Aalbum%3A1KN5Lr40 H56umfa1yzmO5R.

Chapter 32: El Salvador

70. "Crime in El Salvador." *Wikipedia*, 2 August 2024, en.wikipedia.org/wiki/Crime_in_El_Salvador.
71. "Clarion." Vocabulary.com. 2024.
72. "Clarion call." *Merriam-Webster Dictionary*. 2024.
73. Guthrie, Woody. "This Land is Your Land." This Land is Your Land: The Asch Recordings, Vol.1, Smithsonian Folkways Recordings, 1997. Spotify, open.spotify.com/track/3ZjrfGcb3A2PMGA1vRNgSk?si=mGKWn NtPTLGOQD-fuNY1xQ.

Chapter 33: China and Hong Kong: 40th Anniversary Trip

74. "Han dynasty." *Wikipedia*, 2 August 2024, en.wikipedia.org/wiki/Han_dynasty.
75. "Tang dynasty." *Wikipedia*, 2 August 2024, en.wikipedia.org/wiki/Tang_dynasty.
76. "Ming dynasty." *Wikipedia*, 2 August 2024, en.wikipedia.org/wiki/Ming_dynasty.
77. "Quing dynasty." *Wikipedia*, 2 August 2024, en.wikipedia.org/wiki/Qing_dynasty.
78. "List of ethnic groups in China." *Wikipedia*, 2 August 2024, en.wikipedia.org/wiki/List_of_ethnic_groups_in_China.
79. "Hui people." *Wikipedia*, 2 August 2024, en.wikipedia.org/wiki/Hui_people.
80. "Hani people." *Wikipedia*, 2 August 2024, en.wikipedia.org/wiki/Hani_people.
81. "Bai people." Wikipedia, 2 August 2024, en.wikipedia.org/wiki/Bai_people.
82. "Bouyei people." *Wikipedia*, 2 August 2024, en.wikipedia.org/wiki/Bouyei_people.

83. "Yi people." *Wikipedia*, 2 August 2024, en.wikipedia.org/wiki/Yi_people.

84. "Uyghurs." *Wikipedia*, 2 August 2024, en.wikipedia.org/wiki/Uyghurs.

85. "Mongols in China." *Wikipedia*, 2 August 2024, en.wikipedia.org/wiki/Mongols_in_China.

86. "Forbidden City." *Britannica*, The Editors of Encyclopedia, 2 August 2024, www.britannica.com/topic/Forbidden-City.

87. "Great Wall of China." *Britannica*, The Editors of Encyclopedia, 2 August 2024, www.britannica.com/topic/Great-Wall-of-China.

88. Three Gorges Dam." *Britannica*, The Editors of Encyclopedia, 2 August 2024, www.britannica.com/topic/Three-Gorges-Dam.

89. "Xi'an." Wikipedia, 2 August 2024, en.wikipedia.org/wiki/Xi%27an.

90. "Hong Kong Population." *Worldometer*, 2 August 2024, www.worldometers.info/world-population/china-hong-kong-sar-population/.

91. "Hong Kong." *Wikipedia*, 2 August 2024, en.wikipedia.org/wiki/Hong_Kong.

92. "Hong Kong ceded to the British." History.com, 2 August 2024, www.history.com/this-day-in-history/hong-kong-ceded-to-the-british.

Chapter 35: Thailand

93. "Health Concerns Associated with Disaster Victim Identification After a Tsunami --- Thailand, December 26, 2004--March 31, 2005." CDC, 2 August 2024, www.cdc.gov/mmwr/preview/mmwrhtml/mm5414a1.htm.

Chapter 36: Cypress

94. Malki, Elias. *Ambassador of a Higher Power: Bringing Good News to the Middle East.* Charisma House, 2005.

Chapter 37: Finishing Well

95. Quote Fancy. Quote by Matthew Henry. quotefancy.com/quote/1234108/Matthew-Henry-It-ought-to-be-the-business-of-every-day-to-prepare-for-our-last-day. 2 August 2024.

96. "Doin' The Stuff." Vineyard Church Northwest, 2 August 2024, www.vcnw.org/stuff/.

97. Chambers, Oswald. "The Authority of Truth." *Utmost*, 2 August 2024, utmost.org/updated/the-authority-of-truth/.
98. Peterson, Eugene. *A Long Obedience in the Same Direction: Discipleship in an Instant Society.* IVP, 2000.
99. Spurgeon, Charles. *Morning and Evening: King James Version.* Hendrickson Publishers, 2010.
100. Spurgeon, Charles. *Morning and Evening: King James Version.* Hendrickson Publishers, 2010.
101. Maxwell, John C. *The Maxwell Leadership Bible: New King James Version.* Nelson Bibles, 2007.
102. "Jacob Knapp.' *Wikipedia*, 2 August 2024, en.wikipedia.org/wiki/Jacob_Knapp.

Works Cited

Henry, Matthew, et al. *An Exposition of the Old and New Testament.* Vol. 6, Nabu Press, 2010.

Spurgeon, Charles. *Morning and Evening: King James Version.* Hendrickson Publishers, 2010.

The Holy Bible. Amplified Bible. La Habre, California, The Lockman Foundation, 2015.

The Holy Bible. Amplified Bible, Classic Edition. La Habre, California, The Lockman Foundation, 1987.

The Holy Bible. Berean Study Bible. BSB Publishing, 2020.

The Holy Bible. English Standard Version. Crossway, 2012.

The Holy Bible. King James Version. Cambridge Edition, 1969.

The Holy Bible. New American Standard Bible. La Habra, California, The Lockman Foundation, 1995.

The Holy Bible. New English Translation. Thomas Nelson, 2019.

The Holy Bible. New International Version. Zondervan, 2017.

The Holy Bible. New King James Version. Thomas Nelson, 1982.

The Holy Bible. New Living Translation. Tyndale House, 2006.

The Holy Bible. The Living Bible. Tyndale, 1974.

The Holy Bible. The Message Translation. NavPress, 2005.